GEORGE CLOONEY

The Last Great Movie Star

GEORGE CLOONEY

The Last Great Movie Star

BY KIMBERLY POTTS

APPLAUSE THEATRE & CINEMA BOOKS
AN IMPRINT OF HAL LEONARD CORPORATION
NEW YORK

Published in 2007 by Applause Theatre & Cinema Books
An Imprint of Hal Leonard Corporation
19 West 21st Street, New York, NY 10010

Printed in the United States of America

Book design by Clare Cerullo

All interior and cover photos courtesy of Photofest

Library of Congress Cataloging-in-Publication Data

Potts, Kimberly.
George Clooney : the last great movie star / by Kimberly Potts.
p. cm.
Includes bibliographical references and index.
ISBN 978-1-55783-721-9
1. Clooney, George. 2. Motion picture actors and actresses—United States—Biography. I. Title.
PN2287.C546P68 2007
791.4302'8092—dc22
[B]

2007036594

www.applausepub.com

To John, with love

Many, many thanks to my agent, June Clark, Michael Messina, Carol Flannery, Gail Siragusa, Sarah Gallogly, Clare Cerullo, and, of course, John

Contents

Prologue

Oscar Night—March 5, 2006

They've asked me [in the past] to present. But that seems like me trying to force my way into a party that I wasn't invited to. I think you go to the Oscars when you're nominated.

—George Clooney

George Clooney had often told reporters he wouldn't attend the Oscars until he was nominated for one. He didn't expect, though, that one trip to the Academy Awards was all he'd need to take home one of the little golden guys.

After nearly twenty-five years in Hollywood, more than a dozen failed TV shows, a breakout hit TV series that gave him his first big success at age thirty-three, and another decade of critical movie hits (*Out of Sight*) and box office misses (*Batman & Robin*), 2006 was the year that his industry cohorts decided Clooney was a genuine triple threat: he had become the first person in the history of the Academy Awards to receive three different Oscar nominations for two different movies. Two and a half decades in town, and all at once in 2006, Hollywood had decided that Clooney was one of the best actors, one of the best writers and one of the best directors.

And all the big-screen triumphs he was at last enjoying came not because he had motored along the usual path to success in Hollywood.

Instead, Clooney had done things his way, shrewdly switching back and forth between projects with big box office potential and smaller, more independent movies he felt passionately about, working with actors and filmmakers who shared his goals of turning out good work they could be proud of listing on their resumes, and, in a reflection of his personal ethics, making it a priority in his professional life, at every stage and level of the filmmaking process, to treat people fairly along the way.

George Clooney had become a genuine movie star, one of the biggest in the world, one of the most beloved and most respected, and, judging from the crop of those coming up behind him, one of the last real movie stars in Hollywood.

As unlikely as it might have seemed earlier in his career, when he'd felt lucky to land parts in movies like *Return to Horror High* and *Return of the Killer Tomatoes!* and to be playing sixth banana to Mrs. Garrett and the girls on TV's *The Facts of Life*, Clooney had deftly managed to sustain and expand upon a career in an industry that is notoriously fickle. He'd not only become a better actor, one capable of genuinely terrific performances in movies like Steven Soderbergh's slick heist crime dramedy/romance *Out of Sight* and Joel and Ethan Coen's comic adventure *O Brother, Where Are Thou?* He'd also aligned himself with filmmakers who could draw out his best acting efforts, and who had like-minded commitments to making movies that mattered, that provoked, that entertained . . . that, above all, did more than just line a leading man's pockets with an eight-figure payday.

And along the way, he'd remained a loyal friend to those who were loyal to him, a staunch defender of anyone on a movie or TV set who wasn't being treated respectfully, and a charming, open interviewee who cleverly revealed enough about himself to keep 'em wanting more. He had determined how to use his celebrity to draw attention to humanitarian causes. Aside from ruffling the occasional feather with his political beliefs, he'd managed to keep focus pointed on his career and avoid any major personal scandals, despite an infamously long dating dance card that has won him multiple Sexiest Man Alive titles (and a reputation as Hollywood's most confirmed bachelor). His career choices, his commitment to being a good man, his delight at being a guy's guy, his effortless style (he famously never wears makeup for any movie role) and his classic good looks have made him, arguably, the reigning male star of Hollywood, a star in the old-school style of Cary Grant, a Hollywood legend to whom Clooney is constantly compared.

That members of the Hollywood community as a whole were acknowledging Clooney as the star and serious talent he'd become with their nominations for his work at the 2006 Oscars was the proverbial icing on the cake.

His role in the geopolitical oil corruption drama *Syriana* had been a tough one for Clooney. Though the politically active star was excited about the movie's subject matter, he'd gained thirty pounds in thirty days to play Bob Barnes, a veteran CIA agent who's sent to the Middle East to stop illegal weapons trafficking. The extra weight left Clooney feeling awkward in his own skin, and while filming a scene in which his character is tortured he fell over in a chair, injuring his back so severely that he would require surgery, medication, months of rehabilitation and the use of a back brace even two years later. The injury, a tear of the dura mater, the membrane that holds the spinal fluid covering the brain, caused him debilitating headaches that he described as being like "severe ice cream brain freeze that lasted twenty-four hours a day," and short-term memory loss. The lasting effects of the trauma were so severe, in fact, Clooney would later admit that in hindsight the role wasn't worth the pain he'd suffered. "There was not one thing that was fun about it," he said. "It really messed me up. I have these migraines now. I would trade not having done the movie for the pain it's caused me."

Clooney was still in the midst of the *Syriana* health problems while he was putting the finishing touches on *Good Night, and Good Luck*, the drama about legendary CBS newsman Edward R. Murrow and his on-air battles against anti-Communist crusader Joseph McCarthy in 1954.

The movie, which he cowrote with actor and friend Grant Heslov, and also directed and costarred in, had been at the top of his wish list for years, since he'd gained enough power in the industry to get projects greenlighted simply by his involvement with them. *Good Night, and Good Luck* was also a chance to show his love, appreciation and respect for his father, Nick Clooney, a veteran TV and print newsman himself who'd sparked in his son a fervor for all things political, and who counted Murrow as one of his personal heroes.

Making the movie was a culmination of everything the Kentucky native had learned about acting, directing and writing, and with the personal connection to his father, the *Good Night, and Good Luck* production was certainly a pinnacle in his career. Unfortunately, it was colliding with the worst health condition of his life.

There was also the matter of the politically charged nature of both *Syriana* and *Good Night, and Good Luck*, and the drubbing Clooney had taken for his vocal anti–Iraq War stance. He recalls that as children he and his sister Ada were embarrassed when their father would speak up and cause a scene when he witnessed someone being treated unfairly. Nick Clooney was an outspoken defender of civil rights, at a time and place when such a position wasn't necessarily a popular one. He'd instilled in George and Ada the belief that you were responsible for calling out such injustices as racial bigotry, no matter who supported you—or didn't support you.

Nick Clooney had even lost jobs, forcing the family to relocate for his next gig, by speaking up for what he believed in. George Clooney would admit that he and his sister dreaded such showdowns when they were younger, but that his father's integrity and commitment to being on the side of what was right was paramount in shaping the kind of man Clooney wanted to become. As an adult, he would not only look back at his father's convictions with fierce pride, but he would adopt Nick Clooney's personal philosophies for himself. And, like his father, he would find that they weren't always popular sentiments.

Dating back to his involvement with the Hollywood community's efforts to raise funds for the families of the victims of the September 11 attacks, and intensifying with his public ruminations against the March 2003 American invasion of Iraq that kicked off the Iraq War, Clooney had drawn much criticism from the political right. Many, like Fox News talk show host Bill O'Reilly, liked to claim that Clooney's liberal viewpoints and anti-war statements not only made the star a traitor, but would eventually lead fans to boycott all Clooney projects.

So it was at this point, with more than two decades of some very memorable (and some he'd very much like to forget) TV shows and movies to his name, and combating a full lineup of health woes and political foes, that Clooney finally got the nominations—Best Performance by an Actor in a Supporting Role for *Syriana*, and Best Achievement in Directing and Best Writing, Screenplay Written Directly for the Screen for *Good Night, and Good Luck*—that served as his first official invitation to the Academy Awards.

And just twenty minutes after taking his seat at the Kodak Theater in Hollywood for the Jon Stewart–hosted Oscar 2006 telecast, nearly forty million viewers saw Clooney win the first award of the evening, the Best Supporting Actor statue.

"Wow. Wow. All right, so I'm not winning [best] director [later]," Clooney, resplendent in his one and only tuxedo, a one-button Giorgio Armani number, joked as he stepped to the podium to accept his Oscar. "It's the funny thing about winning an Academy Award, it will always be synonymous with your name from here on in. It will be Oscar winner George Clooney, Sexiest Man Alive 1997, Batman, died today in a freak accident at a . . ."

A dose of his trademark humor aside, Clooney also characteristically defended his fellow Hollywoodites against criticism that the industry and its stars tend to be out of touch with the mood of the rest of the country. "And finally, I would say that, you know, we are a little bit out of touch in Hollywood every once in a while. I think it's probably a good thing," he said. "We're the ones who talk about AIDS when it was just being whispered, and we talked about civil rights when it wasn't really popular. And we, you know, we bring up subjects. This Academy, this group of people, gave Hattie McDaniel an Oscar in 1939 when blacks were still sitting in the backs of theaters. I'm proud to be a part of this Academy. Proud to be part of this community, and proud to be out of touch. And I thank you so much for this."

The speech, of course, was praised by many of the actor's fellow stars, while others, the political right, and even some celebrities like director Spike Lee, felt Clooney's words simply amounted to further proof of just how out of touch the industry is. But on a night that was an amalgamation of everything he'd set out to do in Hollywood, of the passion projects that were a reflection of both his work and personal ethics, and of a year that had seen him, literally, suffer for his art, Clooney was ending the night with an eight-and-a-half-pound piece of proof that he had been right to ignore the advice his father had given him about heading off in 1982, in a broken-down jalopy, with $300 in his pocket, to find success in Hollywood.

"I said, 'Oh, Lord! How stupid is that? Are you kidding me?'" Nick Clooney told *Men's Vogue*. "And every phone call he made, I would say, 'Come back to school so you got a piece of paper, a diploma, something to fall back on.' And the one time he absolutely stopped me, which is rare, because I talk a lot, but he said, 'Pop, if I have something to fall back on, I'll fall back.' And I had absolutely no answer for that. It was the last time he heard that cliché from me."

There was no one prouder of George Clooney and his Oscar win than his parents, Nick and Nina, who watched their son's speech from the Clooneys' home in Augusta, Kentucky. "We jumped up and down like teenagers," Nick wrote in his thrice-weekly column in the *Cincinnati Post*. "Even Spags [the family dog] joined the festivities, though I reminded her she hadn't seen either of the movies. We paused only long enough to hear George's singularly graceful speech about the role of movies in our society, then we started yelling again."

Meanwhile, on the West Coast, the younger Clooney had been whisked through the maze of press clamoring for photos and quotes about his win and his politically-tinged acceptance speech, had made an obligatory pit stop at the Governor's Ball, the official post-Oscar celebration bash, and was headed off to a more personal post-awards celebration with his *other* family, The Boys, a close-knit group of pals whom he had befriended in acting classes shortly after moving to Los Angeles, and whose friendships had seen all of them through various breakups, divorces, family deaths, births, health emergencies and career ups and downs. It was meeting up with The Boys, as the friends of Clooney are so famously known in Hollywood, that the newly crowned Oscar winner said he was most looking forward to.

The phone call to Ma and Pa Clooney would came later in the night, when the actor had arrived at one of his favorite Hollywood restaurants, Italian eatery Dan Tana's, which had closed early for the first time in its forty-two-year history so George Clooney could celebrate his Oscar victory with The Boys and celebrity pals like Sandra Bullock, Keanu Reeves, Uma Thurman, Madonna, Mick Jagger, and his on-again, off-again girlfriend, actress Krista Allen.

Wrote Nick Clooney in the *Cincinnati Post*, "We had almost nodded off when, at 2 A.M., the phone rang. 'Well, what did you think?' George asked. . . . Then I asked, 'What party do you go to next?' 'No party,' he answered. 'A car is picking me up in a few minutes and taking me to the airport. In about eight hours, I'll be back in New York. I have to go to work.'"

The industry's recognition of projects he felt a personal stake in, celebrating with the friends and family who'd been his loyal supporters along the way, and having another job to head off to the next day? It had taken twenty-five years, but George Clooney was finally living his dream.

1

Like Father (and Aunt), Like Son

I remember asking him, when he was only five or six, what he wanted to be when he grew up. And his response was "I wanna be famous." We had no idea how serious he was.

—Nick Clooney

The desire to be famous, and the talent, charm and good fortune to make it happen, runs in George Clooney's blood. Not all members of his family, however, have been as well equipped to deal with success as Clooney has proven himself to be.

Siblings Rosemary, Betty and Nick Clooney were born to Andrew and Frances (Guilfoyle) Clooney, both of Irish descent, in the small Ohio River town of Maysville, Kentucky, about an hour southeast of Cincinnati. The Clooney kids' childhood was not a smooth one, thanks to warring parents and a hardscrabble existence that would sometimes force the children to sell soda bottles for cash. Andrew was a painter—"not pictures, houses," Rosemary would later tell friends—and when the Depression hit, paying someone else to give their homes a fresh coat of paint was a luxury few small-town residents could afford. The pressure of not being able to find employment to support his family exacerbated Andrew's drinking habit, and that, along with the family's financial struggles, led to constant fighting that Andrew and Frances thought would be best resolved by splitting up.

That meant the Clooney children, known as smart, pleasant and talented young members of the community despite the instability of their home life, were also separated from each other for much of their growing-up years. Rosemary, Betty and Nick were shuffled back and forth between both sets of grandparents and other relatives when Andrew moved to Washington, D.C., and Frances went off to Lexington, Kentucky, to find a job. Eventually, Rosemary and Betty were left behind when their mother remarried and moved to California, taking only Nick with her. The separation was tough on the children, and each of them dealt with it differently. For Rosemary, it cemented her relationship with Betty as the person closest to her and, she would later recall, the one constant she remembered from her childhood. For Nick, it would cement his resolve to keep his own family together, no matter what, when he grew up and had children of his own.

Rosemary, Betty and Nick were also blessed with striking voices, and each of them found a way to use their talent to wow the adults around them, and to deal with the upheaval in their young lives. For Rosemary and Betty, this meant showing off their beautiful singing voices. The girls often performed at political functions led by their Grandpa Clooney, the town's mayor, while Nick spent his time writing silly songs and honing his love for and talent in broadcasting.

The Clooney kids were egged on in their career pursuits by their beloved Uncle George Guilfoyle, a dashing World War II bomber pilot whose good looks and charm, not to mention killer eyebrows, were passed on directly to another George years later. Uncle George returned to Maysville a war hero, and quickly landed himself a job at the local radio station, where he and CBS broadcaster Edward R. Murrow would inspire young Nick to choose their vocation for himself.

Uncle George was also one of the steady family presences in the Clooney kids' lives, and it was on his advice that Rosemary and Betty eventually decided to take their singing act on the road, after the girls had enjoyed success, and earned some much-needed cash, as singers on Cincinnati's top radio station, WLW. "The audition was Betty's idea," Rosemary laughed about the job that earned each sister $20 a week. "That afternoon we had a quarter to spend. I wanted chocolate malteds, and she wanted to use it for carfare to the station. We flipped, and I lost."

Thirteen-year-old Rosemary and ten-year-old Betty began to travel throughout the area, with Uncle George as their manager, and drew praise for their mellifluous voices all across Kentucky and Ohio. Soon they were hired to perform with professional bands, and, with Uncle George to look after them and try to shield them from the more undesirable elements of life on the road, Rosemary and Betty were singing all across the United States, traveling along in a bus full of older, male musicians, staying in cramped hotels everywhere from Atlantic City to California, and eventually landing in New York City.

And while her new life in New York would set Rosemary on a path to becoming the most famous female pop singer in the country by the 1950s, it also sparked a series of personal and professional decisions that would help spell the end of her reign as the queen of pop, and the beginning of a downward spiral in her personal life, almost as quickly.

Both Rosemary and Betty had fine voices, but to their fellow musicians it was Rosemary who stood out. In February 1948, even Uncle George singled Rosemary out by entering her in an Arthur Godfrey Talent Scouts contest as a solo performer. Rosemary easily won the competition, which included another young singer named Anthony Dominick Benedetto. "That was the only time I ever won anything against Tony Bennett," Rosemary wrote in her 1999 autobiography *Girl Singer*.

Rosemary and Betty had also begun making records with the Tony Pastor Band, and again, though both girls were featured on the recordings, it was Rosemary's voice that gained the attention of those in the music industry. So when she learned that she was being offered a recording contract by Columbia Records in 1949, it was not a surprise to find that the contract was for her solo services. No Betty as the other half of the Clooney Sisters, and no Uncle George as her manager.

"Betty smiled brightly when I started to tell her and interrupted me before I could get the news out," Rosemary wrote in *Girl Singer*. "'I'm tired of being on the road,' she said. 'I want to be one of the girls wearing a formal and dancing while the band plays—not just the girl who sings while the other girls dance.' She hugged me tightly. 'I love you, Rosie,' she said."

Uncle George didn't take the news as well.

He had spent many years helping take care of Rosemary and her siblings in Kentucky, and he had managed to keep her mostly trouble- and heartbreak-free while acting as the Clooney Sisters' manager, Rosemary's occasional love affair with a fellow musician aside. Uncle George, like many in the Guilfoyle and Clooney clans, had talents and aspirations of his own, all of which had taken a back seat to making sure his nieces and nephews were first housed and fed, and later encouraged to make the most of the talents they possessed.

And now, as Rosemary was presented with the career opportunity of a lifetime, she was forced to admit that accepting it would also mean sending Betty and Uncle George back to the Midwest.

"'You know you wouldn't have been able to go on the road without me,'" Rosemary recalled Uncle George saying during a painful meeting between George, Rosemary and Columbia Records execs. "'Yes,' I said. 'You'd never have met any of these people who have offered you a record contract,' Uncle George said. 'Am I right?' 'Yes,' I said. 'And now you want to leave your sister and me behind. You want to be on your own . . . Is that want you want?'

"'Yes,' I said."

Rosemary signed the contract and for the first time in her life began to live alone, in a little furnished apartment at the swanky Parc Vendome apartment building on 57th Street in New York. She cut her first solo record the year she turned twenty-one, and by age twenty-three, she had a huge hit on her hands with 1951's "Come On-a My House." The song cemented her status as a rising superstar, leading to headlining solo performances, magazine covers, gold records and duets with other superstars like Frank Sinatra, and Bing Crosby, who chose Rosemary as his costar for the 1954 holiday movie classic *White Christmas*. Rosemary's popularity, in fact, is difficult to comprehend today, partially because it declined rapidly and steeply once rock 'n' roll took over the radio airwaves, and because there's no current female pop star whose fame, and talent, matches Rosemary's.

But even while Rosemary was enjoying her newfound solo success and her first taste of being on her own, she was still troubled by the things and people she'd left behind. Her parents' troubled relationship, and the years of hearing her relatives on both sides of the family speak negatively about her mother and father, had colored her worldview, specifically her attitudes about men. Obviously, it was difficult to have a sense of security when her childhood had been spent being shuffled back and forth between family members. Out of all the adults in her family, her parents had spent the least amount of time raising her.

It's hardly surprising, then, that when Rosemary was faced with the choice of two potential husbands at the height of her career, she chose the one who was older, more experienced, more worldly, and, unfortunately, less faithful. Oscar-winning actor José Ferrer, fourteen years Rosemary's senior, would become her first husband in 1953. But years of infidelity led to a divorce in 1961, and a brief second marriage to Ferrer lasted only from 1966–67. Like her father, who'd been an unreliable and infrequent presence in her life, the father of her five children had broken Rosemary's heart. Her career, after years of success in the music, movie and TV industries, took a hit when big band, pop vocals were replaced in the public's favor by the tunes of Elvis Presley and other rockers. And, at a time when her personal and professional confidence were shaky at best, Rosemary was among the crowd at the Ambassador Hotel in Los Angeles in 1968 that watched as her friend Robert F. Kennedy, whom she'd campaigned for during his presidential election bid, was murdered.

It was a string of bad decisions, bad breaks and bad coping skills—Rosemary had spiraled into a deep depression and a nasty, out-of-control drug habit—that led, ultimately, to a very public meltdown during a concert in Reno after Kennedy's assassination in 1968. Time in a mental institution, away from her children, made a career comeback all the more difficult, and the fact that she needed to work to support her children, and that the drugs had begin to chip away at her golden voice, just added to the stresses that had pushed the singer to the edge.

As Rosemary herself would later recall, her fragile self-image was predicated on the fact that the public, and an educated, interesting older man, had once loved her. When rock replaced her vocal stylings in the tastes of music lovers, and her husband refused to remain faithful, she took that just as personally. If you believe everything they say when they tell you how great you are, don't you also have to believe them when they tell you that you don't matter as much anymore?

These are the painful lessons Rosemary Clooney learned the hard way, but they would later prove useful to her nephew George. In fact, a good deal of George Clooney's success, and certainly his longevity, is owed to his philosophy that falling out of the public's favor is inevitable. It affects his career choices, certainly his professional ethics, and his work schedule. Temper their enthusiasm for you when you're hot, remember that some day you won't be, and capitalize on every opportunity while you can.

George Clooney has also benefited immensely from an example that is a complete 180-degree turn away from his aunt's tumultuous life. With his sisters having made their mark in the singing world—Betty, to a lesser degree than Rosemary, would also go on to make recordings and star in a local TV show, managed all the while by Uncle George—

Nick had become something of a local celebrity himself. While still earning his diploma at Maysville High School, the youngest Clooney, a charming, handsome go-getter who had committed himself to a career in journalism, began to contribute news reports to a local radio station. After a brief, unsuccessful stint in Los Angeles to try his hand at acting, he moved back to the East Coast and landed a job as a newscaster at a Lexington radio station. He also hosted a teen music show and was elected president of the Bluegrass Press Club, a position that would not only win him respect among his fellow newsmen, but would also bring to pass a fateful meeting with a beauty queen.

2

A Star Is Born

I said, "Would you please pass the butter, and would you marry me?" She picked up the butter, looked at it for a second and said, "Here's the butter, and okay."

—Nick Clooney

One of Nick Clooney's duties as the newly elected president of the Bluegrass Press Club was to act as emcee of the Miss Lexington beauty pageant, and then escort the winner around town as she attended various business and civic functions.

It took just a handful of these obligatory dinners for Nick to decide that Miss Lexington 1959, a lovely young University of Kentucky student named Nina Warren, was the woman he wanted to spend the rest of his life with. He popped the question to Nina after "about the fifth or sixth of those chicken and peas dinners," and two months later, on August 13, 1959, Nina Bruce Warren became Mrs. Nick Clooney.

The new couple moved just as quickly in starting their family. Daughter Ada, named after Nick's grandmother Guilfoyle, was born in May 1960, and one year later, on May 6, 1961, George Timothy Clooney, named after Nick's favorite uncle, was born in Lexington.

Nick Clooney, determined that his children would enjoy a happier, more stable and secure childhood than he, Rosemary and Betty remembered, was still pursuing his newscasting career. That meant the possibility of long days and nights, and odd hours, away from the children, but Nick had a solution: he'd simply take Ada and George, two gorgeous, bright, outgoing children, with him to the studio. "I was determined that my kids wouldn't suffer the way that I and my sisters had suffered," Clooney said. "That's why I took them to work with me all the time. I couldn't stand to be away from them for any length of time."

Ensuring Ada and George grew up in a happier environment also necessitated financial security, but Nick's career, in the fickle world of broadcast journalism, would necessitate many changes of addresses, new schools and friends left behind for the Clooney kids. Taking his children to work with him assured Nick not only that the family that worked together stayed together, but also that the children would understand their father's work and not harbor resentment for the fact that it was going to mean a lot of upheaval in their lives.

By the time Ada and George started elementary school, both were veterans at hanging around radio and TV stations, holding cue cards, operating equipment and even feeding temperature info to their father when he was doing the nightly weather report. The kids would often don funny costumes and perform little song-and-dance numbers, sometimes accompanied by their mother. One of the children, however, had a special love of the spotlight.

Ada was content with passing out refreshments, greeting guests and helping dad and his crew behind the scenes. But like his great-uncle George, George Timothy was a big personality who was eager to share his charm and sense of humor with an audience. Whether it was belting out little songs and telling jokes to help warm up the crowd, chatting with the celebrities who would stop by Nick Clooney's shows or dressing up like a leprechaun at age five to entertain the audience in his on-camera TV debut, George Clooney had an obvious penchant for drawing the audience to him. He made a special impression on local advertisers, including a potato chip company that hired young George to pitch its products during the commercial breaks in Nick's shows. And, as with every born entertainer, George Clooney's first taste of applause only fed his appetite for more. Newsman Nick and beauty queen Nina had a budding superstar on their handswho was learning as he grew just how harsh the entertainment business could be.

Thanks to Rosemary's experiences, the Clooneys had seen firsthand the ups and downs of a career in Hollywood and the music industry. Nick Clooney faced his own trials on the local entertainment scene; despite his popularity with audiences and his colleagues, Nick rubbed some people the wrong way.

More specifically, some people rubbed him the wrong way, and he wasn't shy about letting them know it. Though his children had everything they needed growing up, Nick's frequent job changes meant the family could go from living in "a mansion to a trailer—literally a trailer," according to his son. That meant dinners out were also sometimes an indulgence, so it was exasperating to the Clooney kids when they'd have to leave a meal early, which they knew would happen if someone said something offensive in front of their dad.

"Going out to eat with my family and other families . . . we weren't wealthy at all, and shrimp cocktail was something you really looked forward to," Clooney would later tell an *Esquire* interviewer. "And just as the waiter put the shrimp cocktail in front of you, the man from the other family would say something like 'What's the matter with *those* people?' And my mom would immediately be telling us, 'Eat fast! East fast!' Because we all knew '*those* people' meant 'black people,' and my father was going to make a scene, and we'd all have to leave the restaurant."

Now, of course, Clooney is not only proud of his dad's stance but has adopted it himself, in both personal and professional life. Still, as a kid it could make things tough. It's not always easy for a ten-year-old who's leaving his friends behind and moving to a new school and a new home to understand that dad lost his job because he felt he had to stand up for what he believed in.

Nick had equally high expectations of his children when it came to doing what was right, however unpopular that might make them at the time. Certainly that unpopularity is something his son has become familiar with in recent years, with his outspoken stance against the Iraq War and the political right's responses to his viewpoints. He learned it first and foremost from Nick, who once chastised his son for not standing up for his classmates when the boy came home from school and told his dad that some of his fellow students had been making racist remarks. The ultimate lesson George Clooney took from these experiences, though, wasn't just that the entertainment industry could be a fickle place to make a living. He also learned from his dad that you could forge a career as a performer without compromising your principles, and without turning your back on your family and what meant most to you.

He'd learned from his aunt how not to handle fame. He'd learned from his father everything that would carry him through his career.

3

And He's Off

It was like Gulliver's Travels. *I would go from one school and be the idiot of all idiots and go to the next school and be a genius.*

—George Clooney

When George Clooney's grade school classmates describe him, the preteen Clooney doesn't sound so different from the high school Clooney, the early-career Clooney or, for that matter, the George Clooney of today.

Pals from his Cincinnati school days remember him as outgoing, committed to having fun, and possessing a skill for defusing a tension-filled situation with charm and humor. "One day in English, we were allowed to write a poem outside in the beautiful May weather," a classmate told the *Cincinnati Enquirer*. "After goofing off fifty of the fifty-five minutes, [George and I] realized we better come up with a poem fast. So, looking at the ground, we came up with the landmark poem 'Mud.' 'Mud is black and brown, and it never does frown.'"

Clooney, who had been diagnosed with dyslexia when he was eight years old and suffered a year-long bout of Bell's palsy when he was thirteen, was also the subject of bullies who like to pick on him because his dad was famous on local TV. The Bell's palsy, a condition that causes stroke-like symptoms, struck Clooney just as the family had settled in Augusta, Kentucky, a small town near Cincinnati where the Clooney kids would finish their high school years. But the disorder, which struck him one day as the family was dining out after Mass, left the whole left side of his face paralyzed. "I was convinced I had Lou Gehrig's disease," says Clooney, who had watched the Gehrig movie *Pride of the Yankees* with his father the week before the Bell's palsy attack.

Between the paralyzed face and kids who wanted to knock him down a peg simply because of who his father was, Clooney learned quickly to make the joke, especially the self-deprecating remark, before anyone else could. When he tried to drink out of the left side of his mouth, the beverage would spill out. So he did it often, getting the laugh on his terms.

After almost a year, the Bell's palsy had gone away, and Clooney's amiable ways had made him one of the most popular students at Augusta High. One of the faculty members told a reporter that Clooney, who had grown into a cute, boyish look that would carry him through to the more mature, manly, Sexiest Man Alive look of his thirties and forties, would walk home from school with girls lining the streets to watch him pass by. "Yeah, all twenty-two of them," Clooney laughs.

True, there were only twenty-three students in his graduating class, but Clooney was a popular athlete, beginning his lifelong love of basketball on the Augusta High squad, and feeling so confident in his skills as a member of the Augusta high school baseball team that he tried out as an outfielder with the Cincinnati Reds. "I only lacked skill," he says. "That was the only thing holding me back."

With hopes of a Major League Baseball career dashed, and no other immediate career goals in mind, the son of one of the area's best-known TV personalities followed his salutatorian finish at Augusta High (his then-girlfriend was the class valedictorian) by enrolling as a broadcast journalism major at Northern Kentucky University.

Clooney admits that his college days became more about sowing his oats after a fairly strict upbringing than about any academic pursuits. "I was there for three years, and I was a freshman when I left," Clooney told *Cosmopolitan*. "I was lousy at it. I partied a lot, got drunk a lot."

His experience at the Cincinnati-area university proved useful in a way, though: it eliminated yet another path, which, when you're not proactively pursuing one goal, can at least help you narrow down what you don't want. "I had studied broadcasting and was no good at it," he told *Playboy*. "My father had been an anchorman who was greatly respected. He was really good at what he did, and I wasn't nearly as good as my father. From the beginning I was being compared with him. It's the George W. Bush thing. So, if I wasn't going to do that, then what?"

As he continued to drift, attending classes for three years but accumulating few credits, Clooney worked odd jobs. He played DJ for a Cincy nightclub, sold women's shoes at a McAlpin's department store and even cut tobacco in a relative's tobacco fields. Then came a call from his cousin Miguel Ferrer, one of his Aunt Rosemary's sons.

It was summer 1982, and Miguel and his father, Oscar-winning actor José Ferrer, were shooting a movie in Lexington called *And They're Off*. Don't bother heading to the video store; the low-budget flick was never released, though it would be Clooney's unofficial movie debut. Miguel had invited him to spend the movie's four-month production schedule camping out in his hotel room, and the experience of hanging out on a movie set, and managing to nab a brief one-scene role in the flick, was all the future star needed to finally find his calling in the family business, show business. "I got a bit part and a couple of lines in a movie, and just decided this was really glamorous and exciting and I wanted to do it," Clooney said. "Miguel sort of said, 'Come out to Hollywood and be an actor.' Ignorance is pure bliss. I thought I would do it."

Nick Clooney, however, was not pleased. Having flirted briefly with a movie career during one trip to Hollywood in his single days, and having seen his sister barely live to tell her own cautionary tale about the industry, he felt his son's epiphany about his future was risky at best. "I said, 'Are you crazy, George?'" Nick told *US* magazine. "'You've been around this racket all your life. There are fifty thousand kids out there doing the same thing you are. Don't do it.' Of course, the moral is, always listen to your father."

It was, of course, an understandable stance for his dad to take, and as Clooney has stated throughout his career, luck, with many other factors, has played a big role in his Hollywood success. Given the family history in the industry, it was a reasonable parental concern that he was putting all his eggs in one basket and heading to Hollywood on a whim.

But Nick didn't know just how much his son had taken to heart all the lessons he'd taught him about standing up for what you believe in, working hard, and conducting your life and your business within a personal set of ethics. That, along with an idea that successfully maneuvering Hollywood might just boil down to doing the opposite of what his Aunt Rosemary had done, and a bit of the unshakeable confidence that had allowed him to be able to perform for an audience since he was a toddler, sparked Clooney's decision to head West. So after production on *And They're Off* wrapped, he went back to the tobacco fields to earn some cash, then headed to Los Angeles with $300 and the "Danger Car," a maroon Monte Carlo that was so far on the other side of its better days that Clooney was afraid to shut it off. He made the trip to La La Land in two days, stopping on the side of the road only long enough to catch brief naps while Danger Car idled.

4

And So It Begins . . .

There's this thing about guys that is attractive. There's no question about the fact that there wouldn't be wars if there weren't guys. So, we are stupid; there's no question about it. We do all the dumb things. But there's this thing we also do that I like. There's this camaraderie that I really do love.

—George Clooney

With Danger Car mercifully still running as he steered toward California in 1982, Clooney had already decided what his first stop would be: Aunt Rosemary's house in Beverly Hills.

Though his father hadn't given his blessing to his Hollywood plans, and Aunt Rosemary was still bitter enough about her own showbiz experiences to think his aspirations a bad idea, nephew George was allowed to camp out at Rosemary's house. The experience wasn't always a positive one. He has mostly glossed over that early time in Los Angeles in interviews throughout the years, but Rosemary and her family didn't always make Clooney feel welcome.

First, there was Danger Car. His aunt didn't like the view of the clunker in her driveway, and demanded Clooney ditch the auto. That meant riding to auditions and odd jobs on a ten-speed bicycle, not exactly a trendy mode of transportation for a guy trying to impress casting agents and studio execs.

And there was Rosemary's fragile relationship with her own children. The years of career and relationship ups and downs, plus her rampant drug use and mental health dramas, had alienated Rosemary Clooney from her children, and it wasn't until the late 1970s that she finally got her own demons under control and was well enough to try to forge new connections with her children. Her nephew's appearance on her doorstep, then, meant there was yet another family member who was fully aware of her past and living inside her home. George also may have been a reminder of his father, and of all the years Rosemary and her siblings had missed out on when they were separated as children.

While hitting the audition circuit and taking acting classes, Clooney also worked for a time as Tony Bennett's chauffeur, did odd jobs around his aunt's house, and, during one summer when Rosemary toured with fellow crooners Martha Raye, Helen O'Connell and Margaret Whiting, served as the ladies' chauffeur, driving them across country in Danger Car's last hurrah. But the job made Clooney feel that Rosemary was treating him more like an employee than a family member. George has mostly put a positive spin on his days at his aunt's house, but he has on rare occasion recalled some hurtful evenings when Rosemary's clan would leave him behind. "I will never really be over the sense of how humiliated I was at that time," Clooney said in *Premiere* magazine. "Humiliated in the sense that we would all be sitting around in the living room and they'd say, 'Okay, let's all go to dinner. George, you stay here.'" Adds Miguel Ferrer, "My mother has a way of offering hospitality, and it always ends badly. She'll open up her house and be very generous with the best of intentions. But then she'll get sick of having them around. Then it will end poorly, which is what happened with George."

In Rosemary's defense, there was also skepticism within the family about how seriously her nephew was taking his new vocation. "He ran pretty wild," she said. "I was on the road a lot, but I noticed he had dark circles under his eyes, and he was awful young for that."

Rosemary continued to note that her nephew was as committed to having a good time and enjoying the local scene in Los Angeles as he was to acting classes and auditions, and it didn't sit well with her. Clooney had spent a year living in her home, and, quite simply, he'd overstayed his welcome. It was agreed then that Nick's son, who still hadn't managed to find steady acting jobs yet, would take up residence elsewhere.

And that's when one of The Boys came to the rescue.

The Boys, as any devoted George Clooney fan knows, are the most famous group of celebrity pals in Hollywood. Mark Wahlberg's entourage may have inspired an HBO series, but it's Clooney's Boys, a group that has outlasted every broken relationship, failed marriage, family death and career crisis each of its individual members has endured, who, aside from Clooney's father, mother and sister, have provided his most enduring relationships.

It was in his salad days in Hollywood that Clooney and The Boys formed their bond. Most of The Boys were aspiring actors back in the early '80s, and met in acting classes, when the most famous among them was Clooney. Grant Heslov, a character actor who most recently starred in the Showtime terrorist drama *Sleeper Cell*, lent Clooney $100 for his first set of head shots, and is now Clooney's partner in Smoke House Productions and his cowriter on the *Good Night, and Good Luck* script. Ben Weiss, now a TV director, was introduced to Clooney by Miguel Ferrer, and gave his new Kentucky pal his first insider's tour of Hollywood. Richard Kind, a veteran TV actor who's starred on *Spin City* and *Mad About You*, costarred with Clooney in one of his many short-lived TV shows, *The Bennett Brothers*, and would eventually provide a home for Clooney during his painful divorce from actress Talia Balsam. Actors Matt Adler and Tommy Hinkley met Clooney playing basketball, Waldo Sanchez became his personal hairstylist, and actor Thom Mathews, now a construction company owner, gave the struggling

Clooney a place to crash, and hence a way to stay in Los Angeles, after Aunt Rosemary told him to skedaddle.

His modest digs at Chez Mathews? A closet. But to hear Mathews tell it, his friend made the most of his boxy homestead. "I could never understand how he got girls in that closet with him," Mathews told *US*. "What could he possibly say to get them in there?" George, like his father, was always a gifted talker.

Clooney never overlooked Mathews' loyalty to him, contributing to the household bills with every acting job he landed while living, literally, in the closet, and since that time repeatedly referring to Mathews as his very best friend because of the kindness his pal showed to him when he needed it the most.

Any story told by one of The Boys, in fact, will end with a testament to their pal's loyalty and enduring friendship.

Richard Kind, who by all accounts is not only one of the nicest of The Boys, but also, not coincidentally, most often on the receiving end of Clooney's much-storied elaborate practical jokes, was also on the receiving end of one of Clooney's most thoughtful acts of friendship. When Kind's father, a New Jersey jeweler, died in 1998, he headed back to the East Coast alone. The Boys, all busy with work, were assembled by Clooney, who chartered a private jet to fly the gang to Trenton. Kind was unaware his pals were in attendance when he stood up at the synagogue to talk about his beloved father, but when he looked at the back of the room he saw the faces of all seven Boys looking back at him.

"Richard was in the middle of talking about his father, and he looked up, having no idea, and saw his seven best friends sitting in the back row in black suits," Clooney says. "And he broke down and he stopped, then he said, 'My best friends are here.' Those are the moments you're so proud of, so proud to be a part of it."

5

Hangin' with Mrs. Garrett

One day I decided to audition the way I played baseball. I decided to go in and read for parts not like "I hope, I hope, I hope I get the part," but like I was the best thing that ever happened to them. I mean, I figured they didn't want me to fail. They wanted me to be the guy, right? So I started acting like I was the best actor they'd ever seen. And I started getting parts.

—George Clooney

Having observed his father and Aunt Rosemary's experiences in show business, Clooney made a decision during his first years in Hollywood that would not only set him apart from many of his fellow actors, but would also be one of the touchstones of his enduring success. He came to understand that acting talent alone is not enough to forge a long run in Hollywood. The movie business is, above all else, a business. That Clooney has been willing and able to act as a shrewd businessman on his own behalf, particularly while successfully maintaining the personal ethics under which he chooses to operate, is as much a badge of honor as his Oscar statue.

His first professional job after leaving his Aunt Rosemary's house for the decidedly less luxurious comfort of Thom Mathews' closet was a Japanese commercial for Panasonic. After going to audition after audition, lining up with, as his father had predicted, hundreds and sometimes thousands of other "kids" all trying to make it big, Clooney realized he had to do something to make himself stand out. So he showed up at the Panasonic audition with a six-pack of Sapporo beer, asking if anyone was thirsty—and that, he's sure, is what got him the Panasonic job. Casting directors noticed his charm and his swagger, and appreciated that he had done something to set himself apart from the pack. After all, just how much Oscar-caliber acting skill does one need to display to land a spot hawking stereos? Clooney had figured out something very important about what would get him noticed, and once he cemented that as part of his business plans, he was truly on his way.

"Actors go into auditions thinking, 'Oh God, they're going to hate me, they're going to hate me.' I started to come in selling confidence, not even my acting skills," he told *Playboy*. "The best actor never gets the job when they audition. Never. Especially in television. The guy who gets the job is somebody who comes in and delivers every day . . . So I just changed my attitude. I thought, 'From here on out, I cannot lose a job. I'll do whatever it takes.' So I'd come in with a dog under my arm for some scene. I'd pull a champagne bottle and phone out of my jacket and do the scene. People were like, 'What the fuck is that?' I just thought, 'Fuck it. It's *where* I'm going to hit the ball, not *if* I'm going to hit it.'"

As he began to book commercials and TV guest spots, and even after he had a few recurring roles on series like *Roseanne* and *The Facts of Life,* as well as starring roles in a couple of failed TV pilots, Clooney continued to audition with gusto. During one tryout for a movie role as a punk rocker, he ripped off his shirt to reveal the name of the punk band, drawn in a temporary tattoo, on his chest. He once auditioned for the casting director of ABC by showing up with five pals, including Grant Heslov, who, upon Clooney's cue, brought parts of a bunk bed onto the stage and helped his friend assemble it, followed by Clooney and Heslov reenacting a scene from the Neil Simon play *Brighton Beach Memoirs*. Clooney was signed to a four-month contract at ABC.

Even his unsuccessful auditions proved to be unforgettable. While reading for a role in Francis Ford Coppola's 1992 thriller *Dracula*, Clooney decided he would distinguish himself by speaking in a thick Kentucky hillbilly accent. "This goddamn Dracula thing's comin' in here, comin' down this here slide and blowin' up like a ball-a-fire!" is how he laughingly recalled the audition in *Esquire*. He didn't get the job, but he did make an impression on Coppola. The Oscar-winning director later called Clooney's agent and asked if the actor had mental issues.

Of course, bravado alone wasn't enough to project his career forward. After all, thousands of *American Idol* wannabes have tried outrageous stunts and gimmicks to get themselves noticed and tapped for one of the show's coveted golden tickets to Hollywood, only to be humiliated when told that no such exploits can make up for a lack of basic talent. Clooney wasn't relying on his charm, confidence and good looks to get jobs. He *was* relying on them to show casting agents, producers and directors that he was someone who understood the business, knew that hard work and dedication were valued, and was willing to make those efforts to get his foot in the door. In short, his sometimes over-the-top auditions got him noticed, which helped him build a reputation, which began to help him land more and more jobs.

His first TV series job, playing a bad guy named Lenny Colwell who held three young women hostage during a 1984 guest spot on the NBC private investigator series *Riptide*, earned him his Screen Actors Guild card. He booked the job himself, calling up casting directors and pretending to be an agent representing . . . George Clooney.

His meticulously plotted maneuvering through the TV industry continued to yield work as Clooney landed more guest spots, and, during the 1984 fall season, his first job as a series regular on a Chicago emergency room show called *E/R*. Not that *ER*; this one was a half-hour comedy starring Elliott Gould as an emergency room doctor, a pre-

Seinfeld Jason Alexander as a hospital administrator, and a brash, cocky George Clooney as a brash, cocky young emergency room intern named Ace. Clooney was hired for the medical sitcom by the casting director who'd hired him earlier in the year for the cheesy movie sequel *Grizzly II*, a horror story about a killer bear. He costarred with Laura Dern and Charlie Sheen, but the movie was never released into theaters. The casting director remembered him for *E/R*, however, and though the show lasted less than a season, it cemented Clooney as an actor who would not go unemployed in TV land for years to come.

6

I'll Do It My Way

There comes a point where you go, "I've got to draw the line; this shit, I will not eat."

—George Clooney

To be a steadily employed actor in Hollywood, in films or in television, is no small thing. But George Clooney hadn't traveled all the way to Hollywood with his last $300 to do guest gigs on *Golden Girls* and *Murder, She Wrote*. While he could boast that he was beginning to forge a real career as a working actor, something that would at least show his father that his move to California hadn't been the worst decision he could ever make, Clooney had come to Hollywood with plans for major stardom. *E/R* was a start, but *ER* would prove to be ten fruitful, yet frustrating years away.

The actor quickly followed the canceled *E/R* with a recurring spot on *The Facts of Life*, playing George Burnett, the brash, cocky (yet again) handyman who helped Mrs. Garrett, Tootie, Natalie, Blair and Jo reopen Mrs. G's burned-down bakery as a gift shop during the show's 1985 season. Clooney was again using his natural charm and good looks, as well as his carefully crafted air of bold self-confidence, to play the part, but as the only adult male cast member of the long-running sitcom, he was mostly relegated to being the girls' straight man and providing a bit of eye candy. A season and a half was enough for him; he quit, hoping he'd be on to bigger roles.

One interesting footnote to Clooney's *Facts of Life* experience: Paul Haggis, who would go on to win a screenwriting Oscar for the movie *Crash* the same year Clooney won his Oscar for *Syriana*, was a writer on *The Facts of Life*, and was credited as the script supervisor on the episode that introduced George Burnett to the action.

Next up: a recurring role on *Roseanne*, where Clooney was Booker Brooks, Roseanne's brash, cocky boss and the swaggering love interest of her sister, Jackie. Creatively, the show was indeed a step up from the aging *Facts of Life*, but Clooney found himself once again playing "seventh banana," by his estimation, to a very talented cast of comedy actors.

The show's set was also notoriously tension-filled, thanks to the constant creative tussles between star Roseanne Barr and producer Matt Williams, and though Clooney never had the chance to do much with his supporting role, he did begin to cultivate his set persona, that of a jovial, prank-prone charmer who could lighten the mood and endear himself to even the toughest leading lady. "She was hysterical," he says of Roseanne. "She was the foulest woman I'd ever met . . . and I thought I was foul." Even when he quit *Roseanne* after the first season, the jokester was rumored to have left the cast and crew with a naughty little memento to keep them laughing in his absence: a photo, snapped by John Goodman, who played Roseanne's husband on the show, of Clooney's genitals, "disguised" by a pair of Groucho Marx glasses. The actor has denied such a raunchy pic exists, though he admits that "The Face," as he calls the Groucho glasses-over-the-genitals bit, is one of his favorite gags. Roseanne herself, meanwhile, has confirmed that the Polaroid hung on the set refrigerator for years before mysteriously disappearing one day.

Good cheer among his coworkers, and the fact that he'd clocked some time on the number one show on television (*Roseanne* finished its first year tied with *The Cosby Show* as the season's ratings champ) aside, Clooney was unhappy with the path his career was taking. Though he'd impressed more than one network executive while racking up guest spot credits on *The Golden Girls*, *Hunter*, *Hotel*, *Crazy Like a Fox* and *Murder, She Wrote*, convincing them of his potential to be the next big TV breakout, this apparent success led to another kind of problem.

Clooney costarred with pal Richard Kind in *Bennett Brothers*, a 1987 NBC sitcom about two completely opposite brothers who share an apartment. *Sunset Beat*, an ABC drama pilot in 1990, starred Clooney as Chic Chesbro, the leader of a group of cool Los Angeles cops who go undercover as bikers. Also in 1990, he costarred in the sitcom *Knights of the Kitchen Table*, a flashback-heavy series about a *Friends*-ly group of lifelong pals, including a sole female who would have been one of primetime's first lesbian characters had the show ever made it past the pilot stage. And *Rewrite for Murder* paired Clooney with *Mork & Mindy* star Pam Dawber in a 1991 CBS romance/mystery dramedy that failed to connect with any romantic chemistry between the leads.

But none of the pilots went to series, and Clooney was becoming frustrated. He certainly didn't lack for opportunities; he would star in fifteen failed pilots before landing *ER*. "It's very easy to sit in a room at twenty-three and have everyone go, 'You're the greatest,' and believe it," he told *Vanity Fair*. "Which I think I did for a minute, to be quite honest. I thought I was pretty happening because I had good TV hair."

So why did none of Clooney's pilots make it beyond the one-episode stage? Were they all really that bad? The answer, since most of them have never been seen by the public, is probably yes, though there are many reasons pilots flop. Every year the networks pump millions of dollars into developing a wide range of ideas into pilot episodes, many—actually, most—of which never make it beyond that one episode, no matter how big the stars, producers, directors, writers or development checks attached. But sometimes a pilot doesn't score well with test audiences, sometimes execs determine the show will be too expensive to produce on a weekly basis, sometimes cast members don't have good chemistry with each other and sometimes the material's just not substantial enough to continue beyond a pilot.

Clooney has also pointed out that, appearance-wise, he wasn't exactly in line for the Sexiest Man Alive honors he'd "win" later in his career. The late '80s model George Clooney was ganglier, more boyish, less handsome than the salt-and-pepper-haired epitome of retro, Cary Grant–esque cool who wears a tuxedo like few others can today. Late-'80s Clooney sported a long, wild mane of dark hair and a black leather motorcycle jacket that must have gotten him mistaken for any number of the hair band rock stars who hung out on Sunset Boulevard in the 1980s. "At thirty-one, I still looked like a young man," he says. "Now, though I'm only two years older than Brad Pitt, I look a lot older, which used to greatly frustrate me. It doesn't anymore. As I got older, I saw that it separated me from [movie role rivals] Tom Cruise and Brad . . . I could be in my own category."

Clooney also landed a few movie parts during this pre-*ER* stretch, all in films worth renting years later only for the chance to see the eventual Oscar winner in some embarrassing action flicks. Consider 1987's *Return to Horror High* and 1988's *Return of the Killer Tomatoes* (in which pizza delivery man George actually delivers the camp classic line "That's the bravest thing I've ever seen a vegetable do!"). Packaged with *Grizzly II* (later renamed *Predator: The Concert*), *Return to Horror High* and *Return of the Killer Tomatoes* would make a great DVD box set showing how George Clooney could have become the king of cheesy horror movie sequels, however dubious a title that might have been.

All was not well in Clooney's personal life, either. Never one to have any problems getting dates—as Thom Mathews pointed out, his friend was so smooth he managed to convince women to visit him in his closet home in Mathews' apartment—the last half of Clooney's twenties was marked by a pair of life-changing, longer-term relationships.

First, in the span of less than a month in 1988, Clooney met, fell in love with and began living with actress Kelly Preston. The pair met at a party thrown by their talent agency, and, later that night, "George gave me a ride on his Harley and I was hooked," Preston would tell *People* magazine. Three weeks later, the new couple bought a $1 million house together in the Hollywood Hills.

Because they were two young talents on the verge (two very attractive talents at that), *People* editors were only too happy to feature Clooney and Preston in a lavish, photograph-dotted spread, in which the actors declared their love for each other, with the actress telling the magazine that, career aspirations aside, she was happiest at home cooking for her love, while Clooney asserted that he too was happiest at home, making his own furniture and restoring old cars. For a brief time, that might have been true, but the lovers would soon find that the relationship was doomed to end as precipitately as it had begun.

Clooney was still trying to find a satisfying role in a TV show that would propel him into a movie career, and no such role seemed to be forthcoming. Preston, meanwhile, had landed a major role opposite Arnold Schwarzenegger (Clooney's future *Batman & Robin* costar) in the big-screen comedy *Twins*, bringing her career to an all-time high. While she was off in New Mexico filming *Twins*, and he was stuck in Los Angeles, filming *Roseanne* and quickly realizing that the show would be yet another resume blip that wasn't going to advance his position in Hollywood.

In addition, both stars were on the rebound. Preston had split from her husband of about a year, actor Kevin Gage, not long before the fateful agency party where she met Clooney. Clooney, meanwhile, was still nursing a broken heart over the woman who was going to be the source of even more pain down the road.

Clooney and actress Talia Balsam met while costarring in a play in 1984. Though Balsam, the daughter of Oscar-winning film actor (*A Thousand Clowns*) and *Archie Bunker's Place* costar Martin Balsam, was dating another guy when she and Clooney met, that relationship would soon fizzle and Clooney, having developed real feelings for the actress, began pursuing her. The two dated for more than a year and a half before breaking up. While Balsam concentrated on pursuing her career in the theater, Clooney continued to seek that one career-making role. But the actor had called Balsam the first woman he'd ever truly been in love with, and pals recalled that he was hurt by the split.

As a rebound relationship, then, the Preston/Clooney pairing was probably doomed from the beginning. "I was living with someone and felt sort of cornered," he later told *Playboy*. "I was on a show [*Roseanne*] that wasn't much fun . . . I had a bleeding ulcer. I was in a house I couldn't afford."

Less than six months after the *People* magazine feature declared they were in love, Clooney and Preston were kaput, with him ending the relationship in the middle of a movie theater at Universal Studios. He was left with an ulcer, the expensive house and custody of Max, the potbellied pig he'd originally bought as a gift for Preston.

Fortunately for both stars, they seemed to deal with their split well. They broke up in the summer of 1989, and by the end of the year Preston was engaged to Clooney's *Grizzly II* costar Charlie Sheen, whom she'd eventually leave to marry John Travolta. Also by the end of 1989, Clooney would find a rebound from his rebound, and it was the woman he had first rebounded from: Talia Balsam.

He and Balsam had renewed their friendship after his breakup with Preston, and, having let Balsam get away a few years earlier, Clooney was not going to make the same mistake again. So the couple packed themselves, Balsam's mom (actress Joyce Van Patten) and a few friends into Clooney's Winnebego and headed off to, where else, Las Vegas. "I had gotten out of a relationship that wasn't going very well and married the one girl I truly loved and had loved for years," Clooney said.

The wedding took place in one of Vegas's infamous quickie wedding chapels, complete with an Elvis impersonator performing the ceremony and an obligatory Carpenters ballad playing in the background.

The corny ceremony, followed by a wedding night that found the groom whiling away the hours gambling in a casino, would prove to be an inauspicious start to the new marriage.

After the Vegas trip, the couple headed back to Los Angeles, to the house Clooney still couldn't afford, and to the pet pig that was going to have to get used to a new lady of the house (and vice versa). Clooney was also heading back to a career that was going to get worse before it got better.

With *Roseanne* behind him, he jumped back into the TV pilot fray, again with little success. But one experience was going to prove particularly life-changing for the actor.

In 1990, Clooney was cast opposite *Newhart* star Julia Duffy in *Baby Talk*, an ABC sitcom that was a small-screen adaptation of the big-screen hit *Look Who's Talking* (which, proving just how small a world the Hollywood community is, starred John Travolta, the future husband of Clooney's former love, Kelly Preston). Clooney was, in fact, playing the TV version of Travolta as Joe, a handyman who would become involved with single mom Maggie (Duffy). The show, unsurprisingly, put Clooney in yet another role where he could mug, swagger and charm his way through, without even the slightest chance to stretch his acting muscles at all.

It would, however, give him the chance to prove he wasn't willing to do anything, or remain silent about any treatment he felt unjust, for the chance of becoming famous.

Clooney had originally been cast to star in *Baby Talk* opposite *Hotel* star Connie Selleca, who was replaced by Duffy before the show even hit the airwaves. Producer Ed Weinberger, who'd won multiple Emmys as a writer and producer on classic sitcoms like *The Mary Tyler Moore Show*, *Taxi* and *The Cosby Show*, felt Clooney would have better chemistry with Duffy, so Selleca was dismissed. Even the first set of babies who were to star as the titular wisecracking infant weren't up to par in Weinberger's book, and he replaced them, too.

But the problem, in Clooney's mind, wasn't so much the cast changes as the way Weinberger went about making them. In fact, Clooney claimed, Weinberger treated everyone in a harsh, dismissive, disrespectful manner. Given the actor's penchant for equal treatment for everyone on the set, heads were bound to butt.

It was another personal loss that would finally push Clooney over the edge with Weinberger. Clooney's great-uncle George Guilfoyle, his father's favorite uncle, for whom Clooney had been named, had been very ill. Once a dashing man with a bright future ahead of him, a charming storyteller who was a favorite relative of many youngsters in the Clooney clan, Guilfoyle had spent decades smoking, boozing and carousing, and at sixty-eight, it was catching up with him. Clooney returned to Cincinnati in July 1990, where his Uncle George had been admitted to the Veterans Hospital. It was the last time he would see this great figure in his life. George Guilfoyle died on July 25, 1990, with his great-nephew holding his hand. Clooney was there when his uncle said his last words: "What a waste."

"[He] was a bomber pilot at twenty-two who flew fifteen missions over Germany in the war," Clooney said in an interview. "He was an all-star basketball player, a good-looking, witty guy who dated Miss America. He was on fire with life. . . . But I didn't know him then. I knew him when he was a man who trained horses, became a drunk and slept in a barn. He was a guy who never lived up to his potential."

"As he was dying, I held his hand. He kept saying, 'What a waste,' because he was a sixty-five-year-old guy who had so much promise and didn't do anything with it," Clooney told *USA Weekend*. "I thought: 'The only thing I won't allow myself to do is wake up at sixty-five and go, 'What a waste.' If I get hit by a bus now, everybody will go, 'Well, he jammed a lot in.'"

Back in Los Angeles, *Baby Talk* was finally ready for its prime-time debut, but Clooney had had enough of what he considered to be Ed Weinberger's callous treatment of anyone below him on the food chain.

LEFT: It's in the genes: George Clooney's father, Nick, hosted a short-lived ABC game show called *The Money Maze*, but has been a local news and TV host celebrity in the Ohio and Kentucky area for years.

RIGHT: George Clooney, shortly after anding in Hollywood in 1982. He hadn't yet grown into his Sexiest Man Alive face, but his goofy charm helped him land eading roles in more than a dozen (failed) TV pilots.

Above: You take the good, you take the bad, you take them both and there you have . . . Clooney's first notable TV role, playing hunky handyman George Burnett on *The Facts of Life*, costarring (left to right) Mindy Cohn and Nancy McKeon.

Right: Clooney with a young costar on *Baby Talk*, the 1991–92 ABC sitcom that's most notable for the on-set clash the actor had with producer Ed Weinberger. Clooney quit the show after the tiff, and claims Weinberger told him his career would be irreparably damaged. Instead, Clooney's confidence was boosted when other industry types who'd butted heads with Weinberger offered him work after hearing about the *Baby Talk* incident.

He quit after one season, but Clooney's role as *Sisters*' sexy Detective James Falconer, particularly his chemistry with on-screen love interest Sela Ward, was the breakout role that eventually led him to *ER*. Actor Mark Franken is on the right.

LEFT: The role that launched a superstar: George Clooney as Dr. Doug Ross, *ER*'s sexy pediatrician. His performances would go on to earn two Emmy nominations, three Golden Globe nominations, a *People* magazine Sexiest Man Alive title and tens of thousands of fan letters that poured into NBC and Warner Bros. TV each week.

RIGHT: Clooney wisely deduced that having his character involved in a romance would insure job security, so he talked producers into keeping Julianna Margulies' Nurse Carol Hathaway on the show. She was originally scheduled to die before the end of *ER*'s fast-paced 1994 premiere episode.

Though Clooney was, inarguably, *ER*'s breakout cast member, he's the first to point out that the wildly popular drama was a success because of the entire ensemble, including (left to right) Sherry Stringfield, Anthony Edwards, Noah Wyle, Julianna Margulies, Clooney and Eriq La Salle.

LEFT: During *ER*'s first season, Clooney landed a guest role for his aunt Rosemary Clooney, paying her back for allowing him to bunk at her house when he moved to Hollywood in 1982. Rosemary's appearance, as Alzheimer's patient Mary Cavanaugh, earned an Emmy nomination.

BELOW: Quentin Tarantino and George Clooney as brothers Richie and Seth Gecko in director Robert Rodriguez's *From Dusk Till Dawn*. The first movie Clooney landed after *ER*'s runaway debut garnered mixed reviews but earned praise for Clooney, who dubbed the violent vampire flick a "horr-action" movie.

'Well, I killed that franchise," Clooney joked about his role as the Caped Crusader in Joel
chumacher's campy comic book romp *Batman & Robin*. The 1997 flick, which costarred Chris
O'Donnell, Uma Thurman, Alicia Silverstone and Arnold Schwarzenegger, was such a critical and
commercial failure that it would take Warner Bros. another eight years to restart the Batman movie
ranchise.

ABOVE: Clooney had signed on to star in the superhero movie *The Green Hornet* when *ER* producer Steven Spielberg decided he wanted him to star in his first DreamWorks movie, 1997's *The Peacemaker*, instead. During production of the action flick, Clooney spent his down time playing basketball with costar Nicole Kidman's then-husband, Tom Cruise, but that didn't stop tabloids from later floating stories of an alleged Clooney/Kidman affair.

BELOW: "He's incredibly handsome, and we were taken with each other immediately," Clooney's *Out of Sight* costar Jennifer Lopez said. The movie, which features Clooney's sexiest performance, also sparked his friendship and Section Eight production company partnership with Steven Soderbergh.

One day it all exploded, after, Clooney says, Weinberger fired an actress without telling her directly. She found out she'd been axed when her replacement arrived on the set. Outraged at the director's lack of consideration, Clooney told Weinberger exactly what he thought of him and his lack of respect for those around him.

"Ed, that's enough. You don't pull that shit," Clooney recalled saying to Weinberger. A shouting match continued, and though Weinberger would downplay the whole scenario years later (telling *Vanity Fair* in 1996, "I was unhappy with him. He was unhappy with me. I released him early from his contract"), Clooney felt then, and still feels today, that his next move was ultimately responsible for all the career success that followed. He quit *Baby Talk*, walking off the set after his public blowup with Weinberger.

"To this day, I think that's when I grew up," Clooney says. "I believed I was ending my career. . . . I was living in a house I couldn't really afford. There were things going wrong. I had a bleeding ulcer, and I was putting on weight. Everything was kind of colliding at once. And I thought, 'If I am a man, if I'm a guy, I have to draw a line here.' And from that point on, I was fearless."

Within days, the story of Clooney's verbal skirmish with Weinberger had spread around Hollywood, and the reaction was a pleasant surprise for Clooney. The actor had fully expected that Weinberger would make good on his threat that Clooney would never work in Hollywood again after walking off the set. "What Ed lacked in couth, he made up for in pure anger," the star told a *Movieline* interviewer. "It was the first time I ever thought of doing something else with my life. When I quit [*Baby Talk*], I thought I'd be fired for good. But the minute I stood up to this guy, who was a jerk, things changed. Actors always come from a place of fear that they're never going to work again . . . The truth is the opposite. Suddenly, I could make ballsy decisions, take falls."

Others around town, Clooney would quickly learn, had been on the receiving end of Weinberger's gruff treatment, too, and were impressed that someone, especially someone in the actor's precarious position, had stood up to him. Within days of bolting the *Baby Talk* set, Clooney was called by another Emmy-winning TV producer and writer, Gary David Goldberg, and offered a choice role in the *Knights of the Kitchen Table* pilot, no audition necessary. "I asked them why they were doing this, and they said for the simple reason that it would be fun for them to do that to Ed Weinberger," Clooney recalls. "So that was fun."

In quick succession, he landed an audition for a role in Quentin Tarantino's *Reservoir Dogs*, which he didn't book, but which put him on the up-and-coming director's radar for another movie a few years later. He also filmed a small but notorious role in *The Harvest*, a thriller starring his cousin Miguel Ferrer. Clooney signed on as a favor to Miguel, but the part required him to lip synch to the Belinda Carlisle pop classic "Heaven Is a Place on Earth," while dressed in a wig and gold bra. Clooney's scene would become a fan favorite and an embarrassing bit of video for the TV tabloid shows to run amok with once Clooney became a household name.

He also filmed a cameo for pal Bonnie Hunt's failed sitcom pilot *The Building*, flying to Los Angeles (he was in New York filming the 1993 made-for-TV movie *Without Warning: Terror in the Towers*) on his own dime to support Hunt. "He's the guy who takes care of everything, leads the pack, includes [everyone] in his success," Hunt says. "Success would be horrible for him without his friends around."

And then he joined a TV series that would prove to be the highlight of his pre-*ER* resume: a recurring role on *Sisters*, playing Detective James Falconer, the love interest of the drama's bad girl, Teddy (Sela Ward). *Sisters* was an intense family drama, and finally Clooney was not only surrounded by talented actors but also playing a meaty role himself—one that required more subtle, nuanced performances than the glut of light fare that kept him employed but running in place. Falconer was a detective and recovering alcoholic who met fellow alcoholic Teddy when her daughter was raped at college. After the ensuing trial, the detective and Teddy kept in touch and began dating, becoming a viewer-favorite couple thanks to some intense chemistry between Clooney and Sela Ward.

He stayed with the show from 1993–94. Though Falconer was still a supporting character to the strong female cast, his troubled history gave Clooney a real chance to shine. Falconer came into the relationship with Teddy with a divorce under his belt. His marriage had fallen apart, viewers would eventually learn, because neither he nor his wife could deal with the death of their son, who'd accidentally shot himself with Falconer's gun while the detective was sleeping.

The story line was enough to grab viewers' attention and earn the actor a steady stream of fan mail at the NBC offices, particularly, and in no big surprise, from female viewers.

The show wasn't, however, his cup of tea, and after one season Clooney felt he'd gotten everything he could from being a part of the show. When he left, he forfeited the opportunity to entertain any second thoughts; *Sisters* writers took Falconer out of play permanently, killing him off in a tragic car explosion after he and Teddy had finally tied the knot and begun to settle into a happy married life.

Still, on the brink of the next phase of his career and personal life, Clooney appreciated what a break *Sisters* had been. And the lesson he'd learned from his *Baby Talk* experience with Ed Weinberger had given him the freedom to finally make a serious push for the career he wanted, and to take it to a level beyond second banana status.

7

Hits and a Missus

If I get hit by a truck tomorrow, everybody would go, "Crammed a lot into forty years."

—George Clooney

On a personal level, things were still not going well for Clooney. For all the years of speculation about whether or not the two-time *People* magazine Sexiest Man Alive will ever get married and have children, the fact is that he was married once. And it didn't go so well.

Whether because he married someone he'd broken up with years earlier, or because he did so less than a year after breaking up with a live-in lover, or because his wedding plans involved little more than steering a Winnebego toward Vegas, or because he spent his wedding night gambling in a casino, the marriage didn't start off on the right foot, and it only went downhill from there.

Clooney has spoken many times through the years about the cause of the marital breakup, taking most of the blame for the split. Maturity, or lack thereof, was the culprit.

"[It's not that] I didn't love and adore the woman I married. We'd gone out for a long time, off and on, but what I really wasn't prepared for was the idea that if things start going really badly, you actually need to work them out," he said in *Esquire*. "I was twenty-eight years old. I wasn't as tolerant as I should have been, and I wasn't as willing to fix things as I should have been."

There's also the matter of his friends, The Boys. Quite frankly, Clooney preferred their company. And he preferred the single life, to be able to come and go as he pleased, without having to answer to or take into consideration someone else's wants and needs. Because he is one of Hollywood's most beloved, handsome leading men, and one of the most eligible bachelors worldwide, fans doubt his repeated assertions that he has no plans to marry, that he's just not the marrying type. Who doesn't want to find the love of his life and live happily ever after, after all? What man, especially one as life-loving and successful as George Clooney, wouldn't want a wife and children to share his life with? The answer, of course, is George Clooney. The public and the media's tendency to pooh-pooh Clooney's claim that he'll never marry (or more accurately, that he'll never remarry) is more about us than about him. He's been there, done that, as he's often said—and, like his namesake, Uncle George, George Clooney truly may not be the marrying kind.

His work is his life, and his friends are his family. "The great thing I have in my life is all these friends who are family, who've been family for twenty-five years now," he says. "The same group of guys that won't allow me to get away with anything. They don't care where I get my employment. They all have their own jobs and their own lives and their own families. But every Sunday we watch a movie, play basketball, the families come over, or we might travel together. We work very hard at it. I've worked harder at that than I did at my marriage."

Pal Richard Kind once told an interviewer that "George is not the sort of person to play by other people's rules. And marriage is all about that." Added friend Matt Adler, "I think he really made an effort in [the marriage], and it really hurt him that it didn't work out. And he'll tell you, he wasn't very good at being a husband."

The fact that The Boys have so much insight into Clooney's feelings on the subject adds heft to the notion that, as Balsam has confirmed, he spent much more time with his friends than he did with her. And when his career continued to move along at a much slower clip than he would have liked, specifically when things became so contentious on the *Baby Talk* set, his work problems carried over to home. Home was no longer a refuge from the outside world; instead, it was part of the problem.

And when his Uncle George passed away, Clooney's plan for the future crystallized.

While many people would have assumed that Uncle George's last words—"What a waste"—were his summation of a life spent pursuing a good time, but ending with no wife or children by his side, his nephew didn't see it that way. To him, it meant Uncle George felt he hadn't pursued his dreams as vigorously as he would have liked. It meant he was dying with very little to show for the years he'd been on this planet. And it steeled Clooney's resolve that he wouldn't make the same mistake. That meant what wasn't working was out: bad scripts and unfulfilling career prospects wouldn't be tolerated anymore. He would fix them, and concentrate his efforts on getting the kinds of roles he wanted, and those that would move his career forward.

His marriage also wasn't working, but, by his own admission, he wasn't willing to work on it. So there was only one solution: divorce. After a period of separation, Clooney and Balsam went through a messy court split, with the actor particularly bitter about the legal cost of extricating himself the marriage. "I would say to Talia, 'You tell me how much. What you think is fair. I won't negotiate,'" he said of the tedious and painful procedures of divvying up the marital assets. "Instead, I paid $80,000 in lawyers fees, and that makes me crazy."

Now sans home and minus a big chunk of change, Clooney looked to The Boys for comfort and a roof over his head. He spent several months taking up residence in pal Richard Kind's spare bedroom. Later, when the actor bought the eight-bedroom, two-story Tudor house in the Hollywood Hills that would come to be known as "Casa de Clooney" (complete with a homemade wooden sign announcing the moniker in front), he became the host for all future divorce refugees amongst The Boys. Pal Tommy Hinkley even gave him a dragon statue that sits on the mantel in the Casa de Clooney living room, holding the wedding bands of The Boys' failed marriages.

With The Boys, his Los Angeles family, seeing him through the day-to-day pain of the marriage breakup, Nick and Nina Clooney did their best to support their son, too, never chastising him for the divorce, though they both liked their daughter-in-law very much.

"Talia is a lovely girl," Nick Clooney told an interviewer. "But they probably shouldn't have got married while George's career was on the verge of such a white-hot period. In truth, neither of them was to blame. There was just too much going on in their lives to give marriage the effort it needs. They both wound up getting hurt, which is really too bad."

Clooney was especially appreciative of his parents' reaction, because he so regretted not having made his marriage work despite their fine example. He was also thrilled when, as Nick told *People* magazine, his father decided his son's tough times called for a very special Christmas gift to be delivered to him that year. "George always coveted my '59 Corvette, which I bought to court my wife," Nick recalled. "He always wanted to drive it, and I was reluctant to let him . . . it was a bone of contention throughout his adolescent years. [After the breakup], when things were not going well for him, I had the car refurbished and sent out to California. George said it was the best Christmas he ever had, and he thought it was going to be the worst. He still drives it once a week. It's his connection to family and home."

Meanwhile, as he continued to nurse his personal wounds—which often meant hearty rounds of basketball and beer with The Boys—Clooney also refocused his career plans. Though it had only taken him a year to really get his acting career off the ground after he hit Hollywood in 1982, and though many in the industry considered him to be perpetually on the brink of breaking out, he was only growing more and more unsatisfied with each new role. When a job on a quality series like *Sisters* increased his exposure to network execs and the viewing audience, Clooney was appreciative of the opportunity and the employment, but frustrated by where he didn't see it leading.

The truth was, Clooney had his heart set on a movie career. While he was mindful that actors he admired, like Clint Eastwood, Warren Beatty and Bruce Willis, had started their careers with small-screen roles, he felt like he was stuck in TV land, and was still missing out on the plum roles among the TV offerings. He still believed television was a viable option for him, but only if he could land a series that was good enough to offer him the chance to make a breakthrough performance. That, in turn, would lead to movie opportunities.

Sisters had been a start, boosting his confidence that he could perform well in a dramatic series, and boosting NBC's confidence that he could deliver an audience to a show. Clooney had worked at all three major TV networks, but hadn't been associated with NBC since he'd left *The Facts of Life*. He made a good impression, however, on both NBC execs and the show's production company, Warner Bros., during his days on *Sisters*. Honchos from both companies had made up their minds that they wanted to be in the George Clooney business.

And that is where *ER* came in.

8

A Trip to the *ER*

I did some really bad [TV shows] along the way. . . . It just goes to show that sometimes you get too much credit for things. If one of those crappy pilots had been picked up, I wouldn't have been available to do ER. *And if* ER *had been put on Friday night instead of Thursday, I don't have a film career. It's luck.*

—George Clooney

In any Hollywood career that has seen the successes, and particularly the extreme highs and humble beginnings that George Clooney's has, there are lucky breaks, coincidences, instances of bad timing and wonderful serendipity that come into play. In Clooney's instance, the biggest break of his career came about because of the friendship between a broke med school student and a lowly movie studio intern.

Michael Crichton was a Harvard English major turned Harvard med school student when he decided to help finance his expensive education by writing thriller novels that would interweave the medical knowledge he was learning in school. After several tries, with some of the novels published under the pseudonyms John Lange and Jeffrey Hudson, Crichton's fifth book, *The Andromeda Strain*, became a huge hit in 1969, with Universal picking up the option to make a movie adaptation of the story two years later.

When Crichton visited the Universal Studios lot in Los Angeles to discuss the movie revamp of his book, one of the first faces that greeted him was that of a young studio intern who had gotten himself hired in his lowly position by simply showing up at the studio every day for weeks, acting like he belonged there, and wandering around from set to set, observing the moviemaking process in action.

The intern, a lifelong movie buff who had begun making his own movies as a teenager—"action" flicks where he'd crash his Lionel trains into each other, capture the event on his Super 8 camera and charge the neighborhood kids a quarter to watch his masterpieces—was eventually busted sneaking onto the Universal lot. But execs were so impressed with his moxie and his obvious passion for films that they offered him an intern gig. Which is how Steven Spielberg and Michael Crichton met and became friends.

Though Crichton would go on to earn his M.D. from Harvard, he also continued to pursue his writing career. In 1970, he published his first nonfiction book, *Five Patients*, which follows the titular five patients through medical care. The book, based on Crichton's own experiences working in the emergency room at Massachusetts General Hospital in the late '60s, not only offered the author's commentary on the health care industry at the time, but also captured the mood of the big-city hospital emergency room, with all the drama, gallows humor and breakneck pace that the staff faces on a daily basis. By 1974, he'd turned the book into a screenplay (called *EW* for *Emergency Ward*), but had trouble getting the project into theaters. Studio execs felt the material was ripe for the big screen, but only if Crichton would use it as the basis for a more general medical thriller. He was resolute, however, that the tone of the project was key, and rejected any offer to turn it into something else. "I always felt it was in a special category, a strange thing that was on its own with nothing else like it," Crichton said. "Of course, when there isn't anything else like it, that's a very different animal in the world of entertainment. Something that breaks the rules is looked on with suspicion."

By 1989, the *EW* script, now retitled *ER*, was still floating around, unproduced, when Crichton's old pal Steven Spielberg, the king of the summer blockbuster, was looking for a serious drama to follow his *Indiana Jones* trilogy. Spielberg acquired the rights to *ER*, and determined that it would be his next directing project. But when he and Crichton first met to officially begin breaking down the *ER* movie, Crichton began telling the director about his next novel, a thriller imagining what would happen if present-day scientists could clone dinosaurs using prehistoric dino DNA. Spielberg became so fascinated with the topic that the *ER* meeting turned into a de facto development meeting for a different movie: *Jurassic Park*. "Yeah, it was a great mistake that [Crichton] made, [talking about *Jurassic Park*]," Spielberg laughingly told NBC interviewer Stone Phillips years later. "I'm grateful to Michael to this day for the mistake he made."

Crichton and Spielberg, in fact, were so excited about the dinosaur story that they agreed, on a handshake, to put *ER* on the back burner to pursue the dinosaur movie that would not only become the biggest film of 1993 but would win three Oscars, spark two sequels (with *Jurassic Park IV* scheduled for 2008), earn more than $1.9 billion as a trilogy, and become a Universal Studios theme park ride.

In between the time *Jurassic Park* roared to life and the fall of 1993, both Crichton and Spielberg would go on to other projects, including *Hook* and *Schindler's List* for Spielberg, and *Rising Sun* and *Disclosure*, film adaptations of his books that Crichton helped shepherd to the big screen.

Finally, in the fall of 1993, an executive with Amblin, Spielberg's television production company, got a peek at Crichton's long-gestating *ER* script and decided it would make a better TV series than a movie.

And that's how, thanks to a crucial friendship and the fortuitous interruption of Steven Spielberg's dinosaur jones, George Clooney finally found the project that would make him the TV and movie star he so desperately wanted to become.

9

"I Just Got a Career"

I remember saying to my friends, after I got famous, after the first year of ER, *"I now know I'll never want for an acting job again. I won't have to do anything else if I don't want to."*

—George Clooney

ER, as a weekly TV drama, seemed like a great fit for Michael Crichton's material, the passion project that had been languishing in development hell for more than two decades since it had been written as a nonfiction book in 1970. Steven Spielberg's Amblin television company president Tony Thomopoulos, who conceived the movie script as a TV show, found Crichton initially skeptical, but was finally able to convince the writer of the potential of a TV series that revolved around a group of overworked, overstimulated (and, as it would turn out, sometimes oversexed) emergency room doctors and nurses. But would any TV network go for something so gritty, so fast-paced, so expensive to produce, so sprinkled with unwieldy medical jargon, and, bottom line, so not *Marcus Welby, M.D.*?

It wasn't exactly an easy sell, as, aside from the sometimes offbeat '80s series *St. Elsewhere*, TV execs had traveled a fairly straightforward road with medical dramas. *ER*, on the other hand, promised to be a bit messier, with a suicidal nurse, a drunk pediatrician, an emergency room full of building collapse victims, an inexperienced surgeon performing major heart surgery, an abused baby, and a wide-eyed med student forced to treat patients on his first day, all at a breakneck pace. And that was just in the pilot episode.

Warner Bros., the company that would produce *ER*, agreed to foot the bill for a pilot, which they planned to air as a two-hour made-for-TV movie, based largely on the pedigree of the team behind the show: Crichton, as the writer of the source material and the pilot episode script; Steven Spielberg, whose TV production company had conceived Crichton's book/movie script as a TV series, and who would serve as an executive producer during the first season; John Wells, a veteran TV producer who, after working on the Vietnam war drama *China Beach*, would be deft at handling the frenetic pace of *ER*; and director Rod Holcomb, an Emmy nominee who had also directed the pilot of *China Beach*.

With the staff behind the scenes set, Wells and company were now free to cast the show. Little did they know, they wouldn't have to make the first move to fill one of their most important roles.

George Clooney, having wrung all he could out of his time on *Sisters* and been emboldened when he got nothing but offers of work after risking his career to stand up to perceived industry bully Ed Weinberger, was on the lookout for his career-making role. Warner Bros., the company behind *Sisters*, was eager to keep Clooney in the family, and was even developing a series just for him, a one-hour crime drama called *Golden Gate*. Meanwhile, a casting agent friend of Clooney's had given him a copy of the *ER* pilot script and he wanted in. Badly.

As Clooney saw it, he could take a shot with a series written as a star vehicle, or he could get himself hired on for *ER*, a script so exciting and fresh and unlike anything else on TV that, assuming it actually made it to the airwaves, it had to either flame out or succeed spectacularly. It was not a middle-of-the-road kind of show, which was just fine with Clooney. He'd spent a decade with mediocre success on a string of mediocre (and some not even) shows. He'd rolled the dice by letting Weinberger have it, and he'd quit *Sisters* when he was playing one of the show's most popular characters. He was never going to allow anyone, himself especially, to consider his life to be "a waste," and something told him that getting a role on this new show would prove to be a turning point.

Now Clooney only had to convince John Wells and Wells's cohorts that, despite his many, many failed pilots, Clooney was the man for the job, namely the role of *ER* pediatrician Dr. Doug Ross. "I really fought for the show," he says. "Even if there hadn't been a script, I would have jumped at it—any actor would have—to work with John Wells, Michael Crichton and Steven Spielberg. Then I saw the script, and I realized, 'This is a great, great series.'"

Dr. Ross was perfectly suited for Clooney, and the other way around, too, with Clooney's innate charm the key ingredient to making Ross, a complicated children's doctor who could be self-centered, quick-tempered and given to hitting the bottle to avoid dealing with the consequences of his actions, a character audiences would still root for. "I like the flaws in this guy," Clooney told a *Biography* magazine interviewer. He denied, however, as many critics would charge later, that he was playing an autobiographical role. He enjoyed a drink as much as the next guy, and always makes sure Casa de Clooney is stocked with frosty brews. But Doug Ross's problems with alcohol were not Clooney's. "The alcoholic thing is funny, because I can drink with the best of them," Clooney told *GQ*. "But I'm not even in the same league as most of my family members. And almost everyone in my family, at one time or another, has been a drug addict or an alcoholic. I want the alcohol part of Doug Ross to become a real problem because, as an actor, that's great stuff to do."

Fortunately, Clooney had Warner Bros. execs on his side. *Golden Gate* had been developed for him at Warner Bros. because then–Warner

TV president Leslie Moonves (now the CBS network president) saw in Clooney the potential to be a huge star, on both TV and the big screen. "There is, with George, this match of personality and talent. A lot of times you get one or the other, not both," Moonves said. "With George, what you see on-screen is what you see off-screen. He can be a huge movie star."

With Moonves in his corner, Clooney felt there was no need to sit around and wait for *ER* producers to come to him. The actor called John Wells and told him, the part of Doug Ross was his. Clooney auditioned the day after director Holcomb signed on, and immediately won both of them over. "He was terrific," Wells recalls. "Rod gave him a couple of adjustments, which he did beautifully, and when he walked out of the room, I said, 'Boy, he's great,' and we hired him right away."

Actually, it wasn't right away. As Spielberg would later recall in *Newsweek* magazine, the network had to be sold on Clooney, who was seen as "the albatross in getting a twenty-three-episode order. . . . The network did not want me to hire George for *ER*," the director said. "John Wells went to the front office and screamed and threatened to walk off the show unless George got the part."

Clooney was back in a Winnebego when he finally got the good news that the network had acquiesced and he had been cast as Dr. Doug Ross. He and pal Grant Heslov had taken off on a cross-country road trip. Heslov had just broken up with his fiancée, and as it is the duty of each of The Boys to help the others through such tough times, Clooney and his friend left Los Angeles headed towards the East Coast, stopping along the way to hit golf balls across various state lines. Clooney was at the wheel when his cell phone rang. He took the call, hung up, and turned to Heslov. "I just got a career," he said. He'd been cast as Dr. Doug, and indeed his career, his entire life and the lives of those around him were about to take off on a whole new trajectory.

10

A TV Star Is Born

I give [George] a lot of credit, because he saw that being one of six or seven in a great show was better than being the star of a good show.

—Les Moonves

Aside from the obvious opportunity for exposure to audiences and the decision makers in Hollywood that *ER* presented , Clooney had shrewdly deduced that, more than in a series created just for him, *ER* would allow him freedom to hone his acting skills, without shouldering as much pressure to carry the entire show.

No one would argue that Clooney wasn't the breakout star of the series, and Warner Bros. execs had always foreseen that he would be. Still, one of the unique aspects of the show, and one of its biggest selling points for Clooney, was that it would truly be an ensemble series. Every one of the six leads would have his or her chance to shine, frequently all in the course of a single episode, but with so many characters and story lines whizzing past on screen constantly, he knew that the fate of the show didn't rest solely on his shoulders. Nor would the entire responsibility for promoting the show, and propelling it forward, fall on him.

And after more than a dozen failed series and pilots—with his name prominently featured at the top of the cast list—that never saw a minute of primetime air, being one of the pack wasn't such a bad thing.

Furthermore, Clooney had learned from his experiences with other ensemble casts that being one part, as long as it was a significant part, of a well-crafted project was better than being the star of something not so great. *The Facts of Life* and *Roseanne* were, at various points in the shows' histories, quality TV. Clooney's roles on each of them, however, were mostly forgettable. On series like *Baby Talk* and the short-lived CBS crime drama *Bodies of Evidence*, he was a lead character, but both series, which would rate okay critiques at best, failed to bring him the recognition, and more importantly, job offers, he required to take his career to the next level.

ER, though, provided exactly what he had been looking for: a quality show, run by some of the most respected people in the TV and movie industries; a fresh, provocative spin on the old medical drama genre that was sure to draw audiences in for at least a peek; and a juicy role just ripe for an actor ready to win some cred for his acting chops, without the solo burden of ensuring the show's success. Because designs for a big-screen career were always a part of Clooney's master plan for success in Hollywood, the fact that *ER* was an ensemble show would also make it more likely that, if the show was a success and offers of movie roles followed for him, he would be able to take advantage of those opportunities. It's tough for a show to shoot around a star when he or she is the focus of much of the series' action, but not so when there are five other leads, as well a host of supporting characters, to keep the story lines, and the production schedule, flowing smoothly.

As for his five costars, with the exception of Anthony Edwards, whom audiences knew from his memorable roles as Tom Cruise's best pal in *Top Gun* and the head geek in *Revenge of the Nerds*, most of them were relative newbies to the primetime scene. With Edwards cast, shortly after Clooney signed on, as Dr. Mark Greene, the show's chief resident, staff mediator and general go-to guy, Sherry Stringfield was next. Stringfield spent several years on the daytime soap *Guiding Light* before a brief stint as David Caruso's wife on the first season of *NYPD Blue* inspired *ER* casting directors to sign her up as Dr. Susan Lewis, the emergency room doc who was destined to juggle her career and love life with being forced to raise her niece when the baby was abandoned by Lewis's troubled, hippy-dippy sister.

Noah Wyle had only a small role in another Tom Cruise movie, *A Few Good Men*, as well as a part opposite Christian Bale (who, like Clooney, would also be a future Batman) in the coming-of-age drama *Swing Kids* to boast about when he won his spot on *ER*. But his lack of experience seemed appropriate for the role he'd be playing, that of wealthy med student John Carter, who embarks on his first day at the fictional County General emergency room wide-eyed and totally unprepared for the constant chaos that greets him. Julianna Margulies also had a light resume when she landed the role of *ER* nurse Carol Hathaway, who, despondent about her failed relationship with Clooney's Dr. Ross, tries to commit suicide in the pilot. In fact, Hathaway was originally scheduled to die at the end of the episode, but test audiences' reaction to the character was so positive that she was made a regular. Margulies' previous credits amounted to a handful of guest spots on shows like *Law & Order* and *Homicide: Life on the Street*, plus a failed pilot for *Homicide* producer Tom Fontana and a small role as a prostitute in the Steven Seagal movie *Out for Justice*.

Actor Eriq La Salle was the final piece of the puzzle, and his casting on the show came at the very last minute. La Salle, who like George Clooney had a resume that dated back to the early 1980s and was full of TV guest spots and the occasional movie (most notably the Eddie Murphy/Arsenio Hall comedy *Coming to America*), had been working on another project and was unable to audition until shooting on the *ER* pilot had already begun. He made such an impression during his read-through, though, that two days later he was filming his first scenes as Dr.

Peter Benton, the sometimes arrogant surgeon who was also incredibly passionate about and dedicated to the practice of medicine.

With the cast in place, producers turned their attention to honing the pilot's script and pace to reflect the tone they hoped would help the series attract a wide audience and set a new standard for medical dramas. While, like most other medical shows, *ER* would flesh out the personal lives of the hospital staff, that would not be the main focus of the series. Personal backstories would more often be revealed in dribs and drabs as part of regular conversation while the County General staff was in action in the emergency room. *ER*'s incredibly quick and sometimes choppy action also meant that the sometimes seamless switch between tragedy and humor could be disorienting, but the producers and stars again trusted that there would be a large audience that would appreciate the smart new series.

Now all that was left was to hope for a good spot on NBC's schedule. Though everyone else, including the notoriously fickle TV focus groups, was wowed by the pilot, NBC execs were nervous about how viewers would respond to *ER*'s intricate structure and crowded cast. It was the focus groups that actually helped seal the show's fate. "The powers that be at the time, even after they saw the pilot, thought it was far too complicated, because there were fifty story lines and they weren't tied up," Clooney said. "They thought this was way too complicated for the normal American citizen and that audiences wouldn't catch up. Then they tested it and it tested through the roof. And they thought, 'Well, maybe we were wrong.' You look back at the television shows that have been successful over the years, *Cheers* and *Seinfeld* and *M*A*S*H*, and they are all very smart television shows, and so is *ER*. It just needs to be entertaining."

Finally, NBC showed its faith in the series' potential with the plum time slot it assigned *ER*: Thursday night at 10 P.M., as a part of NBC's Must-See-TV line-up that included the hits *Friends*, *Seinfeld* and *Mad About You*. The two-hour *ER* pilot premiered on September 19, 1994, a

Monday, with a second episode airing that Thursday in its regular spot. The response was immediate and overwhelmingly positive, with more than twenty-three million viewers tuning in to "24 Hours," the pilot that, as the title suggests, introduced us to the County General emergency room at 5 A.M., and wound through an entire day with the staff. On-call doctor Mark Greene, trying to grab a quick nap during a rare moment of down time, is awakened by a nurse who requires his assistance with a drunk and disorderly patient. Greene is annoyed by the request until he finds out who the patient is: staff pediatrician Doug Ross. As Clooney croons a loud, slurred version of "Danny Boy," Greene gives him a sobering concoction we later learn is aspirin. And from Dr. Greene's reaction to Ross, we gather this is a regular behavior for the handsome but obviously troubled doctor. When a new nurse asks if Dr. Ross is always like this, Greene replies, "Only on his nights off." Later, a sobered-up Ross treats a baby who's come into the emergency room with signs of being physically abused. He's furious and disgusted as he rails at the mother, "He's a little kid!" Disgusted, he tells her she should get an attorney. She tells him she is one.

His tour de force performance in that scene had won him the role during his audition. In the course of the pilot, he went from a sloppy drunkard to a flirtatious cad who hit on a young med student and left a coworker so brokenhearted that she may have tried to commit suicide because of him. But he redeemed himself later when he saved an older lady who went into cardiac arrest, helped diagnose a preteen ulcer patient and, of course, called the mother on her abuse of her infant son. Ross's obvious devotion to his patients, despite his personal foibles, won viewers over.

The show and the cast were hits, gracing magazine covers, guesting on talk shows, being bombarded with fan mail. Clooney, in particular, began to receive thousands and thousands of letters at Warner Bros. and NBC, with, not surprisingly, the majority of the missives coming from female viewers who were immediately taken with his bad boy doctor.

He had been down this road before, though. He'd gotten copious fan mail during his time on *The Facts of Life*, *Roseanne* and *Sisters*, too, and, in the self-deprecating manner that is such a part of his charm, downplayed the reaction. "If you stuck a mannequin in my part, he'd be getting all the fan mail, too," Clooney told *People*. "I play a great part on the show. I could be a schmuck all day long and at the end of the day, I save a kid or some old lady's life and I'm a hero."

The star's tempered reaction was understandable, given his experience as a ten-year Hollywood veteran. But as the season wore on, and the show continued to be a critical and commercial hit, there was no denying that *ER* had fast become TV's new watercooler series, and its stars were catapulted to the Hollywood A list. When the Emmys rolled around the next September, the show was awarded eight awards, including an Outstanding Supporting Actress win for Julianna Margulies, the star who'd almost been cut after the pilot. And all six of the show's main cast members earned Emmy nominations, including Clooney and Anthony Edwards as Outstanding Lead Actor in a Drama Series, Sherry Stringfield for Lead Actress, and Noah Wyle and Eriq LaSalle as Supporting Actor nominees. Even Clooney's Aunt Rosemary, whom he'd paid back for letting him crash in her guesthouse with a role as an Alzheimer's patient, had earned an Emmy nomination for Outstanding Guest Actress.

A note on Clooney and Edwards' loss in the Lead Actor race: Mandy Patinkin took home the Emmy in 1995 for his role on *Chicago Hope*, the *other* Chicago-set hospital drama that premiered during the 1994–95 season, on CBS. The show was pitted against *ER* in the Thursday, 10 P.M. time slot, and, with both shows earning rave reviews, it was a ratings battle that TV critics monitored all season, expecting the two shows to be neck and neck all year. In the end, though, there was a very decisive victor: *ER* finished the 1994–95 season ranked second, behind *Seinfeld*. *Chicago Hope* didn't finish the season among the top twenty, even after CBS moved it to Monday nights. *ER*, in fact, for all five seasons Clooney was a member of the cast, never finished lower than fourth in the end-of-season Nielsen ratings.

And so began George Clooney's path to becoming the breakout star of the tube season, one of the sexiest TV doctors ever to hit the small screen, well before Patrick Dempsey's McDreamy ever picked up a stethoscope on *Grey's Anatomy*. Clooney, in the course of the pilot episode, had shown he could deliver more than a toothy grin and a wise-crack. He and the show were a hit. "Right around the third weekend, we had about nine shows in the can, and they picked us up for the total of twenty-six hours in the season," he says. "[And] we started going, 'Okay, I can afford to spend money now.'"

11

Casa de Clooney

This was something I never thought would happen in my career. I've done so much bad television for so long. Basically, it means I've just bought myself a few more years before I end up doing nighttime soaps.

—George Clooney

And spend money he did. Though Clooney has never been acquisitive for the sake of being acquisitive, he has always been willing to spend cash for friends, family and the pursuit of good times. Given his sometimes nomadic existence as a child while dad Nick moved the family to and fro for broadcasting jobs, Clooney is a strong believer both in setting down roots and in financial security. So, though the size of his first major purchase with *ER* money might have come as a bit of a surprise, the fact that it was a house shouldn't have.

Having lost his home after his divorce from Balsam, he started off 1995 with the purchase of the eight-bedroom, two-story home that would become the infamous Hollywood Hills estate known as Casa de Clooney. The house, the previous home of Fleetwood Mac singer Stevie Nicks and one-hit-wonder rapper Vanilla Ice, would serve as the central hangout for Clooney and The Boys, also providing them with a safe place to land during divorces, breakups and other trying times. Featuring a swimming pool, tennis courts and, of course, a basketball court, Casa de Clooney has been featured in numerous magazine and TV interviews, and is still the actor's Los Angeles residence and the home of the Sunday taco-and-movie fests he hosts for The Boys and their families.

His friendships with The Boys, and the fact the group has been able to remain close, are among Clooney's proudest achievements. Any jokes and inferences about Clooney's sexual orientation, because of his devotion to the tight-knit crew, can be put down to ignorance: with the hectic, stressful lives most people lead today, it is difficult for some to conceive of the kind of friendship, with its never-faltering loyalty and commitment to keeping in touch, that the star and his friends enjoy. It's all the more admirable that the friendships have endured through so many breakups, career changes, financial ups and downs, and travels. Because all the friends work at it, he says, these friendships have been the most enduring relationships of his life.

"Probably the one thing I'm most proud of in my life is how hard I've worked at keeping everybody around. It can get tricky," Clooney told a *GQ* interviewer. "Because when you start to get famous, people start to surround you and tell you how great you are; you get this whole crew of friends you don't know, and they're suddenly your best friends. But you have to keep the other people close, and that's work. So [The Boys and I] talk to each other at some point every day. It's not like some sick, fucked-up thing. It's just like 'Hey, man, what's up?' It can be fucked up if that's your obsession. But it's just friendship, The Boys. What it is, is the greatest support group ever. That's what it's about when it all comes crashing down."

With *ER* in full swing and the show a bona fide hit out of the box, The Boys were going to have to start sharing Clooney with a new pack of friends. As one of the most experienced cast members, and the one who, through up-close and personal experience, had the best business sense about Hollywood, Clooney could offer valuable friendship and counsel to his costars. Noah Wyle, in particular, looked to Clooney for financial advice, namely suggestions on how to negotiate the potential minefield of dealing with the "suits" associated with the show and the network. Clooney even gave his younger costar his prized 1960 Oldsmobile Dynamic 88, telling Wyle he hoped the car would bring his young coworker all the good luck and good times it had brought him.

"George is definitely the most loyal person I've ever met in my life," Wyle said. "Friendship, loyalty and good work all mean something to him. He's making a career out of marrying those three, which not many are able to do."

Clooney also took it upon himself to try to keep the *ER* set as lively and drama-free as possible. The show's pace and sometimes tragic story lines, as well as those tricky medical terms the cast had to speak in the heat of the moment in every episode, meant filming days were inherently tension-prone at times. But there was Clooney, strategically hiding a whoopee cushion, skateboarding around the hospital set on an IV stand or toying with one of his costars in an effort to lighten the mood at the precise moment that tempers would flare or frustration would take hold. "It's a very tough show to do, because there are so many things you're doing," Clooney recalls. "You're learning a dialogue—you're learning Latin, basically . . . and you also have to work a choreography out where you have to be a doctor, and you have to do physical things. And even tougher than being a doctor at times, you can't hurt the people you're working on, because they're extras, you know, so you don't really want to crack their chests. . . ."

His castmates appreciated his efforts, no matter how offbeat they would sometimes seem.

"There are times when you just want to say, 'George, take the blue pill,'" Julianna Margulies said. "But every now and then, to look over and see him with a urine container on his head, just makes you feel a little better about your work."

Margulies, after all, owed Clooney a big thank-you for her own career-making role. When the *ER* producers and writers were all set to kill off Nurse Hathaway at the end of the pilot, it wasn't just the goodwill the character had inspired among the test audiences that saved her. Clooney also spoke up, going to New York to visit NBC execs and express his feelings about the character. "I said, 'It's too bad Julianna dies,'" he told *TV Guide*. "In typical network fashion, they then told me, 'She's not necessarily dead.'"

Clooney, to be fair, had ulterior motives. The pilot hints that Carol Hathaway tries to kill herself because she's distraught about her failed relationship with Clooney's Dr. Ross. He saw that there was potential for a big romance between the characters that would only soup up the story lines for both him and Margulies, and ensure their continuing employment on the show. He also knew that if the beautiful nurse died, and the finger was pointed at his womanizing Doug Ross as the reason, it was going to make it that much tougher to sell Dr. Ross as a complicated soul with a genuinely good heart, instead of a straight-up cad. The network, obviously, agreed that Margulies was a key part of the show's future, and Clooney even got to make the call to let her know the show wanted her to sign on permanently.

"He called me just in time," she laughed. "I was just about to cut my hair, dye it red and straighten it for a different job."

And, with her other costars, Margulies confirms that Clooney is the go-to guy when you need a hand. "If I was stuck somewhere in Alaska at four in the morning without any money and I was in jail, I would call George," she said.

Clooney's friend, and *Batman & Robin* director, Joel Schumacher agrees. "George is like everybody's older brother," Schumacher told *Vanity Fair*. "I'm fifty-seven, but if I was in trouble, I'd go see George."

Clooney also became known for the kindnesses he showed other coworkers, and not just the ones who shared magazine covers and saw their names on the screen with his every week.

When a crew member, who was not making anything close to a lead actor's salary, burst into tears one night when she went to leave and found her car had been towed, Clooney hugged her, told her how to retrieve the auto and offered her the cash she'd need to do so.

When producers wanted the cast of the show to have a separate dining area from the crew and the extras, Clooney and Anthony Edwards protested. They hung a giant cartoon of a bossy producer in the dining area, and eventually the powers that be were so embarrassed that they announced everyone on the show, no matter what his or her job was, would be served the same food, from the same craft services area. Clooney and Edwards even took it a step further and convinced producers that the good morale they'd inspire would be worth the price of having two meals each day catered to the set for the entire cast and crew.

When crew members became ill or had deaths in the family, all Clooney's costars recall that he was always the one to begin a cash collection to offer them a bit of financial assistance during their tough times. He was also the instigator of "Dollar Days," where anyone who wanted to participate would stuff dollar bills in a box, with one person's name drawn at the end and declared the winner of the entire boodle. Five years later, when Clooney had fulfilled his contract and decided to leave Dr. Ross and County General behind to pursue his movie career full time, he surprised the crew with a special edition of Dollar Day. He arrived on the set for his last day of taping and "he has this box in his hand. He says, 'Let's do Dollar Day,'" crew member Steve Robertson told *People*. "You really should get in this," Clooney said, grinning as he passed around a box. "I sensed he had sweetened the pot," Robertson said. "People ran to the bank to get dollar bills. I'm not kidding." It was a good call; the Dollar Day prize usually amounted to about $100. To show his appreciation for the pleasure of having worked with them, the departing star dropped a $5,000 check into this Dollar Day box, and one crew member—Robertson, as it turned out—took home an extra $6,100 that day.

Clooney also showed his fellow five *ER* leads his support, questioning a *TV Guide* editor when he felt the magazine was treating Eriq LaSalle, a black actor, unfairly. "Eriq wanted to go after *TV Guide* and rightly so," he told *Movieline*. "He'd done three photo shoots for them, and they never put him on the cover. Maybe you do one and they don't put you on the cover, but not three. The problem was, his complaining made it look like he was an actor who was upset about not getting on the cover of a magazine, as opposed to the bigger issue of racism."

His biggest sign of respect to his costars was in fulfilling his original *ER* contract, sticking around for five seasons, which often meant shooting a movie and the intense *ER* at the same time, and never asking for a raise. For Clooney's five seasons on the show, he earned $42,000 a week (no small sum, obviously), even when his costars would go on to ask for almost ten times as much for each episode. Clooney the businessman felt that he would come out ahead in the long run, as long as he fulfilled the contract he'd signed on with in the beginning. Though heviewed TV as more than a stepping-stone—"I've fought my whole life to get on a show like this," he says. "I'm in a comfortable, comfortable position. I'm going to end up being able to do a film every summer, and that's great luck for me. But I'm not going anywhere. I'm going to ride out the contract and have fun"—he also foresaw that his big paydays would come from big-screen work.

Besides, Nick Clooney's son honored his commitments. He had signed on for five seasons, at $42,000 an episode, and there was no reason to renegotiate those terms. The *ER* producers, Warner Bros. and NBC had given him the shot that he'd long been searching for, and he repaid them by simply doing what he'd promised, contractually, to do. "I'm prouder of that than I am of his great performances," Nick Clooney said. "He kept his word."

12

From TV to Movies

The chasm between television and movies is a huge one. I had been working in television for eight years when I had to audition for a two-line bit in Guarding Tess, *and I was labeled as "television." There is a huge difference. Now, a good percentage of movie actors come from television, but the crossover is still tough.*

—George Clooney

ER would provide Clooney with plenty of opportunities to hone his acting skills throughout his five seasons. In "Hell and High Water," universally agreed to be one of Clooney's finest performances during or since *ER*, Doug Ross interviews to take a job at a private practice after the funds for his County General position are cut. That night, while driving in a downpour to a party, he pulls over in his car, angry and frustrated about the state of his career, and considers smoking marijuana. Just then, a boy walks out of the darkness and pounds on his window, begging him to come and rescue his trapped brother, who's on the verge of drowning in a storm drain. At his lowest point professionally—Ross doesn't want to work in private practice—Doug not only manages to save Ben, the trapped boy, from the storm drain, but successfully performs an emergency tracheotomy with his penknife, and then convinces a news team with a helicopter to fly Ben to County General. It's one of the most frantic episodes in the show's history, and all the more emotional because it involves an endangered child. Clooney pulled it off perfectly, his character responding without hesitation, and with flawless instinct, in a desperate situation that became a reminder of all the best parts of Dr. Ross, to the audience and to the character himself. The scene where a thoroughly exhausted Doug carries Ben out of the storm drain is no doubt imprinted upon the memory of every *ER* viewer.

The fine work he was doing on *ER* wasn't going to make Clooney complacent, however, and, during his second season he began to scope out movie offers. "When I was doing *Roseanne* with Laurie Metcalfe, I'd watch her go off and do small parts in *Internal Affairs* and *JFK*, and I thought, 'That's the perfect way to go,' because eventually the TV series goes away," he told *Entertainment Weekly*. "You need something to fall back on, and that's what my plan was."

He wasn't, as so many critics began to wonder, about to "pull a Caruso" and leave his hit TV show behind in hopes of parlaying his man-of-the-moment status into a high-paying movie career. For one thing, that hadn't exactly panned out for David Caruso, the Emmy-nominated *NYPD Blue* star who'd overestimated his big-screen potential and bounced from *Blue* after one mega-successful season on the gritty hit ABC cop drama. While the show continued for twelve very successful seasons, Caruso went on to star in flopped films like *Jade*, *Kiss of Death* and *Swirlee,* movies that performed so dreadfully that he became box office poison.Hollywood turned its back on him as quickly as he'd turned his back—in a contentious public showdown with TV producer Steven Bochco—on *NYPD Blue*. Caruso's name was mud, and he floundered for years, trying to get his career back, at one point even operating a women's clothing star in Miami. Finally, in 2002, Caruso experienced a TV comeback with the lead role in CBS's spin-off hit *CSI: Miami*. But the actor still serves as a cautionary tale, and, in more unkind circles, a punch line, to stars who seem to be getting too big for their TV show britches.

Clooney was perfectly happy to fulfill his contract with *ER*, and not just because it was the right thing to do. *ER* was his breakout role, and it was a "day job" that provided him security while he tried new things with film roles. He wasn't interested in jumping from a very successful series into a starring role in a major movie. He wasn't interested in a starring vehicle at all, at that point. He was looking for good supporting roles, smaller parts in good films that would get noticed by other dealmakers in Hollywood, and that would benefit his career. He had spent ten years in Hollywood, making an okay living for much of that time, waiting for his big break. This was a patient man. He was finally in a good position, TV-wise, and he was in no hurry to squander his potential movie career by jumping at lots of dollar signs and hitching his wagon to the first script that came along. And they did start to come along, quickly, after *ER*'s debut.

Clooney told *Entertainment Weekly* he had even turned down the very first movie offer that came his way during *ER*'s first season. A studio offered him a cool $1 million for the part, about which he, uncharacteristically, remained cryptic. All he would tell the magazine was that the money wasn't enough for him to risk ending up being the guy who took a "big payday, got a lot of attention and then went into a bad film."

Snapping up such hastily made offers also would have signaled to Clooney that he was starting to believe the hype surrounding his suddenly hot status. He simply wasn't buying it, though, and not just because it's in his nature to be self-deprecating. It all comes back to the experiences of his father and his Aunt Rosemary. If you believe everyone when they tell you how great you are, especially the sudden hangers-on who are only too omnipresent and too eager to get in on the sudden success, then you have to believe them when they start saying negative things about you, too. And Clooney knew that every career takes a downturn, whether because of a change in the public's taste, a badly chosen project, some personal scandal or that audiences simply tire of an actor. "That's the danger, you inhale," he said in a 1997 interview with ABC's *Primetime Live*. "Everyone will tell you you're a genius, which you are not. And you learn that you're never as good as they say you are when they say you're good, you're never as bad as they say you are when they say you're bad. And if you understand that, you win."

That's why it was tantamount, he felt, to plot a career that allowed him to start out small and work his way into bigger movie roles. It was his sense of keeping things in check, keeping his head on straight, but also of knowing, from a business standpoint, what would keep him employed most gainfully, and what would allow him to amass a body of work that he would be proud of. "The goal was to recognize how much money you need to live an incredibly comfortable life," he says. "I don't want to stockpile money and have this list of really bad films at the end of it. You want to be at that charity retrospective when you're seventy and have it not be filled with crap movies."

Clooney had made the decision by this point, buoyed by the obvious opportunties *ER* was going to present, that his career would be his priority. Of course there would be relationships. He never said he wanted to be a monk. But he was very clear that, after the divorce from Balsam, he never wanted to remarry. Whether he truly isn't equipped to handle the give and take of being in a marriage, or simply doesn't want to be in one, Clooney has stated time and time again that marriage is not for him. He's married to his career. It is the focus of his life, and he treats it with the care and planning that might otherwise be devoted to raising a family. He takes it that seriously, and has since those early *ER* days. "I've made it difficult to have a relationship because my first love is work and my second love is my friends," Clooney says. "That will change, I'm sure. There will be someone somewhere along the way who will knock me for a loop again, and I'll be willing to sacrifice everything."

Before Clooney started seriously looking for a movie project, he wanted to clear the path with *ER*'s producers. Though his contract with the show didn't forbid him to make movies, he knew his producers, if they were opposed to his extracurricular acting activities, could make it practically impossible for him to get time off from his *ER* schedule to make movies during the show's regular season. Fortunately, he was not working for a selfish bunch. "If George is on a movie set Tuesday through Saturday, we can slot his stuff for Mondays, at least for a while," John Wells said.

With that matter settled, all Clooney had to do was find a project, and, as it turned out, he didn't have to look any further than the *ER* set.

Director Quentin Tarantino had become the toast of the town with his gritty movies—stylish, action-packed flicks, sprinkled liberally with the filmmaking touches the former video store clerk had gleaned while watching movies day after day at work. In 1992, the crime thriller *Reservoir Dogs* had made him a fanboy and critical favorite, but 1994's *Pulp Fiction* sealed Tarantino's status as a major Hollywood player, winning him an Oscar for Best Original Screenplay and giving him the credibility to get studio execs to greenlight any movie project he proposed.

ER's challenging pace and multiple story lines meant that during the show's first season the directorial duties were divvied up amongst a whole list of names, and the red-hot Tarantino had submitted a request to helm an episode of the red-hot new drama himself. His installment, "Motherhood," was the penultimate episode of the first season, an entry noteworthy for the Tarantino-esque touch of a female gang member coming into County General with her ear hacked off.

While on the set, the director had a chance to renew his acquaintance with Clooney, who had, once upon a time, given a truly awful audition for the role of Mr. Blonde in *Reservoir Dogs*. "I read for the Michael Madsen dancing around scene. I probably would have been horrible, and I thought he was so great in it. It's the best thing I ever saw Michael do," Clooney told *Movieline*. Though he recalls that particular audition as one of his most memorably worst—so bad, in fact, that Tarantino teased him about it mercilessly while directing his *ER* episode—it was one of many high-profile, potentially career-changing big-screen roles George had tried for and missed pre-*ER*. He lost out to Judd Nelson for the role of John Bender, "the criminal," in *The Breakfast Club* (it is difficult to imagine George, even with his mullet-like '80s helmet of hair, dancing around a high school library). And, in one of the lost roles he most lamented, he auditioned several times for the role of sexy drifter J.D. in *Thelma & Louise*, the role that would launch the career of his future friend and *Ocean's Eleven*, *Ocean's Twelve* and *Ocean's Thirteen* co-star Brad Pitt. "There was a turning point after I'd read five times for [director] Ridley Scott for *Thelma & Louise*," Clooney recalls. "That was the closest I'd ever gotten to a big film. I literally stopped and took an honest look at my career. I thought I'd be doing television series the rest of my life."

Back to the future, Clooney was good-naturedly taking Tarantino's ribbing about the blown *Reservoir Dogs* role on the set of *ER*. But he also impressed the director enough that when Tarantino's friend and fellow It Boy director Robert Rodriguez was casting for his new project, the comedy/horror/fantasy/thriller *From Dusk Till Dawn*, Tarantino pointed to Clooney.

Rodriguez had made his mark in Hollywood with the 1992 crime thriller *El Mariachi*, a Sundance Film Festival and Independent Spirit Award–winning movie that the newbie director had shot in just fourteen days, on a budget of $7,000, most of which he raised by volunteering to be a human lab rat for a clinical drug test in Texas. His friend Quentin had shown him several episodes of *ER* with Clooney in action, and the indie filmmaker became a fan.

Then he spotted George sharing his political viewpoints with Bill Maher on the now-defunct chat show *Politically Incorrect*. "He was just sitting back and brooding," Rodriguez said. "After that, I saw him at an Academy Awards party and then I saw him on the cover of a magazine. I showed the picture to Lawrence Bender, and told him I thought [Clooney] looked a little like Quentin."

That would be a key factor in casting the movie, since Rodriguez was specifically looking for someone to play Tarantino's brother in *From*

Dusk Till Dawn. Not everyone initially saw the physical similarities between Clooney and Tarantino; Tarantino, in fact, had pursued another TV star, *Baretta*'s Robert Blake, to play his brother in the movie. But Tarantino felt certain that his and Clooney's personalities meshed well enough, and that the *ER* star would be not only easy, but fun, to work with, and quickly came around to the idea of teaming up with Clooney. An offer was made to Clooney's agent, and the actor accepted, meaning he would follow his first season as the new breakout TV star with a gritty, very un-Doug-Ross-like role in a small film, directed by one of the industry's hottest directors, and written by an Oscar-winning filmmaker (Tarantino). As the future continued to look brighter and brighter for Clooney, he could finally say his career was going exactly as he had planned.

13

From Dusk Till Dawn

The thing I really respect about George is that no one saw him coming. When he was in ER, *he was pretty much defined by it. But he wasn't encumbered by the industry's perception. And now the most powerful directors are calling him. He wasn't handed those opportunities—he put himself there.*

—Brad Pitt

Determined to make the most of this opportunity that had fallen into his lap when Quentin Tarantino decided to direct an episode of *ER*, Clooney took some unusual steps to prepare for his role as Tarantino's onscreen brother. He and the notoriously randy director decided to forge a closer bond by heading out for an evening on the town: barhopping and hanging out at the 1995 MTV Movie Awards. Tarantino's *Pulp Fiction* would win the night's honors for best movie, and the general "anything goes" feel of the MTV awards, plus the rowdy, celeb-packed audience and the obligatory after-parties, gave Clooney and his movie sib a chance to connect. By the time they started production on the movie later that summer, in the scorching, dusty Mojave Desert heat of Barstow, California, there was no doubt they could pull off playing brothers.

"You would have thought they were separated at birth," *From Dusk Till Dawn* assistant director Douglas Aarniokoski told *People*. "They're both so intense, they're both so smart, and they're both so funny. They would just play off each other all the time. It was legendary. I literally would have to go up to both of them and say, 'Gentleman, you have got to walk off the set, because the crew just can't concentrate. They're too busy laughing.'"

The guys' commitment to having a good time was a blessing, not only because it made for a better set, but because it made them more believable as brothers in the horror/vampire movie.

Clooney and Tarantino were playing Seth and Richie Gecko, two wild siblings who kill four people while robbing a bank in Texas, then head south to Mexico with their ill-gotten loot. At the Mexican border, they kidnap a camper-driving preacher (Harvey Keitel) and his children (Juliette Lewis and Ernest Liu) and force them to go across the border to a dive bar called The Titty Twister. Seth and Richie think they're large and in charge until they meet the Twister's regular clientele, who turn out to be vampires, forcing the boys to team up with their hostages to survive the bloody scene. "It's a horror movie/action movie . . . a horr-action," Clooney said. "Of course, the disadvantage of it is that the horror film people are going to be a little ticked off because it takes a while to get to the horror film. And the Quentin fans will be ticked off because they'll go, 'What the hell is this horror stuff?'"

The bigger issue many critics had with the movie was its violence, which many of them felt was gratuitous, gross, and completely unbecoming for a man who had just become one of the biggest stars on TV, if not the biggest, by playing a man who, despite his personal baggage, made his living saving lives, not snuffing them out in a liquor store heist, then celebrating with a trip to someplace called The Titty Twister. "He was already on TV . . . but it turned out the way he is on *ER* is totally unlike him," Rodriguez says. "When I met him, he was just like Seth in the movie, very debonair and fast-talking. So I decided we needed someone hungry and wanting to prove himself. When we got him he was swamped with calls, but we got him first and he worked his ass off for us."

Clooney also acknowledged that the R-rated *From Dusk Till Dawn* was unlike anything he'd done before, but he saw that as a good thing and unapologetically praised the final product."The script was so good," he told *Movieline*. "In the first half of that movie the dialogue is spectacular, it's *Pulp Fiction*. The second half is a much different kind of film, the kind I also enjoy. People who love that film absolutely love it. But the ones who hate it, wow! When I bring it up to some entertainment reporters, you can actually see them twitch. They hate the gratuitous violence. I understand that, but it made me laugh. And my part was so well-written, I saw an opportunity. . . . When a part is well-written, I'm good. I know what my limitations are as an actor, but my strength is putting myself into a well-written part. When I get in trouble is when I have to fix it, or when I have to carry it on personality."

Though the movie itself prompted mixed reviews—the *Austin Chronicle* cheered, "This is horror with a wink and a nod to drive-in theaters and sweaty back seats. This is how it's done," while the *San Francisco Chronicle* decided that "Quentin Tarantino and Robert Rodriguez had their fun with *From Dusk Till Dawn*, and now they need to stay away from each other. For their own good. Forever"—critiques of Clooney's performance as the less violent and less crazy of the two Geckos were generally good. "Clooney makes a terrific debut as an action star. His looks translate beautifully to the big screen, as does his California laconism. He, at least, bears watching," wrote a *Washington Post* reviewer. *Newsweek* called the actor "tremendously smooth," the *New York Times* added that he was "truly dashing," and *Variety* wrote, "What demands attention by a wider audience is George Clooney's instant emergence as a full-fledged movie star. From the first scene, it is clear that the *ER* sensation, who has made numerous forgettable pics in the past, has the looks, authority and action-film savvy to be a new Clark Gable or *Mad Max*-mold Mel Gibson."

Despite the praise critics lavished upon him, Clooney was still typically self-deprecating about his performance, chalking it up to luck. "I was scared to death," he said. "I had to work with Harvey Keitel, and my character was supposed to dominate him. Now, nobody, but nobody dominates Harvey on screen. I did my best, but when I look at the result, I can see him throw in a gesture, raise an eyebrow, or even take a pause, as he takes focus. That's why he's Harvey Keitel, and I'm just a lucky guy with the best job in the world."

He was, of course, selling himself short. True, his strength lies in turning in a good performance with well-written material, and has done so throughout his career. It is no coincidence that in flimsy fare like *The Facts of Life* and *Baby Talk* on TV, or *Return of the Killer Tomatoes!* and *Predator II* on the big screen, Clooney always seemed to rely on his swaggering charm to see him through. In fairness, though, not even the best actor or actress can make bad material look good—though there are plenty of bad actors and actresses who could take a great part and turn in a lousy performance. Clooney has always been his own toughest critic, and the perils of Hollywood, and of buying into the outpouring of adoration that instant fame brings, are always foremost in his mind. His realistic attitude about his talent has been a major factor in his ability to have earned a decent living without having a major hit as an actor in the decade leading up to *ER*, and in the successful acting/writing/directing career he's forged on the big screen since.

Just as important to him as his performance in the movie was his performance on the set. He'd quickly established himself as the "mayor" of the *ER* set, always willing to lending a helping hand to a coworker, or a bit of advice to a costar, always the first one to help relieve a tension-filled workday with a well-placed whoopee cushion or elaborately planned practical joke, and committed to trying to ensure that everyone on a set was having as much fun as he was, and that each and every member of the cast and crew was treated with the same level of respect.

Partly because he was, as he admitted, scared to death about costarring with an actor of the caliber of Harvey Keitel, and partly because he wanted to establish from the beginning that he didn't feel his sudden superstar status on TV entitled him to any special treatment on the movie set, Clooney introduced himself to everyone on the *From Dusk Till Dawn* staff as "George Clooney, television actor." He bought gifts for his costars (Juliette Lewis was especially fond of the glass statue of a hand flipping the bird that Clooney gave her), he played basketball with the crew, he stalked the set with a giant water-gun rifle, and, in general, he endeared himself to everyone involved with the movie. "All of those girls loved him," said Salma Hayek, who played scene-stealing Titty Twister dancer/vampire Santanico Pandemonium. "Not only because he's good looking, he's fun to be with. And he would talk to them. A lot of actors don't talk to the people off the set." Far be it from the charming star to ever pass up the chance to schmooze with the ladies. Douglas Aarniokoski added, "You had to tell [George] where his trailer was. He's the only actor I ever worked with who could tell you every single crew member's name. He was like the camp leader."

On the day the Emmy nominations were announced, with Clooney's Outstanding Lead Actor in a Drama Series nod among them, the movie's cast and crew congratulated him in a way that was totally Clooney-approved. They hung a sign on his trailer that read, "To George Clooney, Emmy Schmemmy. Signed, The Cast and Crew of *From Dusk Till Dawn*."

Clooney even earned a few good-natured laughs from the much more serious Harvey Keitel. "I don't think Harvey's ever laughed so much on a movie set," executive producer Lawrence Bender told *Premiere*. On the first day of production, Keitel finished an intense scene only to be greeted by his costar joking, "That was terrific, Harvey. Reminds me of my early work." Keitel responded, "Oh, fuck you, fuck you," but then got back at Clooney by finding some of the star's early acting head shots, the ones with the shoulder-length flowing hair and big cheesy grins, long before his classic leading-man good looks had hit their stride, and plastered them all over the set. "Jeez, I used to be pretty, too," Keitel teased, asking Clooney to autograph one of the photos for him. "Dear

Harvey," Clooney cheekily wrote. "You show a lot of promise. Next time you get to L.A., call me. I'll help you find an agent."

His lighthearted approach to the filmmaking also helped Clooney get through the final weeks of production, which had stretched into the fall and overlapped with his days on the *ER* set. It made for a physically and mentally exhausting experience, not only because of the work schedule—"I worked seven days a week for over forty days," he told *Entertainment Weekly,* "doing both *ER* and then finishing at three in the morning sometimes for *Dusk*, then making a 6 A.M. call again in L.A."—but also because it required him to channel the energy to portray such polar opposite characters, the violent, murderous Seth Gecko and the troubled but caring lifesaver, Dr. Doug Ross.

"On the movie set, I'd shoot people and want to fix them," he joked to *Premiere*. "[On *ER*], I'd want to give a kid a lollipop and say, 'Put this in your mouth, you little fuck.'"

There was also the stress of managing the inherent difference between working on a TV set and working on a movie set. With the rotating cast of directors on *ER*, each one looking to brand the show by eliciting something unique from the cast members, Clooney realized he couldn't listen to each and every one of them. He was the shepherd of his character, and listening to more than a dozen different directors was only going to make for a very schizophrenic portrayal of Dr. Doug, a character he felt very protective of.

On a movie set, however, the director is, well, the director, and Clooney quickly learned that Robert Rodriguez fully expected the actors to carry out his suggestions. "The first few days on the set of the film, Robert was, 'Do it this way,' and I was, 'Yeah, yeah, yeah, got it,' and I'd do it my way," Clooney told the *Los Angeles Times*. "And he said to me, 'You're not doing it,' and I said, 'You're absolutely right.' I had to learn to be directed again."

That would end up being yet another rewarding part of the *From Dusk Till Dawn* experience for Clooney. When it was over, and he was back on the *ER* set full time, he'd proved he could handle himself on a movie set with intimidating costars and a strong director. He'd reinforced his reputation as a fun, fair and friendly coworker, he'd exhibited a work ethic that few actors, especially ones being touted as the biggest star on television, would even attempt; he'd shown his *ER* producers that he appreciated the flexibility in scheduling that allowed him to make movies while he was starring on the show; and he'd garnered a movie poster full of positive quotes from various movie reviewers across the country.

So what if the movie made a modest $25.8 million (on a $19 million budget)? It wasn't a rousing success overall, but for Clooney it was a personal triumph. He was continuing on his way, and his next big break was right around the corner, from the outstretched hand of a familiar champion of the career of George Clooney.

14

Between the Boob Tube and the Big Screen

The world changed. Steven Spielberg sent me a note, saying, The Peacemaker *is the first film from our new studio and I'd love you to do it. I'd made $250,000 on* From Dusk Till Dawn *and then Steven was offering me $3 million to star in his first movie at DreamWorks.*

—George Clooney

As *ER*'s second season got underway and Clooney wrapped filming on the Quentin Tarantino/Robert Rodriguez collaboration *From Dusk Till Dawn*, there was no denying that, for better or worse, he found himself in the middle of instant fame.

Before *From Dusk Till Dawn* was even released in January 1996, Clooney was already receiving movie scripts from nearly every major movie studio in Hollywood. His "instant" success on *ER* (success that, of course, had been a decade in the making) led them to believe instant movie success would follow. Tempting as it was, he'd held out for a smaller, quality movie with *Dusk*, and the move was about to pay off.

With season two of his five-year commitment to *ER* in progress, Clooney was approached by Universal to star in what the studio hoped would be its next big franchise: an adaptation of the radio program and comic book superhero The Green Hornet. A wealthy newspaperman by day, Britt Reid donned a mask to fight crime as The Green Hornet by night, aided by his trusty sidekick, Kato. The Green Hornet was unlike most superheroes in that his costume consisted almost solely of the mask, a fedora and a crisp overcoat (no green tights, despite what the moniker might imply). That meant his suave, debonair daytime appearance wouldn't change that much when he flipped into crimefighter mode, and Clooney, who had grown more and more handsome each year, was the perfect choice for the role. Britt spent lots of time in well-tailored suits, and Clooney knew how to wear a suit.

Jason Scott Lee had signed on to star as Kato, *Evil Dead* (and future *Spider-Man*) director Sam Raimi had committed to directing, and Universal had ponied up a $3 million paycheck for Clooney, which made the already appealing role all that much better. And after turning in a *From Dusk Till Dawn* performance that would eventually win him raves, not to mention a full season of Emmy-nominated performances on *ER*, Clooney felt confident that he was now ready to handle a starring role in a blockbuster movie.

He wasn't the only one. Less than a month after signing on the dotted line to star in *The Green Hornet*, the star got another offer, and it was one that he would have a hard time refusing. The money was the same—$3 million—but the new offer was a chance to work for Steven Spielberg once again.

Spielberg, one of the executive producers on *ER* during the show's first season, was the talk of the town with news that he and friends David Geffen (the founder of Geffen Records) and Jeffrey Katzenberg (a former head executive at Walt Disney) were launching their own studio. DreamWorks SKG (Spielberg Katzenberg Geffen) was to be a new kind of studio, not unlike the original United Artists, dedicated to making both big-budget and smaller, more artistic films, as well as video games and TV shows. Launched with nearly $100 million from the three founders' personal coffers, as well as a cash infusion of $500 million from Microsoft cofounder Paul Allen, the studio officially set up shop in 1994.

DreamWorks quickly developed its first movie project as the action-thriller *The Peacemaker*, about a terrorist-hijacked nuclear warhead. A lot was riding on the studio's first splash into theaters, and Spielberg knew exactly who he wanted to star in the movie.

"You know, I have a framed letter from Steven Spielberg, saying, 'Here's our first film for DreamWorks. Do you want to do it?' Like I'm going to say no to that," Clooney said.

Convinced not only by his own observations but also by what he'd heard about the caliber of Clooney's performance in *From Dusk Till Dawn*, Spielberg was certain that Clooney was exactly the right guy to play Special Forces Intelligence Officer Colonel Thomas Devoe, the CIA specialist whose Russian contacts and a partnership with government nuclear expert Julia Kelly (Nicole Kidman) would allow him to track down and secure the wayward weapon. Spielberg, who had made blockbusters like *Jaws*, *E.T.* and *Jurassic Park* for Universal, had the clout with the studio to ask execs for the favor of letting Clooney out of his *Hornet* deal, and when the director promised to helm the *Jurassic* sequel *The Lost World*, Clooney was officially went from *The Green Hornet* to *The Peacemaker*, with filming on the DreamWorks premiere film to begin in May 1996, after *ER*'s second season had wrapped.

When it rains, though, it pours, and not long after Clooney had signed on to make *The Peacemaker* during his summer 1996 hiatus from *ER*, he was approached about another project, a Fox romantic comedy called *One Fine Day*. Clooney very much wanted to do both projects—why not test the waters as a big-budget action hero and romantic leading man at the same time?—but there was again a scheduling glitch. Not only did *One Fine Day* begin filming in March, while *ER* was still in full swing, but the movie was also going to be shot on location in New York City, while his NBC drama, of course, was filmed in Los Angeles.

Still, the appeal of the movie drew Clooney in, not just because he would be starring opposite Michelle Pfeiffer, but also because *One Fine Day* was exactly the kind of movie he enjoyed as a viewer. Covering one very busy day in the life of two divorced parents who are being pulled in various career-defining and child-rearing directions, the movie finds newspaper reporter Jack Taylor and architect Melanie Parker crossing paths as they try to get their kids off on a class trip. The uptight Melanie clashes with fly-by-the-seat-of-his-pants Jack, though eventually his charm wins her over, her beauty wins him over, their career crises are averted and the story ends happily with the two 'rents smooching it up in Melanie's living room. Clooney called the movie a throwback to the romantic comedies of Spencer Tracy and Katharine Hepburn.

He would be coming into the project late in the game. Producer Lynda Obst, whose own life was the inspiration for the story of Jack and Melanie's one fine day, had tried to cast several A-list Hollywood leading men opposite Pfeiffer, without much luck. Kevin Costner, Tom Cruise and John Travolta had all been offered the part, and had all turned it down, reportedly because they felt it was a thankless role: between the beautiful Pfeiffer and two adorable kid actors, who was going to notice whatever male star happened to be standing across from them, or so the thinking went.

But when Obst and Pfeiffer, along with *One Fine Day* director Michael Hoffman, watched clips of Clooney in action on *ER* and *From Dusk Till Dawn*, the women were sold. "There's something that women call being a real guy," Obst told *People*. "It's hard to describe, but we know it when we see it and he's it. He has a wonderful ability to make a woman weak at her knees."

Added Pfeiffer, whose sister, actress DeDee Pfeiffer, had dated Clooney when he moved to Los Angeles in the early '80s, "It became clear to me in about ten or fifteen minutes that he was really this character, and that he really had everything that he needed: he was charming and he was funny. He could be a little bit of a dickhead and be charming at the same time. And all of that was important."

So, despite Hoffman's concerns that Clooney had too many TV actor "tics" (a concern that would haunt the actor during his time on other movie sets down the road), Clooney was offered another $3 million payday, and accepted the role of Jack Taylor after *ER* producer John

Wells yet again agreed to shoot Dr. Doug Ross scenes around the star's new, bicoastal work schedule.

Add in the fact that he would later sign on to become the new big-screen Batman later in the year—meaning he would shoot three movies and star on *ER* full time in 1996—and professionally, Clooney was having the kind of year he had hoped for, but not realistically expected to happen, after all those years languishing in bad TV shows and even worse movies.

First though, he had to finish up his second season on *ER*. Critics suggested a bit of his momentum as TV's number one leading man might have been knocked out of him when he failed to win the Emmy Award for Outstanding Lead Actor. Not so. Though *ER* had handily won the ratings war with CBS medical series rival *Chicago Hope*, that show's star, Mandy Patinkin, beat out both Clooney and *ER*'s Anthony Edwards for the Emmy. Clooney and Tony both took the loss well, and the fact that *ER* did win more than a half a dozen Emmys (including an award for Julianna Margulies, as well as honors for the show's editing, directing, writing and casting) was a source of pride for the entire cast.

But there were individual challenges for Clooney to deal with during that second season, beginning with his hair. He had cut his hair short and darkened it for *From Dusk Till Dawn*, and the result, with the remaining locks brushed severely forward, was called "The Clooney Caesar." Jennifer Aniston's shag haircut on *Friends* became "The Rachel Cut," the most popular women's hairstyle since Farrah Fawcett's winged 'do in the 1970s, and Clooney's short new style became the look men copied when he popped up with it for the second season premiere of *ER*.

"I just wanted [Seth Gecko] to look like a guy who never had his hair cut," Clooney told *US Weekly*. "So I took a razor blade, and I cut off all my hair into, like, this Caesar haircut. I did it myself, with a razor blade, and I cut it into this look. But because I was also doing this popular series at the time, the haircut ended up becoming something that I would get known for."

Media outlets breathlessly covered the new 'do, as they had begun to cover everything about Clooney since the first season of *ER*. He began appearing on the cover of every entertainment magazine, and his father, Nick, even recalled the excitement of seeing his son on the cover of *Newsweek* as he and George's mother were vacationing in Australia. "I just went bats," Nick Clooney told *Premiere*. "I was gauche. I was walking up to total Australian strangers, going, 'See this? This is my son! This is my son!'"

Clooney himself, however, took his new tabloid magnate status in stride, even though it meant any time he was spotted in the presence of an attractive female, especially a fellow celebrity, news stories followed suggesting he had a new girlfriend. When he and Noah Wyle guest starred on *Friends*—as doctors, though not their *ER* characters—he was linked to Courteney Cox and Lisa Kudrow. He and Jennifer Aniston both had headline-making haircuts, so he must be dating her, too. He was at The Ivy for a friend's birthday with several other celebs, including Michael Bolton and his girlfriend (and now *Desperate Housewives* star) Nicollette Sheridan. When Sheridan stood up to leave the restaurant and Clooney hugged her goodbye, photographers snapped a photo that was published with a story portraying Sheridan and the eligible bachelor as the hottest new Hollywood twosome. The celebrity magazines and TV tabloid shows, in fact, would go on to link Clooney with models Cindy Crawford, Elle MacPherson (his eventual *Batman & Robin* costar) and Vendela, actress Karen Duffy, even Sarah Ferguson, the Duchess of York, all of whom, he would later claim, he had either never met, or shared only friendships with.

The media hounds and paparazzi irked the generally open and convivial star, however, when they followed him home. "I don't care about a man taking my picture in a public place, but I care if he comes into my yard and shoots in my bedroom window," Clooney said. Before he purchased Casa de Clooney after his first season on *ER*, "The paparazzi found my old house . . . the house is on the street and they [were] climbing the fence." One frightened photog was cornered by superpet Max the potbellied pig, who held him hostage as he huddled in a corner until Clooney came out to see why the watch-pig was making a fuss.

Clooney wasn't totally safe on the *ER* set either, though his biggest crisis was sparked by the shocking accusations of a coworker. While trying to nail an especially intense scene as Dr. Doug, Clooney kept hearing an extra talking. He asked her a couple of times, he said, to be quiet. Yet, when the film began rolling again, the woman, who happened to be African-American, began talking again, loudly enough for the actor to hear and have his concentration blown. Admitting that he lost his temper and asked her to stop talking for a third time, Clooney was not at all prepared for what happened next. The extra went to the Anti-Defamation League and charged the *ER* star with making racially abusive remarks to her in public. "She said I stood around the set in front of thirty blacks, including the ones I work with and am very close with, and said, 'Let's go coon hunting some niggers,'" Clooney told *Premiere*. "And I'm saying to myself, 'Okay, here comes the hell.'"

To add fuel to the firestorm, the Anti-Defamation League leaked the story to the *Los Angeles Times*, and, without Clooney's response, the newspaper ran with the story. "They printed the story without ever investigating anyone," he said, having told a reporter that he could ask anyone on the *ER* set and would be assured that Clooney had never made such remarks.

Clooney probably could have let the situation die a natural death, since everyone who knew him and had worked with him (including his girlfriend at the time, *Head of the Class* actress Kimberly Russell, who is African-American) knew he had been falsely accused. The speech was completely out of character for someone who made such a point of demanding that everyone around him on a TV or movie set be treated equally. Not to mention that he had been raised by a father who had sacrificed jobs and financial security for his family to fight against people who did make racist, hate-filled comments. But Clooney decided that, private perceptions of him aside, what those who didn't know him might conclude from the accusations made the brewing scandal too troublesome to ignore.

His response was typically Clooney-like, employing his penchant for speaking out against that which he sees as an injustice, as well as his love of pulling a good prank. He decided to call the Anti-Defamation League on their own game, by reporting his own case of racial slander. "I'm an Irish-American. I think I've been defamed and I need to know what to do," Clooney said in a phone call to the ADL. He went on to tell an ADL rep that a coworker had made "some pretty terrible claims" against him, to an agency like the ADL, and that the agency had leaked the story to the *Times*. Had he been defamed, Clooney asked the ADL rep. Yes, replied the rep, you've been slandered. And what organization was responsible for this?

"It's the Anti-Defamation League," George replied. "My name is George Clooney and I want to know what you're going to do about it."

The actor took the matter a step further. When the ADL finally launched an investigation of the episode, Clooney asked several extras and crew members present on the *ER* set the day the alleged remarks were made to talk to ADL reps. All testified that they'd never heard Clooney say anything remotely like the comments that had been attributed to him. The ADL, ultimately, found that no racial remarks had been made, and apologized to the *ER* star. The *L.A. Times* also ran a retraction.

Another troublesome, and also untrue, mini-scandal revolving around his job at *ER* was media gossip that Clooney and Anthony Edwards were not getting along because Edwards was jealous of Clooney's instant, wild popularity with viewers, and of the movie offers Clooney was now receiving. Both denied the suggestion repeatedly; Clooney had even told reporters that he felt Edwards had deserved an Emmy award for the first season even more than he had. "[He] should have won [the Emmy]," Clooney said, "It's as simple as that. He captained the best show on television for a year and he should have won for the performance he gave in 'Love's Labors Lost.'"

There was also a lifetime of good blood between the two TV doctors, considering that Clooney had once saved the life of Edwards' baby. During the first season of *ER*, the cast had gathered across the street from the Warner Bros. lot to enjoy a meal at the Smoke House restaurant, a retro, home-cooking establishment that's been popular for years with celebs who work at Warner Bros.

Edwards, or Tony as his castmates called him, had brought his baby son, Bailey, to the eatery, and, in the midst of all the chatter amongst the castmates, the baby began to choke on a piece of food.

"We were all in our doctor's smocks, and nobody knew who we were then," Clooney told *Newsweek*. "Anthony Edwards had his baby with him, and the baby starts to choke on a french fry. And all five of us, in our doctor's outfits, are going, 'Somebody help us!'"

It made for one of Clooney's great talk show storytelling experiences—a talent he'd certainly picked up from listening to Uncle George spin his yarns when the younger George was a boy—but the humorous tale and happy ending that Clooney shared left a few details out.

Edwards would later tell the rest of the story: that it was Clooney who finally had the presence of mind to turn Bailey upside down and gently strike his back until the food was dislodged. The baby was fine, and Clooney, whether relying on his experience on the show, or just basic instinct, had saved the day.

The cast's closeness was just one of the reasons Clooney felt it was ridiculous, and to the detriment of the show and the entire cast and crew, to get caught up in even the suggestion of on-set strife. *ER* had ended its first season as one of the best dramas on TV. If those involved were to prove it hadn't been a fluke, just a flavor of the moment with viewers, they would have to step up their efforts for the show's second season, and that's where Clooney's interests lay. In his mind, the structure, the pace and the intense storytelling had been well established during the first season, and viewers had gotten to know the characters well enough to become invested in them.

But if *ER* was going to remain appointment viewing, the writers and the actors were going to have to give the audience more. "One reason our show took off was because it was something you hadn't seen before. But gurneys bashing through the door—that gimmick is old hat now. This is the year where my character starts to figure out that the way he's skated through life doesn't really work anymore," Clooney told *TV Guide*. "In ['Hell and High Water'] it all comes to a head. I hit rock bottom and I think people will understand all the dumb things I do."

Viewers come to understand after "Hell and High Water" that Dr. Ross's life has been ruled by bitter resentment against his father, a serial philanderer who abandoned Doug and his mom when Doug was a boy. He had no male role model in his life, so the memories of what his father had been were his guiding force into adulthood. When he sleeps with his friend Carter's girlfriend, fights with his friend Mark Greene and rails against the County General administration over a young patient, Doug's emotionally bereft side takes center stage. Then, when he's forced to take a job he hates after being laid off at the ER, and is then confronted with the task of saving a dying boy trapped in a drain during a heavy rain storm, viewers see how desperately Ross wants to be a better man. Future episodes would find Ross tracking down and confronting his father (played by veteran actor James Farentino), who would continue to disappoint the doc. But it also finally gave the character insight into his own development, his own shortcomings and his own lack of emotional maturity, which, in Clooney's five seasons on the show, allowed him the opportunity to really develop and grow the character.

And it continued to prepare him well for his burgeoning big-screen career.

15

"You've Become Elvis!"

Look, if I'm walking out of a cathouse with some hooker on my arm, I deserve it. I'm a celebrity, a public figure, that's fair. But if I'm walking down the street with my girlfriend or my secretary and someone comes up and says, "Hey, does she give good head?"—which is what happens almost every day—there has to be a line drawn.

—George Clooney

Without a doubt, 1996 was the year that would set the tone for Clooney's big-screen career. But it was also the year he would lay down the gauntlet with the media.

His childhood as the son of a newsman left Clooney with an admiration for the kind of journalism skills and integrity held forth by media legends like the late, great Edward R. Murrow. His newfound fame, however, afforded him a completely different view into the realities of how the entertainment media worked, and he didn't find it a pretty picture.

To be fair, Clooney has been more cooperative than many, if not most, celebrities in the give-and-take of media coverage of his career. A quick search of archived magazine cover stories, publicity Q&As and TV interviews will show that there's no lack of coverage of George

Clooney's career and personal life, and much of it comes with direct input from the actor. Even as his star continued to rise, through to his Oscar-winning days and after, he's always sat down with a variety of entertainment journalists, and has a reputation among them for being more straightforward and forthcoming in those interviews than the average celeb. He may sometimes tell his stories again and again, but it's as much a product of his love of storytelling as it is his attempt to placate reporters with a well-rehearsed sound bite. His TV show and movie costars have often pointed out that they've heard the same tales of debauchery about Clooney and The Boys, but they laugh every time they hear them, because Clooney clearly relishes sharing them so much, and is such a charming and witty storyteller. "I just picture George's brain as this incredible filing system of funny anecdotes about the things he's done," Anthony Edwards told *US* magazine. "Even if you've heard the story five hundred times, he tells it so well that you can't help but laugh."

But with the paparazzi now creeping into his backyard and outlets like the tabloid TV shows trying to spin stories out of situations where clearly none existed—like his alleged fling with Nicollette Sheridan—Clooney felt it was time to take a stand before what he felt was careless coverage got out of hand.

"Every single day, some photographer or other tries to get into my face and embarrass me," Clooney told *Cosmopolitan* magazine. "I was with my buddy the other day, and a photographer came up and was like, 'Hey George, is that your gay lover?' And you sit there, going, 'Yeah, sure this is my gay lover,' and if you punch the guy out, you give him a story and a lawsuit, which is all he wants in the first place."

The target of his ire: the syndicated tabloid TV show *Hard Copy*, a sort of *National Enquirer* for the tube. Long before cell phone cameras were ubiquitous and everyone ended up on YouTube, *Hard Copy* distinguished itself for employing guerilla methods to obtain often-embarrassing video of celebrities doing and saying things they wouldn't want to have televised. The more embarrassing or outrageous the video, and the bigger the stars those videos featured, the more money the paparazzi made from them, and *Hard Copy* led the way with this footage.

From the moment *ER* became a huge hit and he became the show's breakout star, Clooney was a favorite celeb for the *Hard Copy* producers to feature. Often, the footage was a result of the photographers trying to provoke him into some sort of angry reaction, as was a common behavior to get celeb footage. They'd see him with a female and make derogatory remarks about her, trying to get him to defend her. "I walked outside with a girl who's overweight, and a photographer goes, 'Hey George, who's the fat chick you're walking with?' So you curse a guy like that out, and he sells the story to *Hard Copy*."

They had tried to break into his home, he said. And, in one pathetic attempt to make something out of nothing, *Hard Copy* had aired a clip from the movie *The Harvest*, an independent 1993 movie in which Clooney had taken a small role as a favor to his cousin Miguel Ferrer. The role, that of a lip-synching transvestite who sings the Belinda Carlisle song "Heaven Is a Place on Earth" while wearing a blonde wig, falsies, a miniskirt and a gold bra, would have been totally forgettable except for *Hard Copy*'s decision to air footage from the film, with the intimation that maybe the clip was an indication of what new TV heartthrob George Clooney really liked to do in his spare time.

Still, that wasn't the final straw for Clooney. That came one night, early in 1996, when he was dining at an L.A. restaurant with a friend. He looked over at the table next to him and saw a couple that appeared to be celebrating a birthday. There was even a cake, and waiters singing birthday wishes to the couple. But Clooney happened to notice that the duo also had a small video camera on the table, and that the camera was on red, meaning it was recording. Not only that, but it was pointed not at the alleged birthday party, but at Clooney. Such a ruse was a common tactic the "stalkerazzi" employed, and the actor recognized it as such immediately. He leaned over to their table and asked them to turn the camera off. When they didn't, he was not at all surprised to see the footage of the "party," and of him asking the couple to turn the camera off, being aired on the next episode of *Hard Copy*.

Clooney was livid, and he did what he always does when he gets angry: he wrote a letter. He and his father, he's said, are frequent writers of letters to the editor.

This little missive, typed on his beloved old-school IBM Selectric manual typewriter, was addressed to Linda Blue Bell, a Paramount executive who worked on both Hard Copy and another, more celeb-friendly syndicated tabloid show, *Entertainment Tonight*.

"I said, 'Look, you guys have always been very nice to me [at *Entertainment Tonight*],'" Clooney said. "'I do an interview with you once every two weeks. But I'm not going to help you make money so you can use it to buy a paparazzi video of me.'"

Clooney got a response quickly, and from the head of the creative affairs department for Paramount Television. *Hard Copy*, he was told, would not only agree to never air footage of the *ER* star again, but the exec promised to investigate the show's methods of obtaining paparazzi footage in general. Clooney agreed to call off his threatened boycott of *ET* if the exec was willing to put the promise to keep him off *Hard Copy* in writing, and a letter to that effect was sent to the star. Clooney framed the letter and put it on his wall, and also continued to monitor whether or not the exec would keep his word by recording *Hard Copy* every night to make sure his face didn't pop up on it. It didn't. For several months.

Meanwhile, Clooney had much on his plate work-wise, as the year was proving to be exciting, fruitful, and, though he certainly wouldn't complain about the influx of work being thrown his way, incredibly exhausting.

While heading into spring and winding down on the second season of *ER*, the busy actor began commuting cross-country every week to New York City in March to begin work on his romantic dramedy *One Fine Day* with Michelle Pfeiffer.

The movie was being shot at more than forty different locations around the Big Apple, including the Upper West Side, where residents were still angry about their lives being disrupted by the recent shoot for Barbra Stresiand's *The Mirror Has Two Faces*. Even the presence of the soon-to-be Sexiest Man Alive did not quell the New Yorkers' frustration with the film crews, and they responded by calling in fake bomb threats to disrupt production and try to get the movie's location moved elsewhere.

Clooney, meanwhile, had his own crosses to bear. Not only was he exhausted by the multi-coast work schedule, but, while filming scenes in Central Park, he quickly learned he was allergic to a fertilizer used there. He also suffered a broken eye socket in a spirited game of basketball with the crew. He had a few days' down time on the movie set but had to get creative to cover the injury on TV. "I was still shooting *ER* at the time, and I had to do things like hold a baby in front of my eye until the swelling went down," he told the *Los Angeles Times*.

On-screen, *One Fine Day* was going along swimmingly. Clooney and Michelle Pfeiffer had instant chemistry, and he had no trouble conjuring up inspiration for playing an old-time newspaper reporter, out for the big scoop. "Jack's a bit of an idiot," Clooney said of the character he says he based partly on his dad, and partly on Brian Keith's performance as Uncle Bill on the TV show *Family Affair*. "He's a very good reporter. I grew up with those guys, I know them. They always have some sort of food stains on their coats. They're great at one thing and lousy at everything else."

He and Pfeiffer also bonded with the young actors who were playing their children, Jack's daughter Maggie (Mae Whitman) and Melanie's son Sammy (Alex D. Linz). His playfulness with the kid stars was evident on the screen, especially in scenes where he was able to play a big kid himself, much to the obvious delight of his young costars.

He was used to working with babies as *ER*'s pediatrician, but it turned out older children found him as charming as his females costars did. It also helped that he'd made a deal with Whitman and Linz: every time he said a curse word in front of them, he had to give them a dollar, prompting him to joke at the end of the shoot that he had coughed up enough cash to pay the kids' way through college.

He got along so well with the younger cast members, in fact, that Michelle Pfeiffer made a $10,000 bet that her costar would have a child before he turned forty. "George is all talk. He's the kind of guy who'll have several kids when he gets into it," she said. The actor accepted the bet, and, of course, won. He had enjoyed being with the kids on the movie set, but the experience had just reinforced his feeling that he was a better uncle than a potential dad. "I'm a fun uncle. I get all the fun because they only see me once in a while," Clooney told *People*. "Then I come into the trailer and their parents have to take them home and discipline them and do all the things I don't want to be responsible for."

Clooney was also getting more comfortable with negotiating the differences between acting for TV and acting on the big screen, all the more trying since he was once again, as he had while filming *From Dusk Till Dawn*, doing both simultaneously. *One Fine Day* director Michael Hoffman got over his initial reservations about Clooney's TV actor tendencies very soon after filming began. "He's like watching Cary Grant," Hoffman told *Vanity Fair*. "Men will like him because he's a respectable and viable advocate for their position. And women obviously love him."

Aside from those grumpy Upper West Siders, New Yorkers liked him so much that they would often pool into crowds during location filming, prompting producer Obst to tell her star, "Oh my God, you've become Elvis!"

When filming wrapped, Clooney felt certain he'd turned in a good performance, and when the movie was released in December 1996, the critics agreed. The movie, written by Neil Simon's daughter Ellen Simon, didn't fare quite as well, with reviews calling it an "uninspired formula movie" (Roger Ebert) and "bedraggled" (Salon.com), and ReelViews' James Berardinelli suggesting it "lacks focus and direction, and that makes it one fine mess." At the box office, it would make around

$46 million on a $33 million budget, but the lukewarm reviews didn't tell the whole story. *One Fine Day* was released during a particularly heavy holiday season that pitted it against box office favorites like *Jerry Maguire*, *Beavis and Butthead Do America* and the first *Scream* movie.

But, as with *From Dusk Till Dawn*, while the movie itself was ultimately considered less than a success, Clooney's performance earned reviews that only added to studio execs' feeling that just as he was the hottest star on TV, he was soon to be the hottest actor on the big screen. *Variety* said Clooney is "the rare major actor who, like Clark Gable, holds equal appeal for men and women, and here he shows a light touch that offers further evidence of considerable range and ability to dominate on the big screen." Salon.com said "rakish, rumpled and effortlessly charming Clooney is the single big surprise of *One Fine Day*. . . . Yeah, [he's] infantile—but damned if Clooney, with his relaxed goofiness, doesn't make this regular-but-sensitive-guy routine work."

Before the multitasking actor had much of a chance to mull over his performance in *One Fine Day*, during which the second season of *ER* had wrapped, he was off to begin production on *The Peacemaker*, the first DreamWorks movie, and the one for which Steven Spielberg had called in a personal favor in order to cast Clooney.

The movie was based on a nonfiction article in *Vanity Fair*. The *VF* piece had investigated the former Soviet Union's disposal of its nuclear warheads after its disarmament program was implemented. But, disturbingly, as the writers of the article found out, greedy military officials often stole the nuclear weapons and sold them on the black market to the highest bidders. *The Peacemaker*, then, would revolve around scientist Julia Kelly's (Nicole Kidman) concern that just such events have taken place (with the action shifted from the former Soviet Union to post-Cold War Bosnia), which calls into action cynical, hard-nosed U.S. army colonel Thomas Davoe (Clooney) to use his military connections to try to track down the MIA WMDs and stop a terrorist who's out to exact revenge for the death of his daughter.

Emmy-winning *ER* director Mimi Leder was handpicked by Spielberg to helm her first motion picture, and though she was dealt a personal blow at the time—her father, filmmaker Paul Leder, died of lung cancer as the movie was in pre-production—she decided to see the project through, urged on by pal Clooney.

So, having wrapped *One Fine Day* on May 17, Clooney hung around New York City and began filming *The Peacemaker* on May 21. Though it meant no summer vacation for the hardest-working man on TV, he wasn't complaining. Because he would have to be back in the United States to start the third season of *ER* in the fall, Leder and crew didn't have time to shoot the movie chronologically, which would have required starting the movie in Europe, coming back to New York, and then finishing in Europe. Instead, they filmed *The Peacemaker's* dramatic final half-hour first, outside the UN building on the east side of Manhattan. "It was extremely difficult to start with your emotions so high and geared in fast motion," Leder told *Premiere*. "We were constantly questioning ourselves: have we gone too far?"

Leder's other concerns about the shoot included avoiding action movie clichés. The movie's villain, Dusan Gavrich (Marcel Iures), for instance, plotted a terrible act of vengeance, but the audience was shown his motivation: the death of his wife and child, as well as what he considered to be the ruination of his country by larger powers. "You understand why he's doing it and it makes sense," Clooney said in a TV interview with Larry King. "It doesn't mean you would do it. It doesn't mean it's right. But you understand him."

Despite the attractiveness of the leading man and woman, the script also avoided the usual conventions of such casting by not having the two to fall in love while trying to thwart Gavrich's plot. Off-camera, Clooney got along well with Kidman, as he always does with his female costars. Having heard about the bet Michelle Pfieffer had made with her costar—the $10,000 assertion that he would have kids by the time he was forty—Kidman made the same deal with Clooney. She, too, of course, would lose, but when Clooney eventually received their checks, he sent both of them back to his actress pals, along with a note (no doubt typed on his IBM Selectric) offering double or nothing on a bet that he wouldn't have kids or be married by the time he was fifty. Check back in 2011 for an update on that one.

The fact that his character didn't have any romantic scenes with Kidman's government scientist probably took a bit of pressure off Clooney in terms of the set atmosphere. Kidman was still married to Tom Cruise at the time, and Cruise, not busy with a film of his own, was a constant presence during filming. He and Clooney got along well, playing basketball together in Clooney's down time on the European sets (the movie filmed in Macedonia, Slovakia, Croatia, the Czech Republic, Poland, Russia and Austria) and, with Kidman, spending their July Fourth holiday together in London for the premiere of Cruise's first *Mission: Impossible* movie. Having to film a hot make-out scene with Kidman might have been a buzzkill on Clooney's budding friendship with her A-list hubby.

As enjoyable a time as they had making the movie, the result was, at best, forgettable. Neither Kidman nor Clooney turned in bad performances;they simply didn't have well-fleshed-out characters to portray. The action-heavy movie devoted little time to developing the characters' backstories, and that, combined with all the techno-babble, foreign politics and terrorist activity (this was, after all, pre–September 11, before Americans had been confronted with terrorist activity on their own soil), left little for audiences to invest in.

The movie ultimately took in $41 million at the U.S. box office, but against a $50 million budget, it was considered a flop. The *Los Angeles Times* concluded that "What *The Peacemaker* doesn't do well . . . is bring much in the way of emotion or character development to the table," while *Entertainment Weekly* added that the "essential spark of surprise is missing. The mechanics of 'breathless' suspense are blanketed by an atmosphere of creeping caution," and Toronto newspaper the *Globe and*

Mail called *The Peacemaker* "A ticket to terminal boredom."

As for Clooney's performance reviews, they were mixed. The *San Francisco Examiner* said, "[What] he doesn't have much of is variety. There is only so much winking an audience can bear before gastrointestinal disturbance sets in." The *San Francisco Chronicle* was harsher, declaring, ". . . his rugged good looks spell movie star, but his body language spells Don Knotts, without the wit." On the flip side, the *New York Times* called Clooney "naturally well cast as a charming roué," and the *Los Angeles Times* said, "Both Kidman and Clooney give dependable, movie-star performances in these James Bond-ish roles." Not rave reviews, but no one blamed the two leads for the movie's poor performance, either.

The question that seemed to puzzle most critics and Hollywood reporters was why and how the subpar movie had ended up being the much-anticipated first film project from the new DreamWorks studio.

As for Clooney, even with another season of *ER* and two more big-screen movie roles under his belt, the year still held a couple of major surprises, one the movie role of a lifetime, and the other, his most serious relationship since his ill-fated marriage.

16

Being Batman . . . and a Boyfriend

I basically buried a franchise.

—George Clooney

Just how valuable a Hollywood player did Warner Bros., the studio behind *ER*, think George Clooney was? Valuable enough so that they hatched a plan to keep their star and his big-screen ambitions in the family.

By the time Clooney was finished with his second season on *ER*, he'd already completed two movies and had another one lined up for his summer 1996 hiatus. It was clear to the studio that Clooney was committed to parlaying his TV star status as far as it would take him in Hollywood, and the smartest thing for Warner Bros. to do was try to keep him on the WB lot as much as possible. First, he was a hot property all over Hollywood, even though none of his movies had yet panned out as big box office hits. Second, the thinking was that if Warner Bros. could keep him happy with movie roles, he might also be more willing to re-up his *ER* contract when his original deal for five seasons on the show expired.

And that is where the idea for George Clooney as the Caped Crusader came in. Stepping into the shoes of one of the most beloved of all comic book superheroes, Clooney signed a three-movie deal with Warner Bros. worth a reported $25–28 million, with the next *Batman* feature as the first movie of the pact.

Michael Keaton had kicked off the *Batman* movie franchise for Warner Bros., starring in 1989's Tim Burton-directed *Batman* and the 1992 Burton-helmed sequel *Batman Returns*. Though Keaton would go on to be very popular in the movies, initially fans were dead set against Burton casting him, writing thousands of letters to Warner Bros. proclaiming what a mistake the studio had made. Like the more recent recasting of Daniel Craig as the newest James Bond, which also caused a flood of anti-Craig sentiments until fans actually got a look at the new 007 in action, fans of Gotham City's legendary superhero were forced to admit they'd misjudged Keaton. Burton had originally cast him in the role of wealthy businessman Bruce Wayne/Batman because he felt Keaton was the perfect actor to pull off the dark, brooding aspect of the character, and especially after Keaton held his own against Jack Nicholson as the villainous Joker, *Batman* fans agreed that Burton had been right on with hiring Keaton.

Two movies in, though, Keaton decided he wanted to pursue other types of roles, and the Batsuit was passed along to Val Kilmer.

Kilmer, in 1995's *Batman Forever*, was equally well cast as the moody hero. But the production proved to be tension-filled, with Kilmer, who has a reputation for being a difficult coworker, and director Joel Schumacher constantly butting heads. When it was time to plan the 1997 follow-up, *Batman & Robin*, Kilmer had already signed on to star in *The Saint* for Paramount, and the scheduling conflict was an opportunity for Schumacher to bring in a new Batman.

Enter George Clooney.

No matter how the final product, the worst-reviewed *Batman* movie in the series, turned out, there was every reason to believe Clooney would be able to handle the part. His Doug Ross was nothing if not dark and brooding, and his classic good looks would make for the perfect Bruce Wayne. Schumacher had even mocked up a potential Clooney-as-Batman storyboard by drawing a cowl on a photo of the star in a *From Dusk Till Dawn* ad. It worked, he thought.

The problem with *Batman & Robin*, or rather the biggest of many problems, was the script. It was terrible.

Written by eventual Oscar-winning *A Beautiful Mind* screenwriter Akiva Goldsman, the story was flimsy, overwrought and filled with cartoony characters who were more in line with the campy 1960s live-action *Batman* TV series than the previous string of big-screen dramas that had delighted established *Batman* fans and made millions of new ones.

Clooney, too, had to shoulder some of the blame for the change in tone. He had lobbied producers to make the character a bit lighter in the new movie, arguing that audiences had seen as much of the moody Batman as they could want. He felt fans wanted to see more of a comic book story, a campier, lighter movie, than the first three *Batman* movies had delivered.

He was wrong.

"I thought it was a bad script," he later admitted to *Movieline*. "*Batman* movies have always been the story of the bad guys. Bruce Wayne sits around, going, 'It's so hard to live because my parents were killed when I was little.' We, as an audience, go, 'O.K., you're rich, you're schtupping the most beautiful babes in Gotham City, you've got a mansion and the coolest gadgets. Get over it.' Other than that, it's been about the Joker or the Riddler. There wasn't much for me to do, and I didn't do it very well."

Touché, though, really, what exactly is an actor to do with a movie that begins with a shot of your rubber Bat nipples and pans up to a lingering shot of your rubber Bat butt?

Of the many culprits in the failure of the fourth *Batman* movie, including director Joel Schumacher's obsession with a neon palette and costar Arnold Schwarzenegger's inability as Mr. Freeze to deliver his endlessprofusion of ice puns in a manner that was decipherable, George Clooney's performance as the Caped Crusader should actually be pretty far down on the list.

Schumacher's over-the-top comic book adventure was a Day-Glo mess, with everything, including the flaming green fire, making the movie seem like more of a cartoon than an actual animated movie would have. And the dialogue. The script seemed to have been written for the sole purpose of forcing Uma Thurman to utter as many cheesy double entendres as possible. Her Poison Ivy was a plant-loving scientist named Pamela Isley who turned villainous after being sacrificed by a fellow scientist out to sell an evil invention to the highest bidder. The new, super-sexed-up Ivy then spent the rest of movie slinking around Gotham trying to exact her revenge on the human world, purring ridiculous come-ons like "Come join me, my garden needs tending" and "Some lucky boy's about to hit the honey pot. The winner will receive an evening of my company. I'll bring everything you see here, plus everything you don't."

Then there were the Mr. Freeze-isms, as Ah-nold attempted to make the malignant Freeze both sympathetic (his motivation for evil-doing was to find a cure for his comatose wife) and clever. Neither worked, despite, or rather because of, lines like the Freeze greeting "Ice to see you!" "I'm afraid my condition has left me cold to your pleas of mercy" and "Allow me to break the ice. My name is Freeze. Learn it well. For it's the chilling sound of your doom."

As over-the-top as the villains were in the movie, Clooney was right in his assessment that, despite being the titular superhero, the movie was not really about Batman at all. It was a complaint previous Batmen had made, and one of the reasons that had figured into both Keaton and Kilmer's decisions to quit the series. Batman's role continued to shrink with each subsequent movie, and when the decision was made to make a less dark and deep Caped Crusader in *Batman & Robin*, little did Clooney know that, in supporting the shift, he was also leaving himself with little to do in the movie. And no, as nearly every critic and moviegoer would agree, he didn't do it very well.

Batman/Bruce Wayne's main story line in the movie revolved around thwarting Freeze and caring for Alfred, Bruce/Batman's beloved and loyal servant, who was dying a slow and painful death. The illness was meant to highlight the father-son bond between Bruce/Batman and Alfred, who'd raised him after his parents were killed when he was a child. But, as Clooney himself had recognized, he is not at his best when given bad material, and the only thing that really made viewers believe there was a father-son bond between the two was the fact that, as fans of the TV series, the comic books, the previous movies, they *knew* there was a father-son bond. Clooney's performance was stilted, and, as he'd been made aware by many directors, including Steven Spielberg, he had a tendency to rely on his TV-actor charm—that head of his is constantly bobbing when he's trying to convey emotion—as the go-to acting maneuver. And in *Batman & Robin*, along with all the other problems, it simply didn't work.

And then there was the matter of the Batsuit. The costume weighed forty-five pounds and was, by design, three sizes too small, but that didn't even begin to suggest how uncomfortable it was to film an entire movie wearing the suit.

"Although the movie's fun to do, it's a miserable gig right now, because the suit is awful," the Batsuit's wearer told E! Online at the time. "It's made of hard rubber and weighs about fifty pounds, but the hardest part is that your eyes and ears are covered and your nose is plugged up. I think the most I can keep it on for is fifteen minutes, and then I'm out of it and just soaking wet. If you really had to wear this thing, everybody would kick the hell out of you. I mean, the most elaborate stunt I've been able to do is walk to my trailer."

With all that going against it, it didn't come as too much of a surprise when the reviews of the movie were merciless.

"It's a gee-whiz kiddie movie imagined by pervy grown-ups who get a giggle out of mixing bloodless fight scenes with close-ups of rubber-wrapped butts and baskets," wrote *TV Guide*. "Screenwriter Akiva Goldsman has written quips, not characters and Joel Schumacher still seems miscast as a Bat-action director," added *Newsweek*. "It looks bad: cluttered surfaces, production design reminiscent of overblown

Broadway musicals, editing too fast for the eye to catch up, poor staging of fast action," surmised *Slate*. "*Batman & Robin* drags itself through icicle-heavy sets, dry-ice fog and choking jungle vines, before dying in a frozen heap. Unfortunately, that demise occurs about twenty minutes into the movie, which leaves you in the cold for approximately 106 minutes," wrote the *Washington Post*.

Clooney's performance didn't win raves, either, though most reviewers acknowledged he wasn't given a lot to work with.

"Clooney fails to make much of an impression as The Batman, but to make an impression amongst all the garish theatrics, he would pretty much have to shout his dialogue in rhyming verse, backwards," wrote *The Onion*.

"A non-brooding Batman? All Clooney can do under the circumstances, with those curly dark lashes and wry brows, is speak slowly and smile philosophically. . . . Michael Keaton's Batman was serious. Val Kilmer's was downright depressed. Clooney's is detached and bemused," said the *San Francisco Examiner*, also remarking on Clooney's "stiff cornball delivery and tendency to smile during the most tragic moments."

Added *Variety*, "Physically, Clooney is unquestionably the most ideal Batman to date . . . (but) Clooney is unable to compensate onscreen for the lack of dimension on paper."

In the end, the June 1997 release would cost Warner Bros. $125 million to make, and would earn back a relatively paltry $107 million at the domestic box office. The franchise was dead for sure, at least for the next eight years. But George Clooney didn't singlehandedly put the nail in the temporary coffin of the *Batman* franchise. *Batman & Robin* did.

While the movie didn't turn out to be the commercial hit those involved would have hoped, Clooney did come out relatively unscathed, and hindsight has only made him less accountable for the movie's failures.

Besides, the movie's production had been very pleasant for everyone involved, and for Clooney, specifically, because he was in love.

While on a relaxing trip to Paris in August 1996, during a brief break from *The Peacemaker* production, Clooney had gone out on the town with a Paris newspaper reporter. While knocking back a few refreshments at a club called Barfly, the actor spotted a pretty waitress, Céline Balitran, who was also studying part-time as a law student.

The thirty-five-year-old Clooney was immediately smitten with the blond, French-speaking twenty-one-year-old, and asked his newspaper friend to arrange a meeting. "The next day he calls and says, 'How can I get to know this beautiful girl?'" the reporter told *People*. "So I suggested he take her for a moonlight walk by the Chateau de Versailles, because it's very romantic. 'Great idea,' he said. Then, after three months of not one word, a few weeks ago I got a call from Céline saying, 'Thank you, I'm in love with George in Los Angeles."

Clooney had swept Balitran off her feet, keeping phone lines burning with hours-long calls when he headed back to the United States. It didn't take long for her to agree to visit him in L.A., and during that trip, after he told her they should start dating, she moved into Casa de Clooney.

"Between George and me it was love at first sight," Balitran told a French magazine. "I know this must seem a bit innocent for today, but George represented for me everything a woman could desire. Charming, funny, intelligent, extremely handsome. . . . Two and a half weeks [after meeting him], I left for Los Angeles."

More of a homebody than someone anxious to be out on the Hollywood party scene with her man, Balitran said she and Clooney were happiest visiting flea markets, going to the movies and enjoying quiet dinners at home, where she had been given free reign to redecorate, or, as one of The Boys put it, finally "decorate."

The fact that he was in his first serious relationship since his divorce, or at least the first relationship where he'd cohabitated with his girlfriend, added to the already spectacular year the actor was having in 1996, and made his hectic work schedule all the more bearable.

He began filming *Batman & Robin* while he was working on the third season of *ER*, and though both projects were filmed on the Warner

Bros. lot, his schedule still added up to a one-hundred-hour work week at times.

Balitran often visited him on the *Batman* set, where, as usual, he was the arbiter of fun, a welcome relief for those who'd been a part of the previous *Batman* movie production, where things had gotten so tense between star Val Kilmer and director Joel Schumacher that the two men had gotten into a shoving match at one point after Schumacher chastised the actor for yelling at crew members. "Val is the most psychologically troubled human being I've ever worked with," Schumacher told *Premiere*. "The tools I used working with him—tools of communication, of patience and understanding—were the tools I use on my five-year-old godson. Val is not just high-strung. I think he needs help. I say this to you only because I have said this to him."

Schumacher was so happy to be rid of Kilmer that he would even make some cheeky remarks about the tailoring of the Batsuit, saying there would have to be a bigger codpiece put into the costume for the new Batman. "Please leave my penis out of it," Clooney joked, trying to remain out of the fray of the Batman battle.

With Clooney, "what you see is what you get," Schumacher said, meaning Clooney had a sense of humor and took it upon himself to make sure everyone making *Batman & Robin* had a good time, even though he was the one working two full-time jobs. And having fun on any Clooney set meant practical jokes.

While close pal Richard Kind is his favorite patsy in real life, on the *Batman & Robin* set Clooney went right for his on-screen sidekick Robin, a.k.a. actor Chris O'Donnell. O'Donnell was particularly hot at the time, having already been introduced as Robin in the previous film and getting a meatier role this time around, as a headstrong youngster starting to demand a more equal role beside his superhero mentor. Clooney, good-naturedly, felt this made O'Donnell ripe for a gag or two.

He and Schumacher, having witnessed O'Donnell pull up to the set beaming with pride over his new BMW convertible, ordered dozens of bags of microwave popcorn from craft services and had them dumped into the car, filling it all the way up to the windows with the snack food. On another occasion, they left O'Donnell, in Robin mode, suspended forty feet in the air while the crew went on break. And Clooney enlisted O'Donnell's singing voice to help him when he'd tease another costar, Alicia Silverstone, by singing X-rated versions of Andrew Lloyd Webber tunes from *Cats*.

He also spent down time on the set with Balitran, though they had become a favorite paparazzi target, and one of the resulting video clips would lead Clooney to declare war on the entertainment media.

For nearly six months after he and Paramount had agreed that he would not boycott *Entertainment Tonight* if the company's other tabloid program, *Hard Copy*, refrained from airing any more footage of him, Clooney had monitored the show to make sure it remained Clooney-free. It did.

But in September, the temptation to get in on the coverage of commitment-phobe Clooney's new love affair must have been too much, and *Hard Copy* ended up airing a thirty-second clip of Balitran visiting her boyfriend on the *Batman & Robin* set. It was a run-of-the-mill bit of video, shot by a paparazzi, but it was the principle, not the content, that set Clooney off. Paramount had made an agreement with him, and he had faithfully lived up to his end. But, perhaps thinking enough time had passed that Clooney would just let it slide, *Hard Copy* could no longer make the same claim. Out came the IBM Selectric.

"So now we begin," he typed in a letter to Paramount. "Officially. No more interviews from this day on. Nothing from *ER*. Nothing from *One Fine Day*, nothing from *Batman & Robin*, and nothing from DreamWorks' first film, *The Peacemaker*. These interviews will be reserved for all press but you. *Access Hollywood*, E!, whoever."

It was a bold move on his part, especially so early in his film career, to cut off any press coverage, and his declaration that he was boycotting *Entertainment Tonight* and *Hard Copy* most likely would have backfired on him if his fellow celebrities hadn't supported him. After all, he could control what he personally did, but he couldn't direct how his costars, on the big and small screens, would react to the boycott. They did support his stance, though, and in short order his Warner Bros. TV cohort Dean Cain, of ABC's Superman drama *Lois & Clark*, pulled the plug on a scheduled interview with *Entertainment Tonight* in support of his basketball pal. Clooney's *ER* costars wrote a letter of their own to *ET*, reiterating Clooney's letter from months earlier that they would not talk to *ET* since money that show made was used to purchase paparazzi videos for sister show *Hard Copy*. Soon, A-listers like Jim Carrey, Madonna, Tom Cruise and Steven Spielberg announced that they supported Clooney's efforts to make Paramount TV change the way it operated *Hard Copy*. The star was thrilled. "I'm not punching anybody, and I'm not suing anybody," he told the *Los Angeles Times*. "If it works and there's some change, great. If it doesn't, I did it to take a stand."

Paramount TV gave in, sort of, to the band of celebrities, promising not to purchase any footage of celebrities' children or of celebs being provoked into any sort of confrontation by a member of the paparazzi. That might have been enough to quiet things down for a while, though Clooney continued his crusade against the paparazzi. He told Oprah Winfrey on her daytime talk show that he felt no one would take the potential dangers of dealing with the paparazzi seriously until someone was physically hurt.

Sadly, Clooney's fears about a tragic paparazzi car chase—sparked by a story his *Batman & Robin* costar Arnold Schwarzenegger had told him about being chased off the road with his children in the car—came to fruition the next year, when Princess Diana died in a car crash as she and her boyfriend were trying to evade a pack of photographers.

Clooney took the opportunity to speak out again, publicly, on the paparazzi, even calling a press conference to announce that he felt it was necessary for the Hollywood community to approach Congress about changing the law to make the more outrageous behaviors among the paparazzi illegal. Some celebs supported him again, and it became a hot-button topic when the public became outraged by the death of the internationally beloved Diana.

It also made Clooney not so popular with celebrity event photographers. Not that he minded so much, but when he and Balitran showed up for the red carpet premiere of *The Peacemaker* a few weeks after Princess Diana's death, all the photographers held their cameras in the air and refused to take his picture.

As his father would remind him later, when he'd become involved in public squabbles with members of the political media, you can't dish it out without expecting a reaction, and he had gotten a lot of reaction to his anti-paparazzi campaigns.

All in all, with three major movies under his belt, Clooney was enjoying one of the happiest times of his life, and one of the most important periods in his career: he was starring in the number one TV show in the country; he was, at last, in a happy relationship; he had successfully taken a stand, and been supported by his community, against what he felt was unjust treatment by the paparazzi; and the final product of the *Batman & Robin* production had taught him something very valuable, something that would drive his future plans for his movie career.

"They pay you to do publicity for a film, but I draw the line in lying about it," he told *Movieline*. "You find ways to talk around it. You say it's the biggest movie I've ever seen, and working with these guys was one of the greatest times of my life. You say everything but the fact that the movie is an hour too long and just doesn't work.

"I decided after *Batman & Robin* that I wanted to be sure I could go in and say, 'I'm really proud of the film.' So I didn't do a job for a year. I just focused on finding the right script."

17

Enter Soderbergh

I wouldn't have been prepared for the down period if I hadn't gone through it for a long time beforehand. You realize there are other elements, including luck. I'm no better an actor in Out of Sight *than I was in* Batman & Robin, *which I had shot six months earlier. And I was killed for* Batman & Robin *and praised for* Out of Sight. *The second and third rounds in your career are the ones that define you.*

—George Clooney

Clooney had told reporters that the reason he had never attended the Oscar ceremony, and had, since the first year of *ER*, refused offers to be a presenter on the Academy Awards telecast was that, as a TV actor, he felt he didn't have the right to insinuate himself into the movie world. But, with three major movies under his belt, and very good reviews for two of them, he had absolutely earned the right to call himself a movie star and to take advantage of all that title meant.

For Clooney, though, the focus was on how to become an even bigger movie star, which to him meant not starring in more summer popcorn movies—*Batman & Robin* had taught him that quality should be the main factor in selecting any future projects—but finding a really solid, well-scripted movie that would allow him to show what he could do with such a part.

Meanwhile, he was also taking seriously his role in helping to keep *ER* the number one show on television, and he had an idea to keep the show fresh. He and Anthony Edwards had been discussing the possibility of doing a live episode of the show. *ER*, they felt, with its quick pace and plot twists and turns, would be the perfect material for a live airing, keep viewers on the edge of their seats wondering what the regular cast members would be doing, what gross or tragic medical mishaps would roll into County General throughout the episode, and whether Clooney and company would be able to pronounce all those multisyllabic medical terms without the benefit of multiple shots.

At first, producer John Wells balked at the idea, given the complexity of shooting just one regular episode of the show. But Clooney and Edwards continued to work on him, and he took them seriously enough to broach the idea with the network. The verdict: they loved it, and the show's fourth season premiere, an episode titled "Ambush," would be aired live on September 25, 1997. Despite Clooney's threat to mention the release of his new movie in the middle of an operation during the live telecast, the episode went off without a hitch. Revolving around a film crew making a documentary about life in an emergency room, the episode found Dr. Morgenstern (William H. Macy) suffering a heart attack and Alex Kingston joining the cast as Dr. Elizabeth Corday. As Clooney and Anthony had predicted, viewers tuned in in record numbers, sixty million of them to be exact, setting a new high for the number of viewers to tune in for a series' season premiere.

With his time winding down on the show—just one more season left on his five-year contract—the TV star was also looking for his next big movie break, and it came in the form of a stylish dramedy adaptation of the Elmore Leonard dark comedy novel *Out of Sight*.

Clooney was hooked on the script after reading less than ten pages, and signed on right away. The movie told the unusual love story of a sexy female federal marshal and a lifelong (but not always –successful) bank robber whom she is charged with putting in jail. Jack Foley and Karen

Sisco meet when he breaks out of prison and takes her hostage while making his getaway. They're locked in a car trunk together—very up close and personal—and, despite their, to say the least, different stations in life, their attraction to each other is mutual and immediate. Jack continues on with his escape and leaves her unharmed, but she spends the rest of the movie trying to track him down, ostensibly to return him to the hoosegow, though not before enjoying a scorching hotel romp with him.

With Clooney signed on as Jack, he and director Steven Soderbergh, best known at the time for his 1989 indie hit *Sex, Lies and Videotape*, set about casting the movie's female star. It was a role that demanded a unique actress who, as a daddy's girl/federal marshal, could be tough, almost masculine, in her love of weaponry and bringing down bad guys by any means necessary, but who would also generate such chemistry with Clooney that this committed officer of the law could plausibly not only consider not only an affair with a criminal, but even break several laws herself in order to get her man.

And when Jennifer Lopez walked in the door to audition, both Clooney and Soderbergh immediately knew they'd found their Karen. "This is it. This is the end," Clooney told *People* magazine about his reaction to Lopez's audition. "And immediately, literally instantaneously, she was the girl."

For her audition, Lopez was asked to enact the trunk scene, with Clooney's old leather couch sitting in for the car; he said she'd nailed it perfectly.

The duo clicked immediately when filming began. Lopez was professional, Clooney says, and displayed none of the diva-like behavior she had been accused of in the past. If the film was going to be believable, the two stars had to enjoy working together, and they did.

"We really hit it off," Lopez said. "He's incredibly handsome, and we were taken with each other immediately. Sometimes there's no spark, but the most beautiful thing is when it happens magically. George and I had that."

The criminal activity, Soderbergh's stylish camera work and the movie's stellar supporting cast, which included Don Cheadle, Ving Rhames, Michael Keaton, Dennis Farina, Catherine Keener, Albert Brooks, Steve Zahn and Luis Guzmán, were all part of what makes the crime dramedy fun to watch, but Clooney's scenes with Lopez were truly memorable. *One Fine Day*, as well as his relationships on *ER*, had shown that Clooney was romantic lead material, but his steamy, slow-build flirtations with Lopez were as sexy as the actor has ever been, before or since, on screen. He and Lopez are so well suited as a couple on screen, with their golden complexions, dark, smoky eyes and perfect hair, that you almost start to imagine what pretty babies they'd make together in real life.

"It's essential for the film that the chemistry between me and Jennifer works," Clooney told *She* magazine. "You can't plan that, it's down to luck. There are lots of married couples who work together, but find the chemistry isn't there on the screen. We got lucky."

Added J. Lo about the cool, sexy love scene in *Out of Sight*: "It became a game. By the end, we were ripping our clothes off because the anticipation was too much."

The *Out of Sight* production, which took place in L.A., Miami, Detroit and the Angola Prison in Louisiana (with five hundred real-life inmates used as extras), was the usual friendly, Clooney-esque atmosphere, with lots of joking, camaraderie amongst the cast and crew, and plenty of basketball. Soderbergh said one scene in which Clooney has to portray his character as a bad hoops player was torture for the actor, because it was filmed in front of the Angola inmates. "To be bad in front of five hundred cons was mortifying for him," Soderbergh joked.

It was also during filming on *Out of Sight* that Clooney found out he'd been named *People* magazine's Sexiest Man Alive for 1997. Soderbergh teased him about the honor by having T-shirts printed and distributed to the cast and crew that featured a current photo of the sexy man on the front, and a picture of a toddler-aged Clooney on the back. The actor, of course, appreciated the ribbing, but he viewed the *People* "award" with mixed feelings.

"They're saying a very nice thing about you, but the connotation is always that you're an idiot or you're untalented," Clooney told *Access Hollywood*. It was an unwarranted worry, if he was, in fact, worried about the *People* title, because of the many ways people in Hollywood might have described Clooney, unintelligent and untalented weren't likely to be among them.

All in all, the *Out of Sight* experience had been a positive one for everyone involved, especially for Soderbergh and Clooney, who bonded so well that they would go on to form a production company together.

For Clooney especially, the movie, which filmed much more under the radar than *One Fine Day*, *The Peacemaker*, and certainly *Batman & Robin*, was finally the film that proved his big-screen potential to anyone who still harbored doubts. Not only did critics rave that *Out of Sight* was the best movie adaptation of an Elmore Leonard novel to date, but Clooney's suave, nuanced, slightly cocky, slightly hangdog performance as the heist man with a heart of gold (stolen gold, of course), was deemed spot on, with no qualifications that he was a TV actor playing the part.

> "Clooney is the most impressive he's been on film" —*The Washington Post*

> "Clooney finally comes to his own as the debonair bank robber, a role that combines his good looks and easygoing, laid-back charm." —*Variety*

> "This is Clooney's wiliest, most complex star turn yet . . . and his performance is slyly two-tiered: Foley is all charming moxie on the surface, a bit clueless underneath." —*Entertainment Weekly*

> "Looking leaner and hungrier and less pleased with himself, Clooney turns Jack Foley into a memorable rogue hero, a smart crook who's never been smart enough to stay out of the joint." —*Newsweek*

> "What I liked most about George as an actor is that he's very low key. And that's the way I hear my characters in my books. They say things straight and don't get too excited about anything. I want it as real sounding as I can. And George did a great job of that." —Elmore Leonard

The June 1998 release got lost in the shuffle of big summer blockbusters and failed to make back its almost $50 million budget, but *Out of Sight* finished atop many critics' best-of lists at the end of the year, while the National Society of Film Critics awarded it Best Film, Best Screenplay and Best Director honors, and script adapter Scott Frank was nominated for an Oscar.

"I call it the Jack Kennedy syndrome," Clooney would later tell *Esquire*. "The first thing he did was the Bay of Pigs. A complete failure. But he never tried to hide from it. He admitted his mistake, and he moved on. *Batman & Robin* was terrible, and I was terrible in it. *Out of Sight* came out the next year, and I think it's the best film I've been in."

For both fans and non-fans of George Clooney, the movie remains an underrated gem. "It didn't do well, but that wasn't our fault," Clooney said. "We did everything right."

18

The *Three Kings* Brouhaha

Life's too short.

—George Clooney

Studios continued to throw roles in summer blockbuster movies his way. But Clooney was still having to hustle to land the kinds of roles that, post-*Batman & Robin*, he'd decided to focus on: movies he could tell reporters he was proud of in the obligatory press junkets that go along with major movie releases.

Following his work on *Out of Sight*, landing the lead role in David O. Russell's war drama *Three Kings* should have been a given, but director Russell didn't see it that way at all.

A gritty, action/dramedy, *Three Kings* was also written by Russell. The story revolved round a group of Persian Gulf War vets who, after the war is over, plot to steal and return home with gold that was originally stolen from Kuwait. The four friends get their hands on the booty, but before they can abscond with their ill-gotten goods, they find a group of people whose lives are in danger, and who need their help more than the vets need the gold.

Clooney wanted the part of Major Archie Gates, the special forces op who would mastermind the vets' plan to swipe the gold, hidden in a Saddam Hussein bunker and reachable via a map that was found hidden in the anus of an Iraqi soldier killed by Sgt. Troy Barlow (Mark Wahlberg) in an act of confusion of the rules of engagement after the war's end.

Clooney, a lifelong fan of war movies, war-related biographies and magazines, and, as he's become famous for, the politics behind war, thought Russell's *Three Kings* was one of the best modern war scripts he'd read. The movie, beyond the basic postwar theft story, made points about the parties on both sides of the war and the political motivations of each side, as well as the multicultural differences between the warring countries and the ethics, or lack thereof, of everyone involved. The smart, darkly funny script was, said *Chicago Sun-Times* critic Roger Ebert, a "weird masterpiece, a screw-loose war picture that sends action and humor crashing head-on into each other and spinning off into political anger."

Clooney desperately wanted the part, because it fit his criteria of being a quality film he would be proud of in the end, and also because he knew it was yet another chance to really shore up his big-screen skills. His days on *ER*, or at least on his initial contract with the show, were numbered, and he wanted to be in control of what direction his career would take once Dr. Doug Ross was no longer an operator at County General.

"It's a black comedy like *M*A*S*H* and *Catch-22*, films that I liked growing up," he said. "It's a hysterically funny story, and I thought it was told without being preachy."

So it was all the more frustrating to him that he was having to work so hard to get in with Russell and *Three Kings*. Russell had actually named Nicolas Cage as his first choice for the role. He also had considered Clint Eastwood and John Travolta, who both passed on the script fairly early on, and even Dustin Hoffman, who liked the part but was deemed too old by studio execs. The studio, Clooney's home turf of Warner Bros., wanted Mel Gibson, despite the fact that Clooney still had two movies left to make on his three-picture deal with WB (and another

Batman movie was almost certainly never going to happen, at least not with Clooney donning the cowl and cape again). Even though the studio agreed to sign off on Clooney starring in *Three Kings*, it was a hard sell to Russell, who frankly saw the budding movie star as nothing more than a very handsome TV star.

But Clooney was a cool and confident customer, and, convinced he was the right man for the movie (and that the movie was the right move in his career), was not above putting on a full-court press to make Russell see things his way.

The actor recalled to *Entertainment Weekly* that he flew to New York City and showed up at Russell's hotel room, ready to convince the director of indie comedy favorites *Spanking the Monkey* and *Flirting with Disaster* that Archie Gates was his role.

"He opened the door with his video camera," Clooney told *EW*. "It's very annoying. And he says, 'Does this bother you?' And I said, 'It will only if I don't get the job. If I end up in *The Making of Three Kings* and I'm not in the movie, then I'll look like an asshole.'"

Eventually, after a couple more trips to talk with him in New York and Nicolas Cage's decision to star in the Martin Scorsese thriller *Bringing Out the Dead* instead of *Three Kings*, Russell agreed to cast Clooney in the movie. The fact that just winning the part had taken so much effort, not to mention that by this time he considered Russell to be an odd duck, probably should have been a warning sign for Clooney of things to come.

Even though Russell had agreed to give Clooney the part, he'd seen *From Dusk Till Dawn* and was only willing to acknowledge that he thought the actor had "a little glimmer." The fact that *Three Kings* was being shot in the hot Arizona desert in spring and summer, and that Clooney was doing another double production schedule (*ER* was still finishing its fourth season), also contributed to the subconscious bitterness and resentment simmering between the director and his star. "I worked until four-thirty in the morning on *ER*, got on a jet, went directly to the

(*Three Kings*) set, and worked for twelve hours," Clooney told *Premiere* magazine.

With the situation already fraught with tension, the production only got worse when it turned out that Clooney and Russell had radically different ideas of how a movie set should be run. Clooney, as usual, and despite his brutal moonlighting schedule, wanted to have fun, wanted to bond with his costars (Wahlberg, Ice Cube and Spike Jonze made up the rest of the foursome out to find Saddam's gold stash) and wanted everyone on the set to be treated with respect. Russell, on the other hand, was first and foremost concerned with getting his vision of the movie on film, and, by Clooney's account, wasn't interested in input from anyone else, or in whose toes he might step on along the way.

Clooney's description of just how out of control his relationship with Russell would become starts with a set of conditions Russell attached to Clooney's employment in the movie. According to Sharon Waxman's book *Rebels on the Backlot*, Russell had all but come right out and told Clooney that he didn't consider him capable of playing the role. "You have a lot of habits, you ought to break them," Russell told his star, referring to Clooney's well-documented habit of bobbing and weaving his head on camera, especially on *ER* and in any role where he's trying to convey cockiness. Archie Gates promised to be just such a role, and Russell, to be fair, was understandably concerned about Clooney's "tic."

Russell's solution to the actor's tic, however, ticked Clooney off. The director also had an office on the Warner Bros. lot, and asked that, in his *ER* down time, Clooney come to the office and work on his acting skills. "I want you to be very still in this role," Russell instructed the star, telling him to sit quietly in the room and go through a series of yoga breathing exercises.

To say that man's man George Clooney had little patience for the yoga breathing exercises as a means to improve his acting is an understatement. Clooney had once told a reporter he was embarrassed to admit that, in a desperate effort to treat the bleeding ulcer he'd developed after his divorce from Talia Balsam, he'd sought the services of an herbal specialist. And now, after he'd become TV's leading leading man, and had already embarked on what was a burgeoning film career, here was this strange guy telling him to breathe quietly to become a better actor.

Clooney was also frustrated with Russell's work process. Tasked with memorizing two sets of scripts at the same time, he was frustrated by any last-minute script changes, because it threw an extra, and he felt unnecessary, burden onto his already taxed-to-the-max schedule. Russell, on the other hand, didn't like his creative process held hostage to anyone else's schedule or expectations, and he felt totally justified in tinkering right up until it was time to shoot a scene.

Russell was also the one who had suggested working with Clooney privately, "because I don't think you're going to want to have me changing these habits in front of a hundred people." Yet, Waxman reports in *Rebels on the Backlot*, once filming began, Russell was constantly making comments about Clooney's acting "habits" in front of the cast and crew, and Clooney, each time, would be visibly annoyed.

And the relationship only continued to devolve.

Clooney says Russell was temperamental with the crew and spoke to them disrespectfully; Russell says Clooney was more concerned with being a jokester than with showing up to the set prepared every day.

Clooney says Russell made the cast do multiple takes time and time again, with direction as specific as how to move a finger, after rewriting dialogue on the fly; Russell admits it, but defends his quest to make the best movie he could make.

Clooney had gone to Russell and told him that Warner Bros., concerned about fallout from the politically charged movie, had tried to pull the plug and get Clooney to drop out of the project; Russell came to see Clooney not as having been loyal to him or the movie, but as being cold and resentful at finding out just how many other actors Russell had pursued for the Archie Gates role before being forced by the studio to hire Clooney.

It went on and on, and in one final attempt to redirect the working relationship that seemed, to almost everyone around, to be irretrievably off-course, Clooney wrote Russell a three-page letter, not even bothering to go to the IBM typewriter, but writing this time by hand.

As reprinted in *Rebels on the Backlot*: "You have created the most havoc ridden, anxiety ridden, angry set that I have ever witnessed. And here's the joke of all jokes. I still don't think that you're a bad guy or a bad director. I think you are a horrible communicator. You don't always know what you want, but you know what you *don't* want. OK. Make that clear. We'll all help you get there. In order for this to be a creative process you have to allow others to have input."

Waxman reports that Russell never responded to Clooney's letter, a move that the actor no doubt found ungentlemanly. The movie was also tumbling over budget, the desert heat was an irritant to everyone, and a few days after Clooney's letter had been ignored, and after several near-scuffles between the director and actor, the proverbial straw that broke that camel's back led to an all-out brawl on the set.

The showdown came near the end of the shoot, on a particularly tense day. Wahlberg was hyperventilating and blacking out, Waxman says, in a scene in which his character has been shot in the chest. Hundreds of extras were scattered across the set. Helicopters, part of the movie story line, were flying above. And Russell was filming a scene in which a solider is supposed to knock Ice Cube to the ground. The soldier was being played by a local ROTC recruit, not an actor, but when he approached the Cube takedown without the aggressiveness Russell wanted, the director got rough with the extra, Clooney claimed. Others defended Russell, saying he was frustrated and simply demonstrated for the extra exactly how he wanted the move to play out.

What is sure is that, at this point, Clooney and Russell full on didn't like each other, had a boatload of resentments against each other, were tired, hot, anxious about the production, eager to turn in good performances as star and director, and perfectly willing to let each other know exactly how they were feeling, in front of the entire cast and crew.

According to Waxman, Clooney pulled Russell aside and told him, "Don't you push those people aside!"

> RUSSELL: What are you fucking talking about? Why don't you do your job?
>
> CLOONEY: You're being an asshole. Don't you fucking touch those people!
>
> RUSSELL: Hit me, pussy!
>
> CLOONEY: I'm gonna fuck you up!

By this point, the two men were nose to nose, and Russell headbutted Clooney. The actor put his hands around Russell's throat and began choking him. An assistant director quit the movie in disgust at the display, and walked off the set. Clooney only let go of Russell's neck, he says, when his friend Waldo, one of The Boys and Clooney's personal hairstylist, "grabbed me by the waist to get me to let go of him," Clooney told *Playboy*. "I had him by the throat. I was going to kill him. Kill him. Finally, he apologized, but I walked away. By then, the Warner Bros. guys were freaking out."

Clooney says Russell was sour throughout the rest of the shoot, which finished, mercifully, uneventfully.

"Some days George was right, some days David was right," third party Ice Cube told *Premiere*. "But when it's all said and done, you've got to look at David as the person with the whole movie locked in his mind. We would complain about shooting a scene thirteen, fourteen times, but if we didn't get what the director wanted, you've got to do it again. . . . [Clooney and Russell] showed that they both were interested in making the best movie they could."

Afterwards, Russell told Waxman, he and Clooney agreed not to talk about the fight in the media. Clooney, he says, broke that agreement right away. Russell had told *Premiere*, during press events for the movie's release, that he and Clooney "are friends. . . . It's a movie, and part of the process is that there're going to be misunderstandings. It was really nothing."

Clooney talked not only to *Premiere* and *Entertainment Weekly*, Waxman reports, but to his friends and coworkers in Hollywood who, without being acquainted with Russell, took the actor's opinions about him as fact. Clooney had called Russell a weirdo, and Clooney's cohorts, she says, accepted the characterization as truth. Clooney continued to speak about the fight to the media, and after he told *Vanity Fair* in 2003 that he "would not stand for [Russell] humiliating and yelling and screaming at crew members, who weren't allowed to defend themselves . . . my job was then to humiliate the people who were doing the humiliating," Russell responded, "George Clooney can suck my dick."

The brouhaha was still making headlines eight years later, as video clips from another Russell production, 2004's *I Heart Huckabees*, hit viral video Web site YouTube.com in 2007. The outtakes from the *Huckabees* shoot show Russell verbally abusing actor Lily Tomlin, calling her names, spitting out expletives, stomping around the movie set, kicking things, knocking things over, and, in general, confirming the kinds of behaviors Clooney had hinted at from the *Three Kings* set.

In fact, Clooney was immediately suspected as the source of the clips, though he quickly denied he was the culprit. "That tape has been going around for about two and a half years," Clooney told *Entertainment Weekly*. "Everybody's seen it. . . . The last thing in the world I would have done is stick it on the Internet. There are pranks I like to play, but [posting this kind of footage online] falls into the world of screwing with people's careers. I'm not sneaky. I like 'em face-to-face." Clooney, who was so adamant that he was not responsible for putting the video onto YouTube that he offered a $1 million prize to anyone who could prove otherwise, did admit that the video of Russell's outrageous behavior on the *Huckabees* set provided a bit of vindication for him.

"I felt bad for Lily," he said, "but I also felt a little vindicated for anyone that thought that had anything to do with me on [*Three Kings*]. Maybe [the video being released] is good. Maybe it'll make people behave themselves on sets."

In the end, Clooney decided life was too short to ever consider working with Russell again, and it's safe to say that that is probably the one thing on which he and his *Three Kings* director agree.

It's a shame that the movie will probably always be remembered most for the Clooney/Russell battles, because it is among Clooney's finest performances. In fact, whether or not he would agree, Clooney almost certainly owes Russell a bit of gratitude for the marked improvement in his subsequent performances.

Despite the brusque manner in which he conveyed his opinions, Russell was right about Clooney's "TV actor tics," especially the bobbing head that was maddeningly never still. It was apparent on *ER*, though less bothersome because of the show's hectic pace and quick cuts. It was there in *One Fine Day*, especially in scenes when Clooney was trying to convey some bit of earnest sentiment. And it was most annoyingly pronounced in *Batman & Robin*, when his character had little else to do. Whatever Bruce/Batman was feeling—sadness over the declining health of Alfred, anger at the ungrateful, disrespectful treatment from his sidekick Robin or bemusement at the quip-laced antics of Mr. Freeze and Poison Ivy—it found expression in Clooney's constantly moving head.

That almost every trace of that has been excised from his big-screen performance since *Three Kings* is likely due in some part to Russell's direction. It had been pointed out to Clooney before, but never so directly and, frankly, so rudely and so publicly. But because it was such a sticking point, and not something the actor could dismiss as an unfounded concern on the part of the "weirdo," it's not unreasonable to think that Russell's constructive (in result, if not intention) criticism of that particular aspect of Clooney's acting bag of tricks has stuck with the star.

Either way—and despite the film's failure to live up to expectations at the box office (the final budget had ballooned up to around $75 million, and its domestic box office take topped off at $60 million)—the movie would go on to earn positive reviews for both director and star Clooney.

19

Breaking Up—*ER* and Balitran

*I can't sleep; I can't breathe . . . this is real anxiety. If [*Fail Safe*] is a failure, it's my failure.*

—George Clooney

Despite his busy schedule, Clooney had taken time to think about his future on *ER*, and after all the hours he'd logged not only working on the show and a movie set simultaneously, but traveling back and forth during those productions, he decided his first contract, the one that had made him the Hollywood player he'd long planned to be, would be his last with the show.

Clooney was satisfied with what he'd accomplished with the character; Dr. Ross had evolved from an alcohol-soaked, hotheaded womanizer who often acted without much thought about consequences to himself or those around him into a more thoughtful, responsible doctor who was not only capable of being supportive (and faithful) to his true love, Nurse Hathaway, but who had come to understand that his complicated relationship with his alcoholic, absentee father did not necessarily dictate the kind of man he would become. From befriending and trying to protect teenage prostitute Charlie (recurring guest star Kirsten Dunst) to proving his friendship to Hathaway while he waited out her relationships with Dr. Taglieri and paramedic Shep, the playboy pediatrician had become a grown-up.

His last episode as Dr. Doug Ross would air during the February sweeps period—the four-times yearly periods when networks try to pump up their ratings to use to set ad rates—and was being filmed mid-January. Clooney had asked just a couple of things: one, that his character not be killed off (he wanted the option of returning for guest spots) and, two, that the crew not make a fuss over his departure from the set. There was a cake, though, of course, and the final "Dollar Day," the star's way of saying goodbye and thank you to his coworkers.

As for Dr. Doug's last hurrah, in "The Storm, Part II," which aired on February 18, 1999, the character went out in a classic Ross way. The maverick doc had swiped some experimental drugs to help a child stricken with Lou Gehrig's disease, and when the inevitable fallout ensued, he decided he'd had enough of County General policies, and packed his bags and headed for Seattle and a job with an HMO. Ross had tried to persuade girlfriend Carol Hathaway (Julianna Margulies) to go with him, but when she refused, he left alone, unaware that Hathaway was pregnant with his twin daughters.

"[George] didn't cheat the network, the producers or his friends on the show," producer John Wells told a newspaper when Clooney announced he was leaving. "George literally lost millions of dollars by staying with *ER*. [He] has done the thing few people do in this business."

Ross and Hathaway would be reunited the next season when Margulies also left the show. Clooney made a cameo appearance in the episode, which, though rumored in gossip columns, was kept a surprise even from NBC execs. As the final minutes of "Such Sweet Sorrow" unspooled on May 11, 2000, Carol flies to Seattle, finds Doug on a fishing dock behind his house, and embraces him in an emotional reunion as the Don Henley song "Taking You Home" fades into the credits.

"It was all very sneaky," says the actor, who with Margulies made a stealth trip to Seattle, where a couple was paid $10,000 for the use of their house to film the scene. "Even my agent didn't know until I told him as we took a plane to Cannes (to promote *O Brother, Where Art Thou?*). He was talking into a phone saying, 'He'll never do it.' I said to him, 'Well, I did do it.'" John Wells had gone to the trouble of providing fake scripts (minus a Clooney appearance) to the network, paying bonuses to the crew to remain mum and even hiding the film in his refrigerator at home in order to keep the Ross/Hathaway reunion a surprise for audiences.

Before his final *ER* appearance (to date, anyway), Clooney had also shepherded another TV project to the airwaves, producing (via his Maysville production company) and starring in a live TV remake of the 1964 Cold War drama *Fail Safe*. The ambitious venture, a remake of one of his favorite movies, which had been directed by one of his favorite directors, Sidney Lumet, revolves around a crisis in which the U.S. President has ordered that nuclear bombs be dropped on Moscow, setting off what, in effect, would be World War III. And even though the President comes to the conclusion that ordering the attack was a mistake, thanks to an electrical malfunction it's too late to call it off.

"It was Camelot—there was an innocence," he told *TV Guide* about why he has such a fondness for retro fare like *Fail Safe*, and, later down the road, the Rat Pack remake *Ocean's Eleven*. "I loved the politics, I loved the singers. I'm nostalgic for black and white in a way, and I don't mean black and white, the colors. I mean black and white, the feeling. I like things simpler."

Clooney had gotten a charge out of filming the live *ER* episode he and Anthony Edwards had proposed, and had been thrilled with the reaction it produced. Now he saw *Fail Safe* as the perfect material with which to take another shot at live television. It was also another chance for him to do something that he found personally interesting. Not content to ever again sit around waiting for the right things to fall into his lap, he was going to use every bit of clout he had in Hollywood to make projects that, as he had said after the experience of having to promote *Batman & Robin*, a film he didn't think was very good, he could be genuinely proud of.

"People will watch us like they're watching the Indy 500," Clooney said. "They don't go to see you go around in a circle three hundred times; they want to see you crash and burn!"

The risks and potential payoff of live TV were also appealing to Clooney because he felt only the best actors and crew could make such a heady venture work, and he turned to his friends and past coworkers to make sure *Fail Safe* the remake would come off as well as the classic original. Henry Fonda had played the President the first time around, and Clooney called on Richard Dreyfuss to fill those shoes for the live remake. Clooney himself took the role of head pilot Jack Grady, and friends Noah Wyle, Don Cheadle, Harvey Keitel, Brian Dennehy, Hank Azaria, Sam Elliott and four of The Boys—Grant Heslov, Tommy Hinkley, Thom Matthews and Matt Adler—rounded out the cast.

The movie was shown in black and white and produced on two Warner Bros. soundstages when it aired on April 9, 2000, and reaction to the broadcast was overwhelmingly positive. The story, originally based on a novel by Eugene Burdick and Harvey Wheeler and adapted for the remake by Oscar-nominated screenwriter Stephen Frears (*The Grifters* and *The Queen*), remained, unfortunately, as timely in 2000 as it had been in 1964—and, despite the many technological advances in communications equipment and weaponry between the original movie and Clooney's live CBS remake, the tension and powerful ending remained as shocking as it had been in the original. The movie was also recognized during awards season with Golden Globe and Emmy nominations, nabbing two technical Emmy Awards.

With things trucking right along in the actor's career—he was now at the point where he felt free to turn down even the biggest movie roles if he didn't see the potential in them, as he'd done with *Wild, Wild West* and *Jack Frost*, among others—his personal life had taken another downturn, one that probably put the seal on his commitment to remain single.

Clooney and Céline Balitran had been, by all accounts—even those from his *ER* coworkers, his parents, and The Boys, all the people who knew him best and spent the most time with him—very happy for a spell. But Clooney never stopped answering reporters' queries about his romantic future with the declaration that he would never marry again or have children, even when he and Balitran seemed to be at their happiest. He also continued to show—in his interviews and by his actions—that his career was his number one priority. There was hardly ever a window in his schedule that didn't include working on a TV project, planning other projects, setting up projects with this production companies or going off to actually star in a film.

Balitran, no matter how in love she was, had to realize that she didn't come first in her boyfriend's life, and most likely never would. She'd also spoken openly about her desire to be married and have kids, and Clooney's public declarations that he had no such plans for his future, it couldn't have been lost on his girlfriend. As she spent more and more time alone at Casa de Clooney, she must have sensed that she was going to have to radically downgrade her expectations if she planned on remaining in the relationship.

By the spring of 1999, she made the decision that she could not, in fact, compromise all her dreams for her own life to stay at home and wait for Clooney to drop in between movie shoots. The two broke up, after three years of dating and cohabitating, with the twenty-four-year-old Balitran being the one to actually pull the plug.

"The truth is, it just became tougher and tougher for us to make it," Clooney told *Esquire*. "She lasted as long as I think she was going to last. It was like, 'I don't really think I want to play anymore.'"

There was much tabloid speculation about the end of the affair, with the most ridiculous assertion being that Balitran had given Clooney an ultimatum about Max, the now 150-pound pet pig who, gossipers claimed, did not get along with the new mistress of the house.

Balitran herself, who was photographed with other men not long after her split with the star became a topic of public and tabloid speculation in the fall of 1999, talked about the breakup with French magazine *Oh La!*, saying she and Clooney were still friends, and confirming that they had wanted very different things out of life. "I wanted to have a real family with children, even though I think I'm still a little young for this," she told the magazine. "And I also wanted a simpler life, quieter than the one in Hollywood. But George didn't want to hear about family life. I know that it will never be the right time for George. I respect his choice, but it's the reason George and I could not go on together."

Clooney, who had developed a bleeding ulcer after his last major breakup (the divorce from Talia Balsam), seemed to take the split much more in stride this time. He did spend a few weeks staying at the home of pal Grant Heslov, because Casa de Clooney was still so fresh with memories of Balitran and the decorating she'd done. But by the next summer, during an interview with *Vogue*, he was sloughing it off in his typical humor-as-defense mechanism way. His pal Hinkley had tried to guess what he was going to order while the gang was out to dinner. "You're getting the French dip," Hinkley said. "I had a French dip, and it cost me three years of my life," Clooney quipped.

In the same interview, though, he also expressed guilt over the end of the relationship with Balitran, considering that she had left her entire life behind in France, at age twenty-one, to move to Los Angeles at his prompting.

"She pulled up roots and came here for me," he said. "So I felt it became something of my responsibility to make sure that even though we're not still together, her life is not bad because of that. . . . So I made sure she had a great place to live. And I made sure that she had cash. And I still talk to her and make sure that, you know, she has a lawyer who will help her with her visa. We still keep in contact . . . [and], quite honestly, I don't want to be sitting in the lap of luxury and hear, 'Well, Céline had to go back to Paris because of the lawyers, or because her visa kicked out or she didn't have any money.'"

"Yeah," he added, "I'm a much better ex-boyfriend than I am a boyfriend."

At age twenty-four, Balitran probably understood more about Clooney than the actor understood about himself. Her assertion that "it will never be the right time for George" was insightful; Clooney's commitment to his career has only gotten stronger through the years, and despite a string of flings—Renée Zellweger, actress Jennifer Siebel, *Monk* star Traylor Howard, Canadian bartender Maria Bertrand, *Charlie's Angels* movie star Lucy Liu, *Melrose Place* star Brooke Langton, British TV hostess Mariella Frostrup, Italian heiress Gianna Elvira Cantatore and Teri Hatcher among them—and even a couple of longer-term dating scenarios, with British model Lisa Snowdon and actress Krista Allen (who was rumored to have made a short run at living with the star at Casa de Clooney until, as one of his friends put it, she became clingy)—post-Balitran, it seems clear that George Clooney, who turned forty-six in 2007, may very well win that $40,000 double-or-nothing bet with Michelle Pfeiffer and Nicole Kidman.

"If you hang out with George for even ten minutes, you would sense a sadness to him," Tommy Hinkley said. "He believes you have a choice. You either have a career, or you have love."

ABOVE: His much-ballyhooed feud with director David O. Russell got most of the press, but *Three Kings*, starring Clooney, Ice Cube (left) and Mark Wahlberg, is notable for featuring one of the uture Oscar winner's most controlled performances.

ELOW: Tim Blake Nelson (left), Clooney and John Turturro in 2000's *O Brother, Where Art Thou?*, a uirky take on Homer's *Odyssey*. Clooney calls it the first in his "trilogy of idiots" movies (followed y *Intolerable Cruelty* and the upcoming *Burn After Reading*) with filmmaking brothers Joel and Ethan oen.

ABOVE: The A-list of the A-list: Julia Roberts costarred as the ex-wife of Clooney's Danny Ocean ir the 2001 Rat Pack remake *Ocean's Eleven*. So believable was their on-screen chemistry and so wild were their offscreen shenanigans that rumors spread that a Roberts/Clooney affair was the cause of her break-up with then-boyfriend Benjamin Bratt. The pretty woman and the sexiest man alive bot denied the gossip.

BOVE: *Solaris* received mixed reviews from critics, who found the movie confusing, and was a ommercial flop, but there's no denying Clooney's chemistry with costar Natascha McElhone. In ne biggest departure from the story line of the original Russian film, Clooney's Kelvin is a man ho never gets past the death of his wife, and instead decides to live with a re-creation of her.

EFT: A rare shirtless scene: Clooney with costar Natascha McElhone in 2002's *Solaris*, the Steven oderbergh-directed remake of a 1972 Soviet flick. The movie features another scene that's much-oogled, in which the actor's bare backside is exposed.

LEFT: George Clooney, executive producer of *K Street*, the 2003 semi-improvised HBO satire about Washington, D.C., lobbyists. The show also led to a reunion of sorts: the cast included Clooney's ex-wife, Talia Balsam, as well as her second husband, actor John Slattery.

BELOW: Clooney, pictured here with costars Robert Downey Jr. (left) and David Strathairn, cowrote, directed and starred in *Good Night, and Good Luck*, the 2005 story of legendary newsman Edward R. Murrow's takedown of witch-hunting Senator Joseph McCarthy.

ABOVE: Clooney, with Frank Langella and David Strathairn, in action as director on *Good Night, and Good Luck*, a job that would earn him a Best Director Oscar nomination. The movie, which also won him a Best Writing Oscar nomination with cowriter and friend Grant Heslov, was the star's tribute to his broadcast journalist father, whose idol was Edward R. Murrow.

BELOW: The accolades were nice, but a back injury Clooney sustained during the filming of *Syriana*, writer/director Stephen Gaghan's geopolitical thriller, left him with pain so debilitating that he admitted the praise and, later, the awards, weren't worth the physical trauma he endured. "I would trade not having done the movie for the pain it's caused me," he said.

And the Oscar for Best Performance by an Actor in a Supporting Role goes to . . . George Clooney for *Syriana*. Accepting the first statue handed out at the 2006 Oscar ceremony, Clooney drew criticism from some and cheers from others with his speech, which praised the movie industry for talking "about AIDS when it was just being whispered," and talking about "civil rights when it wasn't really popular."

he Oscar winner, backstage at the Kodak Theater, clutching his little golden prize. The March 5, 006, ceremony marked the first time Clooney had even attended the Academy Awards fest, saying e didn't feel like he belonged until he was a nominee.

Above: (Left to right) Matt Damon, George Clooney and Brad Pitt looking Rat Pack cool in 2007's *Ocean's Thirteen*, the sequel that finds Danny Ocean's gang seeking revenge on a new Vegas mogul: Willie Banks (Al Pacino), who's double-crossed Danny's friend Reuben (Elliott Gould).

Right: The Oscar winner plays an attorney roped into cleaning up the unsavory messes of his firm's high-powered clients in the 2007 legal thriller *Michael Clayton*, the final production of the Clooney/Soderbergh Section Eight collaboration. The movie marks the directorial debut of Tony Gilroy, who wrote *The Bourne Identity* and its sequels, starring Clooney's *Ocean's* movies pal Matt Damon.

20

"The New Cary Grant"

His head is shaped like a star's—Cary Grant, Tony Curtis, Tyrone Power all had that head. He's got great skin, his hair falls right. He's the Velvet Man: he always looks like he's wearing velvet.

—Carl Reiner, on George Clooney

With a string of dramatic parts under his belt, Clooney decided his next project would be lighter fare. And in keeping with his resolution only to take on smart, quality movie roles, Ethan and Joel Coen's *O Brother, Where Art Thou?* was a dream.

The filmmaking brothers, who'd won an Oscar for their 1996 *Fargo* script (and had been nominated, with that movie, for Best Picture), made exactly the kind of movies Clooney personally enjoyed: smart, quirky, dark comedy, with great dialogue and richly written characters. *Raising Arizona*, *Barton Fink* and *The Big Lebowski* were also on their resume.

O Brother, Where Art Thou? was certainly no departure from the siblings' typically stylized flims, as an updated retelling of Homer's *Odyssey* set in the American South during the Great Depression. Clooney, who had signed on to the project without even reading the script so eager was he to work with Ethan and Joel, would play con man Ulysses Everett

McGill (referred to as Everett in the movie), who escapes from a prison chain gang with dopey pals Pete (John Turturro) and Delmar (Tim Blake Nelson) with a plan to claim some buried treasure previously hidden after a robbery. In truth, Everett is plotting a reunion with his wife and seven (!) daughters—a reunion that needs to be hurriedly arranged since the ex-Mrs. McGill is set to wed another man in Everett's absence.

Ironically, the nostalgic film also caused Clooney to hark back to his 1980s TV days as a "hair actor," because Everett is given to a cheeky bit of vanity where his 'do is concerned. One of the funniest running bits in the movie revolves around Everett's proud declaration that he's "a Dapper Dan man," referring to the goopy pomade that sets his dark locks just so across his head.

> EVERETT TO A SALESMAN: Hold on, I don't want this pomade. I want Dapper Dan.
>
> SALESMAN: I don't carry Dapper Dan, I carry Fop.
>
> EVERETT: Well, I don't want Fop, goddamn it! I'm a Dapper Dan man!
>
> SALESMAN: Watch your language, young feller, this is a public market. Now if you want Dapper Dan, I can order it for you, have it in a couple of weeks.
>
> EVERETT: Well, ain't this place a geographical oddity. Two weeks from everywhere!

"It's all about my hair, this movie," Clooney joked to *Esquire*. "I'm in love with my hair. Which seems perfect for me."

The movie was the best example yet of the actor's comedic abilities, and the goofy grin he forms to deliver Everett's best lines is particularly memorable, since it can't be an easy thing to make a face that handsome look that silly.

He'd also sought out a personal source to help him perfect his hillbilly twang. "My Uncle Jack has a tobacco farm in a tiny Kentucky town, near where my mom grew up," he said. "He's a pretty heavy-duty Kentucky boy. I called him up and told him that I was going to do this movie that takes place in the South. It had been a while since I'd been in Kentucky and heard the accent. So I sent my uncle the script and said, 'I want you to just read the script into a tape recorder, the whole script, and then I'm going to use that. I'll get you a credit and pay you some money.' And now, at the end of the movie, there's a special thanks to Jack Warren."

Even Francis Ford Coppola, who had been so weirded out by Clooney's choice of a hillbilly accent for his *Dracula* audition years earlier, would have to have been impressed with Clooney's performance in *O Brother, Where Art Thou?*

"People talk about George as the new Cary Grant or Clark Gable. Well, he has style, but he is very much an actor of today," Ethan Coen told *McCall's*; ". . . people underestimate him. He is subtle and very clever. He is never predictable. He will always surprise you."

Clooney was his usual eager-to-please self on the movie's Mississippi set, playing basketball with the crew, telling and retelling his stories and, all would agree, not showing any signs of the tension that might have been awaiting him back in Los Angeles, since it was during this period that he and Céline Balitran went their separate ways.

He even tried his hand at singing for the movie's best-selling soundtrack—his aunt was the honey-voiced Rosemary Clooney, after all—but had to admit that his own crooning tool wasn't quite up to Aunt Rosemary's standards, and requested that his vocals be dubbed.

"We were both staring at our shoes," Joel Coen joked about his and brother Ethan's reaction to hearing Clooney's version of the movie's theme song, "I Am a Man of Constant Sorrow." "George has a good voice, but it's not suited to that kind of mountain music, which is hard to just walk into. You have to be brought up in it, because it's a very particular sound."

Even Uncle Jack's hillbilly sampler tape couldn't work that magic.

Not long after he wrapped the Coens' movie, Clooney was off to Massachusetts to star in *The Perfect Storm*, an adaptation of Sebastian Junger's bestselling nonfiction book about the tragic fate of the Gloucester fishermen of the *Andrea Gail*. Clooney would portray the *Andrea Gail*'s captain, Billy Tyne, whose entire crew was killed when the boat got caught up, 575 miles out in the sea, in a vicious storm.

Clooney had been a huge fan of Junger's book, and, looking to fulfill his contract with Warner Bros., he lobbied for the part, which was first offered to Mel Gibson. "I finally got it when Mel fell out," he says. "I love seeing men going into certain death, you know? Saying, 'This is our duty, and we're going to do it.' I loved that about this story. They went knowing, 'There's a good chance we won't make it. But if we do, we're rich. And if we don't try, we're broke.'"

Junger was personally thrilled with Clooney's casting for the part. "It's guys like Clooney who are the successful captains," Junger told *Vogue*. "The kind who can charm the work and the courage out of the men, who understand that the men are lonely, they miss their girlfriends, they're scared. . . . The other kind of captain is a tyrant. [George would] have been a terrible tyrant."

As the subject matter suggests, the production was tough and very waterlogged. Wolfgang Petersen, who knew how to make a thrilling action adventure after helming great films like *In the Line of Fire* and *Air Force One*, had big plans for *The Perfect Storm*, and, by necessity, they all involved water. Lots and lots of water.

In fact, during filming, the cast even got caught in the tail end of a real storm, an offshoot of Hurricane Floyd, which created fifteen-foot waves and very, very rough water.

"Some of the movie was shot on a soundstage, but a lot was shot in a very real boat off Dana Point, in rough seas," Clooney told *Playboy*. "Everyone was throwing up, though it didn't get to me. We got the shit kicked out of us out there. For one scene, I was yelling at [costar] Mark

Wahlberg, and in between words in the take he would turn around and go, 'Aaaaarrrh.'"

Petersen was quick to point out that his lead actor was fully committed to the role, with Clooney even insisting on performing some of the most dangerous stunts himself.

"For the actors, it's a bit frightening when these huge masses of water come all over you, but of all the actors, George was probably the least intimidated," Petersen told *Biography*. "I think he actually enjoyed fighting the elements, so to speak. And imagine the fishing boats—they have these things like wings that go out left and right to stabilize the boats, and in one scene at the height of the storm, he has to crawl out and fix something at the very end of the wing, and most of these shots he actually did himself [without a double]. It was pretty astonishing."

Much was made of the fact that Clooney's was the only character in the movie who didn't have a Boston accent, and people still question whether or not it was because he couldn't perfect one. It wasn't. Factually, a Boston accent would have been an error, because Billy Tyne, while based in Gloucester during the fishing season, was actually from Florida. He didn't talk with a Boston accent, so neither did Clooney, who is actually known to be a very gifted, and dead-on accurate, mimic.

Off set, Clooney was, as always, the life of the party, even drinking with the local residents at the local landmark Blackburn Tavern and the Crow's Nest, the bar featured in the movie and operated in real life by the mother of Bobby Shatford, the doomed *Andrea Gail* fisherman played by Wahlberg. The cast and crew would spend many evenings socializing with the townfolk, many of whom were friends and family members of the men who had died aboard the *Andrea Gail*. The interactions helped foster an attitude among the cast that extra care should be taken with their portrayals of the *Andrea Gail* crew.

Some members of the real Billy Tyne's family would later file a lawsuit against Warner Bros., claiming Tyne had been defamed because, they asserted, the movie suggested he was responsible for the decisions that had ultimately led to the deaths of the crew members aboard the *Andrea Gail*.

"The tricky part about this movie is that we're walking a fine line between entertainment and also dealing with real people's lives," Clooney says. "So you can't just go, 'My ex-wife's an idiot,' because the lady actually lives in this town."

On the lighter side of the production, Clooney wasn't the only one pulling practical jokes on the set. He was even the butt of a few, the best of which was perpetrated by costar John C. Reilly, playing *Andrea Gail* crew member Dale "Murph" Murphy. While filming one particularly tense action sequence, Reilly took advantage of Clooney's weakness for needing cheat sheets to remember all his dialogue. Aware that Clooney had taped some cards with his dialogue written on them to the steering wheel of the boat, Reilly mischievously moved his costar's cards. Once the action began, and the actors were being tossed to and fro by the fast-whipping waves, Clooney began to glance frantically towards his crib sheets to deliver his lines. When he didn't find them, Reilly reported, he began mixing nonsensical sounds into the dialogue he could remember, to cover for what he couldn't.

As usual, he was always up for being the instigator of a good joke, too. "We were shooting at sea once when it was pretty rough weather and a lot of people got seasick. Our still photographer was really pretty sick and had to run away and bend over the railing," Petersen recalled. "So George asked someone to take a photo with her camera—he dropped his pants, put his rear to the lens, and then quickly put it all back together. She has no idea, and then a couple days later when she developed the material, she found that shot. He did that kind of stuff all the time. He was always in for a joke. I like a set where people are in a good mood, and boy, if you have a partner like George on the set, it's just fun all over."

Finally, with work on both movies completed—and Clooney having made a couple of cameo appearances in pal Robert Rodriguez's kid adventure *Spy Kids* and the *South Park: Bigger, Longer & Uncut* movie—it was time to promote them.

O Brother, Where Art Thou? wouldn't hit theaters until December 2000, but it was premiering at the Cannes Film Festival, and that meant Clooney was headed to France.

If anything finally made him feel like he was being welcomed into the Hollywood film community, it was the trip to Cannes, where the Coens' picture was among the contenders for the prestigious Palme d'Or ('Golden Palm') honor. Though ultimately the film didn't ultimately win, it was well received by the crowd, as was its star, who drew crowds wherever he went.

Throughout the festival, whispered stories about Clooney circulated among his fellow celebrities as he held court at his hotel bar, drinking vodka without regard to the hangovers in store, accepting congratulations from those who'd seen and appreciated his performance in *O Brother*, and (inspiring most of the chatter) spending time with several beautiful women, including his *Batman & Robin* costar Uma Thurman, Charlize Theron, actress Traylor Howard, Winona Ryder and British TV star Mariella Frostrup. Clooney, and the movie, were, to say the least, a hit at Cannes.

Once back in the States, it was time to premiere the real-life adventure *The Perfect Storm*, and Warner Bros., in a shrewd marketing move, had scheduled the premiere event to be held in Danvers, Massachusetts. Tickets were sold to the invitation-only screening, with the raised funds going to the Gloucester Fund, a nonprofit organization started to benefit local residents, many of whom rely on the dangerous fishing industry to make their living.

Locals turned out in droves, and weren't disappointed to catch a glimpse of stars George Clooney and Mark Wahlberg entering the

Danvers Loews Theater, along with director Petersen. The same couldn't be said for critics, who, for once, liked a movie more than they liked Clooney's performance in it.

The *Chicago Reader* reviewer said, "The movie—whose most persuasive drama always seems to occur when captain George Clooney is off-screen—is scary and exciting." From *Variety*: "With the exception of Reilly, who in his full beard looks like a cuddly rat who would be at home on any vessel, [the] cast is merely adequate." And, unfairly, since Clooney had deliberately gone without a New England accent for the film, the *New York Times* said, "Mr. Clooney conveys a darkly heroic gravity, but his lack of even a trace of a New England accent makes him seem socially out of place in a cast whose other members get the regional dialect more or less right."

When it came time for audiences to vote, via ticket sales, on the movie, the results were still less than overwhelming. *The Perfect Storm* would earn its $140 million budget back, and then some, with a $182 million domestic total, but, in terms of pure box office draw, none of Clooney's movies had yet proven to be an unqualified, runaway hit.

The numbers for *O Brother, Where Art Thou?* in December would be better, but still not of blockbuster proportions. The reviews: positive, for the movie, the directors and Clooney, whose performance earned him his first Golden Globe Award, for Best Performance by an Actor in a Comedy/Musical Motion Picture. But the modestly budgeted movie (around $25 million) earned back $45.5 million, only enough to be considered respectable, and not enough to put Clooney in the category of a Tom Hanks or a Samuel L. Jackson (whose films, on average, make them among the most bankable stars in Hollywood) in terms of the money his films could consistently be relied upon to earn. It's quite a testament to Clooney's talent and his popularity that he was considered among Hollywood's A-list despite his still unproven money track record.

Of course, that was about to change, anyway.

21

The Rat Pack Redux

Clooney—in his roles and in his life—is a man's man, without being too over-the-top (like Schwarzenegger or Stallone), too sensitive (Hanks), too outré (Spacey), or too boy toy (Pitt, Cruise). He's already being compared to Clark Gable and Cary Grant for his lethal combination of elegance and virility, without any great suggestion of depth (or Brando-ish, Bogart-ish darkness). He's more likable than Bruce Willis, less neurotic than Russell Crowe.

—*Vogue* magazine writer Lisa DePaulo

Clooney realized that, if he was going to be able to stick to his resolve to make only movies he would be proud to promote, he would have to figure out a way to get projects made himself. And that, in a nutshell, was the spark for his partnership with *Out of Sight* director Steven Soderbergh in the production company the two would call Section Eight (a cheeky reference to the U.S. military discharge that's issued on the basis of mental illness, which TV fans will remember as the main goal of *M*A*S*H*'s Klinger).

The two had bonded over their shared vision of the kinds of movies they wanted to make when they worked together on *Out of Sight*. Clooney appreciated the way Soderbergh operated, the kind of set he ran and his enthusiasm for breaking out of the studio popcorn movie mold;

and Soderbergh respected Clooney's enthusiasm for making movies, his positive presence on a movie set and his acting skills. Soderbergh had inherited Clooney as the star of *Out of Sight*, as Clooney had already signed on to the project when Soderbergh boarded. He wasn't unhappy with the Clooney casting, though it's probably fair to say he was pleasantly surprised at just how good Clooney's performance turned out to be.

"We're friends, and we share similar tastes in material and the two of us together can attract a different quality of project," Clooney said. "I started out [in Maysville Productions] with a nice guy who had the old producer ideal—you get thirty-five projects in development and do two or three of them. I looked at all the projects and said, 'I wouldn't do any of these.' When that deal was up, I said to Steven, 'Look, let's do movies we want to do.' It was a way for me to protect Steven, and for Steven to protect me. He's got great taste."

Added Soderbergh: "I like what he does, and he trusts me, I think. George and I are so alike. We have no patience for drama. We have no interest in people who are not sincere and don't care about what they're doing. That makes it easy to work together."

The duo's first joint venture was near and dear to Rat Pack fan Clooney's heart: a remake of the Frank Sinatra/Sammy Davis Jr./Dean Martin heist adventure *Ocean's Eleven*. As Clooney and Soderbergh saw it, they'd marry the idea of the buddy/heist movie with Soderbergh's stylish filmmaking and an A-list-powered cast to ensure that the movie would make enough money to reward its stars with handsome paydays on the back end, and to feed the coffers of Section Eight. The partners' master plan: make big popcorn movies (albeit stylish, quality popcorn movies) for cash, then funnel the profits from those movies towards smaller, niche films that might not pay off in big box office dollars but might attract some nominations come Hollywood awards season and lead to more funding for future niche flicks.

"Steven calls me . . . and says, 'I just finished [reading the script for] *Ocean's Eleven* and I know how to do it,'" Clooney told *Movieline*, continuing,

> I've known Steven [at this point] for four years and I've sent him twenty scripts and he not only passes, he says, 'No way dude.' He's a snob. Next day we walk in to see [producer] Lorenzo di Bonaventura at Warner Bros., and he greenlights it on the spot. We start talking to Brad Pitt and he's in. Steven had just finished *Erin Brockovich* with Julia Roberts, and he sends her the script with $20 tucked in and a note saying, "I hear you get twenty a picture now." She's in. Then everybody starts calling, you can't imagine the names. We're going to have a terrific cast, everybody working below rate. We said, "If we all get paid, we can't make the movie, so why don't we all just take a big chunk of the back end, work cheap and see if there's any money at the end."

Casting the movie turned out to be a fairly easy task, then, though the sheer talent Clooney and Soderbergh gathered was, frankly, more impressive than the 1960 original, which features Frank Sinatra, Dean Martin, Sammy Davis Jr., Peter Lawford and Angie Dickinson. In Clooney's version, he would play leader of the pack Danny Ocean, a lifelong thief who'd just been released from prison and hatched a scheme to gather his all-star criminal cohorts to pull off a bold heist that involved robbing three Las Vegas casinos (the Bellagio, the MGM Grand and the Mirage) at once. And, in what would give the movie something in common with the previous Clooney outing *O Brother, Where Art Thou?*, Danny's motivation is not just money, but also winning back the hand of his ex-wife, Tess (Julia Roberts), who was dating Terry Benedict (Andy Garcia), the owner of the casinos Danny planned to fleece.

The assembly of crackerjack safe crackers, acrobats, pickpockets and masters of disguise who'd split the $150 million with Danny included his old pal Rusty (Brad Pitt), a card sharp; Linus (Matt Damon), an expert pickpocket; Basker (Don Cheadle), a pyro technical expert; Reuben (Elliott Gould), who'd been swindled by Terry and was willing to front the cash to prep the heist; squabbling brothers Virgil and Turk

(Casey Affleck and Scott Caan), the getaway drivers; Frank (Bernie Mac), a card dealer who gains entry to the casinos by applying for a job; Livingston (Eddie Jemison), the gadget guru; Yen (Shaobo Qin), the Chinese acrobat who will maneuver his way around the vault where the cash is stashed; and Saul (Carl Reiner), a retired scammer who will dress up in fancy duds and pretend to be a wealthy businessman staying at one of Benedict's hotels.

The resulting movie is a fun, clever and exciting do-over on the original, and critics overwhelmingly agreed that it easily topped the Rat Pack's version for retro cool style. "It's a scrumptious and dizzy-spirited lark, a what-the-hell-let's-rob-the-casino flick made with so much wit and brains and dazzle and virtuosity that the sheer speed and cleverness of the caper hits you like a shot of pure oxygen," said *Entertainment Weekly*.

Released on December 7, 2001, during the first holiday season after the September 11 terrorist attacks, the film offered moviegoers a much-needed diversion from the events of the previous few months. And enthusiastic audiences in turn delivered Clooney his first bona fide box office smash. The slick adventure, which had come in with an $85 million budget, earned more than $183 million domestically and an astonishing $450 million worldwide.

That tidy sum was good news not only for the actor and Soderbergh, who had proved they could make high-quality mainstream movies that would pay off quite literally, but also for their cast members, who had agreed to forgo up-front salary for a chunk of the profits.

Of course, in true Clooney style, the cast had gotten more than a nice payday. They'd also had a great time making the movie; in the spirit of Sinatra and the Rat Pack, they were a constant presence on the Vegas strip during down time on the production. The camaraderie that's apparent in the final movie is a carryover from the set, which became the quintessential Clooney-led practical joke fest. Producer Jerry Weintraub was the number one victim of the frat boy antics, which ranged from Clooney and company covering all his doorknobs with Vaseline and wrapping his toilet—on a night when he'd returned home lateafter imbibing quite heavily—with plastic wrap, to the actors scheduling daily 5 A.M. wake-up calls that Weintraub had never requested. In one meticulously planned gag, Clooney and the gang sneaked into Weintraub's Bellagio hotel suite, covered him head to toe with M&Ms as Weintraub remained asleep, and then arranged for him to be startled by one of those 5 A.M. phone calls.

At last Clooney had found someone who could go toe-to-toe with him in the practical joke arena: namely the equally mischievous Brad Pitt. Pitt's attacks against Clooney were, at first, subtle, as he would tell interviewers that Clooney was sensitive about his hairpiece (he didn't actually wear one) and his complexion (Clooney, famously, is so confident in his looks that he says he's never used makeup on camera). Pitt would tell reporters, with a completely straight face, that Clooney was upset becausehe wanted to be a two-time *People* magazine Sexiest Man Alive, like Pitt.

And then there were the Clooney/Pitt farting contests, one of which, during a flight on a small private studio jet that also carried *Ocean's* screenwriter Ted Griffin, is remembered as pure torture. "When you're at thirty thousand feet and you can't crack a window, it can be particularly upsetting," Griffin said. The winner of that little match, by the way, was Pitt.

"I had this feeling about George and Brad, because they have very similar attitudes about themselves and about work," Soderbergh said of the costars' chemistry. "They're unpretentious, they're self-deprecating, they treat people well and never want to appear as the cliché of the self-obsessed actor. They both like to laugh."

The friendships that were forged on the set of *Ocean's Eleven* were one reason—along with the chance to earn some cash, of course, for themselves and Section Eight—that a sequel to the movie was quickly planned.

The emphasis, unfortunately, was on *quick* planning, because the script, as nearly everyone involved would later admit, simply wasn't up to the standards of the first. A thin pretense about the crew having spent most of the money they'd made from the Benedict heist—money the vengeance-minded casino owner was now demanding they pay back, with interest—and needing to pull off another major heist was the reason for getting the boys together again in *Ocean's Twelve*, and the plot just spiraled downward from there. The story line included a pseudo-clever, but also incredibly contrived, bit in which Tess, played by Julia Roberts, pretends to be Julia Roberts to distract some hotel employees, and a cameo-making Bruce Willis, and buy the guys some time.

"The studio was panicked [about the Roberts scene]," Clooney told *Entertainment Weekly*. "[Warner Bros. president] Alan Horn, who's a good friend, called up and said, 'I really think this is a bad idea.' But the closer we got to shooting, the more we all realized, 'If there's ever been a film that sort of steps out and points and makes fun of all these things, it's this.' And it required Julia's absolute, unbelievable commitment to it."

Meanwhile, a side plot involved giving Pitt's Rusty an ex-girlfriend (who's also a Europol agent) and seemed like another contrivance, just for the sake of providing a role for Catherine Zeta-Jones. Finally, the main heist plot itself was so convoluted and stretched thin that it frankly made little sense.

In fact, when Clooney was discussing a second sequel—the summer 2007 adventure *Ocean's Thirteen*, which takes the gang back to Las Vegas—he joked to a reporter that the poster for *Ocean's Thirteen* should simply read: "*Ocean's Thirteen* . . . better than *Ocean's Twelve*."

Behind the scenes, however, the *Ocean's Twelve* production was another good experience for the crew, with prankster action continuing between Clooney and Pitt. Clooney would reroute throngs of fans who greeted him outside the cast's hotel by alerting them that Brad Pitt was coming out just behind him, siccing the crowd on his unsuspecting buddy. Pitt would give back even better. In perhaps the greatest gag—or at least the best one that the cast members will admit to—from any of the *Ocean's* movie sets, Pitt distributed a memo to the entire crew, supposedly written by Clooney, that instructed everyone that Clooney was only to be addressed by his character's name, Mr. Ocean. The crew complied for several days, until Clooney finally figured out what was going on. His retaliation: a bumper sticker on Pitt's car that read "Small penis on board."

"One of the benefits of making a second film is that [the actors] know their characters so well," Soderbergh told *Premiere*. "There's a chemistry that you can't fake. And it comes from genuinely liking each other and spending time together when we're not shooting. They are just so generous towards each other. They're always willing to share the scene, which is crucial to a movie like this."

One of the other big appeals of the second movie, for everyone involved, was a planned shoot on location in Europe, including a nice long stint in Italy, where the whole cast could enjoy the use of Clooney's famous Lake Como estate, Villa Oleandra.

The eighteenth-century estate, located in the northern town of Laglio (population nine hundred), was an impulse buy for the actor. He and some friends, including Cindy Crawford and her husband Rande Gerber, had been vacationing nearby in 2002, and passed Villa Oleandra while on a motorcycle trip. Clooney was instantly smitten with the grand home; to him it represented the perfect place to get away, to enjoy life, to be with his family and friends—and the perfect investment for all the money he'd worked so hard for many years to amass. The purchase of Villa Oleandra, with $10 million taken from the stock market investments he'd dumped in protest when George W. Bush was elected in 2001, was "the best thing I've ever done in my life," Clooney would say, clearly proud of this most tangible of the rewards his fame and Hollywood status had brought him.

The property was pure luxury, with fifteen bedrooms (including a master suite so big Clooney finds it too intimidating to sleep in), multiple terraces, a gigantic kitchen and dining room table, a separate kitchen area just for making pizzas, a swimming pool, a well-appointed gym (where he would go to drop the weight he'd gain for his role in *Syriana*), beautiful grounds that overlooked Lake Como, and incredibly detailed painted ceilings that almost look like they were copied directly from the Sistine Chapel. "[These were painted] before they had television, so you just watched your ceiling," Clooney joked while giving an ABC news crew a tour of the spread.

Photos of Clooney, Pitt, Damon and their castmates lounging around the estate, walking along the beautiful water and jumping off Clooney's boat were constantly featured in the weekly celebrity magazines throughout the *Ocean's Twelve* production. Given their dedication to having as good a time making the movie as they'd hoped movie fans would have watching it, it might have made for a better release if *Ocean's Twelve* had consisted of footage of the cast whooping it up on Lake Como.

It certainly couldn't have garnered any less positive reviews than the final cut of *Ocean's Twelve* did, with *Rolling Stone* summing up the sequel perfectly: "Clooney and company work it too hard this time. You can tell they're huffing and puffing to stay afloat. But all I hear is: glug glug glug."

As the box office take showed, the sequel was also poorly received among audiences, with the $110 million budget returning only $125 million in domestic ticket sales.

In between the two *Oceans*, Soderbergh and Clooney pursued other projects, both jointly and solo. Clooney took a small but memorable role in the 2002 crime comedy *Welcome to Collinwood*, about a group of bumbling thieves. He played Jerzy, the wheelchair-bound safe hacker—and yes, he told a reporter, he recognized a career trend of playing characters on the wrong side of the law. "They're more fun to play," he shrugs.

He also reprised his role as the cheeky Devlin (who gets himself elected president) in Robert Rodriguez's *Spy Kids* sequel, *Spy Kids 3-D:*

Game Over; produced the forgettable Mark Wahlberg-Jennifer Aniston musical dramedy *Rock Star*; and reunited with Joel and Ethan Coen for *Intolerable Cruelty*, a romantic comedy in which Clooney stars as a superficial divorce attorney (we meet him as he's talking on a cell phone and having his teeth whitened at the same time) who finally meets his match in the equally ruthless, gold-digging wife (Catherine Zeta-Jones) of one of his clients. Clooney joked that his character, Miles Massey, was just a suit-and-tie version of Everett, the "idiot" he played in his other Coen brothers romp, *O Brother, Where Art Thou?* Clooney claims that, when he works with the Coens on another movie, the 2008 dark comedy *Burn After Reading*, it'll complete a trilogy of sorts. "This will be my third idiot," he told *Vanity Fair*. "[The Coens] call it my trilogy of idiots."

Also between their *Ocean's* flicks, Clooney starred in the Soderbergh-directed sci-fi romance/drama *Solaris* (a remake of the 1972 Russian film *Solyaris*). The odd, somewhat confusing 2002 psychodrama, told partially in flashbacks and set mostly aboard a space station, will be mostly remembered for two things: one, as one of the few misses on Soderbergh's resume of critical hits. And two, for a scene in which Clooney's naked posterior is on full display. A little Google-ing is all it takes to find the evidence.

Clooney made his directorial debut, too, with the movie adaptation of Chuck Barris's quirky autobiography *Confessions of a Dangerous Mind*. Barris, written off as a producer of throwaway TV fare like *The Gong Show*, *The Dating Game* and *The Newlywed Game*, claimed in his book that he was actually a CIA assassin, with the cheesy TV producer gig as his cover. The movie, though earning back less than half its cost at the box office, was a critical hit for Clooney as a director, and for star Sam Rockwell, whom Clooney had to fight to cast. Rockwell, Clooney's costar in *Welcome to Collinwood*, was perfect as Barris, but the studio, Miramax, had wanted to put a bigger name in the small project (Mike Myers, Ben Stiller and John Cusack were on the studio's wish list for the part), and it was only after Clooney agreed to act in the movie as well as and direct it, for a mere $500,000, and to make an appearance in the studio's *Spy Kids* sequel, that Rockwell got the green light. That Clooney had managed to persuade A-list pals Julia Roberts and Drew Barrymore to appear in the movie as well, and keep the budget at a relatively modest $29 million, didn't hurt its journey to the big screen, either.

Most importantly, *Confessions of a Dangerous Mind* proved to Clooney that everything he'd learned being an actor and a producer on movie sets had prepared him to direct. He borrowed liberally, he admitted, from the directors whose works most inspired him, as an actor and a movie fan.

"I think 'stole' is the better word," Clooney told a *Variety Life* interviewer. "I stole a ton from Steven [Soderbergh]. Other people as well. After *Confessions*, I sent Mike Nichols an apology 'cause I stole shots from him. I sent Sidley Lumet an apology letter, too. Not to mention all the stuff I stole from Joel and Ethan [Coen]."

Clooney also had a reunion of sorts with his ex-wife, Talia Balsam, in 2003. He and Soderbergh produced a short-lived political satire/improv series for HBO, called *K Street*, and Balsam and her current husband, actor John Slattery, starred in the series. It was a chance for the former spouses not only to work together, but to get reacquainted a decade after their painful divorce.

"It was really nice to reintroduce myself to her," Clooney said. "Now we can look at ourselves as two people who had a reason to be together at a point in the past. We were able to get past the rough times in the past, just make jokes and have fun."

As for Clooney's personal life during this period, it coincided with an increase in the number of weekly celebrity magazines, which meant more fervent coverage of his continuing bachelorhood and of his intensifying belief that it was his responsibility to speak up when he saw some wrongs that needed to be righted.

His dating life, for the most part, consisted of short-term flings, though the tabloids were more interested in perpetuating stories about relationships that he adamantly denied were anything more than friendships. When his costar from *The Peacemaker*, Nicole Kidman, split with husband Tom Cruise in 2001, speculation began that a Kidman flirtation with Clooney had been part of the cause, even though Clooney would insist he hadn't even seen Kidman since he spent time with her—and Cruise—on the 1997 movie set. Likewise, when Julia Roberts broke up with boyfriend and actor Benjamin Bratt in 2001, the tabloids suggested that part of the reason for the split was that Bratt felt very threatened by the friendship Roberts and Clooney had formed while filming *Ocean's Eleven*. Clooney's cheeky response: "I didn't have time [to break up Roberts and Bratt]. I was too busy breaking up Tom and Nicole's marriage."

When the actor wasn't fending off false reports of his part in marital infidelities and breakups, he had to work to disentangle himself from various celebrity feuds.

After the September 11 attacks, the entire Hollywood community, regardless of their feelings about the politics involved, rallied together to plan a telethon to raise as much money as possible for the surviving family members and others affected by the terrorist attacks. Soon the telecast, which the four major TV networks had agreed to underwrite and broadcast simultaneously, was overrun with celeb volunteers, which sparked an idea by Clooney. Instead of simply having the famous folks show up to speak to viewers on camera, organizers could schedule them to work the phone banks, too. Even at such a somber time, Clooney knew that the opportunity to call in and offer a pledge to Robert De Niro, Brad Pitt, Julia Roberts, Al Pacino, Jack Nicholson, Halle Berry, Tom Cruise, Goldie Hawn, Tom Cruise, Tom Hanks or Clooney himself would encourage Americans to dial in. The telecast producer thought it was a great idea, and the telecast, titled *A Tribute to Heroes*, aired on September 21 with an A-list gallery at the phone banks. Clooney then became more and more involved in the planning of the show, which included celebrities reading tributes to those who had perished in the attacks and touching performances by musicians singing tear-inducing songs.

Because his involvement in the telethon was so visible, Clooney, by no plan of his own, became the de facto celebrity spokesperson for the fundraising event. When Fox News commentator Bill O'Reilly was looking for someone to explain why the monies raised by the telecast—some $30 million that was earmarked for the United Way's September 11 Telethon Fund—weren't being distributed in what he felt was a timely manner, he turned to Clooney to shed some light on the matter. By the beginning of November, Clooney had agreed to talk with O'Reilly about the event, telling the broadcaster that he was out of line in suggesting that the celebs who'd volunteered their time for the telecast had only done so for the free publicity.

As the events of September 11 led into George W. Bush's declaration of war on Iraq in 2003, Clooney became more and more outspoken about his opposition to Bush's policies, a position that would again get him lumped in with a group of left-wing Hollywood types who became the butt of many conservative pundits' ire. Celebrities like Clooney, Tim Robbins, Susan Sarandon, Barbra Streisand, Sean Penn and, in the most famous incident, the Dixie Chicks, were called unpatriotic for speaking out against the war and against Bush, and Clooney admitted he had worried briefly that his critics might be right when they said he'd kill his career with his public discourse on all things political.

"[Miramax head] Harvey Weinstein rang me up and asked, 'What the hell is going on?' and so I called my dad," Clooney told *Men's Vogue*. "'Am I in a little dutch here?' And [my dad] said, 'A lot of people have gone to jail for saying things they believed in, lost their jobs, their livelihood. You're getting scared because you lost a few popularity points. Stop being a baby. You're a man . . . take it.' And he was right."

The actor later told *Variety*'s *VLife*, "I demand my right of freedom of speech. I demand my right of dissent. But I've also got to be willing to let people say bad things about me when I make those demands. You have to take your hits and be a grown-up about it."

Clooney *has* drawn criticism from some fans (and non-fans) for his outspoken views. But, as his next two big-screen projects would prove, even if it may have cost him a few ticket sales, his personal politics did nothing to trip up his climb to the top of the Hollywood power list.

22

Syriana and *Good Night, and Good Luck*

> Syriana *isn't an attack on the Bush administration. It's about questioning sixty years of failed policies in the Middle East.* Good Night *deals with the responsibility of the fourth estate. These aren't films that try to answer questions, they're films that ask them. That's the whole point.*
>
> —George Clooney

When screenwriter Stephen Gaghan was writing the 2000 epic drug drama *Traffic*, the Steven Soderbergh–directed film that would go on to win four Oscars, including a screenplay statue for Gaghan, he also had the idea of writing a movie about the oil industry and its multi-layered effect on the American government.

A few years later, in the aftermath of the September 11 attacks, former CIA operative Robert Baer wrote the memoir *See No Evil*, which details his personal experiences in the Middle East, including his up-close understanding of the complicated global relationships that have been forged because of the world's dependence on oil. Among other revelations, Baer's book recounted his attempts to get Bill Clinton's administration to covertly support a coup against Saddam Hussein from within the Iraqi government. It also delivered Baer's summation, after more than twenty-five years as a CIA op stationed all over the world, that the agency was headed towards a state of ineffectualness in which pencil-pushing desk jockeys were tying the hands of field agents and their attempts to protect America from terrorists.

Section Eight partners Clooney and Soderbergh optioned the movie rights to the tome before it had even hit bookstores in January 2002, and, renewing Soderbergh's relationship with Gaghan (Soderbergh had won Best Director honors for *Traffic*), the three began plotting a movie based partly on Baer's book and experiences, and partly on a year of firsthand research that would take Gaghan all over the world.

The screenwriter's travels included spending time with Baer himself, and, after determining that he wanted the movie to reach beyond the scope of Baer's book, Gaghan decided to write the script in the same style he had used to cover the illegal drug trade in *Traffic*. He'd weave together four loosely related stories into one movie, with a character based on Baer serving as the centerpiece of the picture.

The device of connecting separate story arcs and characters as Gaghan had done with *Traffic* was termed "hyperlink" cinema by movie critics, and, perhaps because it requires a deft touch to effectively pull off, several movies that have used the technique have gone on to critical acclaim, including the racial drama *Crash*, which earned a screenplay Oscar for Clooney's old *Facts of Life* cohort Paul Haggis in 2006, and the Brad Pitt thriller *Babel*, which won Oscar nominations for director Alejandro González Iñárritu and screenwriter Guillermo Arriaga in 2007.

That didn't mean getting Gaghan's script, which would come to be called *Syriana*, greenlighted, or financed, was going to be easy. The early development cycle was, after all, less than a year after 9/11, and the country was more interested in staving off future terrorist attacks than in seeing a dramatization of what geopolitical ideologies might have played a role in the events of September 11.

"When we started [*Syriana*], nobody was encouraging us," Clooney told *Entertainment Weekly*. "We jumped in on our own. And there was no reason to think it was going to get any easier."

Warner Bros. execs would agree to be the movie's producing studio only as long as Clooney agreed to a starring role. He quickly went after pal and *Oceans Eleven* and *Twelve* costar Matt Damon to take on the role of Bryan Woodman, an energy analyst whose business trip to push his company's services to a Middle Eastern oil emir (Alexander Siddig) end in a family tragedy.

The film's other headline role, then, was Clooney's, and it was one that would bring him both great rewards and great pains. In the interest of getting the movie made and funneling more of the budget towards the final cut, he agreed to work well below his usual eight-figure salary, for a $350,000 fee.

"People talk about cutting their fees, but George does," Gaghan says. "He's not just doing vanity projects—these are things that have intellectual, philosophical heft. You have to want to do something different, and I don't know many people like that in any walk of life."

Clooney's Bob Barnes is a tragic figure, both committed to his job and trying to balance his all-consuming work with raising a son who doesn't care that Dad's absences and frequent moves, dragging his son along with him from country to country, are part of Dad's effort to help save the world. Barnes is also struggling to make sure he can put his son through college (CIA operatives, even those who face danger on a regular basis, are government employees, meaning they're paid government wages), and, for all his world travel and decade of experience with "office" politics, he's still surprised when the government leaves him to look like the patsy.

To more authentically represent Baer's stockier appearance, Clooney felt it was important to pack about thirty pounds onto his usually trim frame. Unfortunately, he had little more than a week and half between the end of the *Ocean's Twelve* production and *Syriana*'s August 2004 start date, which meant altogether he'd have little more than a month to pack on the pounds before he had to begin filming his scenes.

"I bulked up to 207 pounds from 175," Clooney said. "I only had ten days between *Ocean's Twelve* and *Syriana*. It was like this marathon pie-eating contest. I went to my house in Italy, and I ate nine meals a day and drank beer. It was horrible. When you're in Italy with all that great food you want to look forward to a meal, so to be just pounding the food down was horrible."

The result was a remarkable change in appearance—the potbellied, full-faced, bearded actor was almost unrecognizable under the extra weight, a prospect that, surprisingly, didn't faze the studio, which had insisted that Clooney star if they were going to back the movie.

"The studio was willing to take it on politically, but like any studio, they needed a star," Clooney told *Rolling Stone*. "It didn't matter whether I was going to be fat and bearded, they still needed a star. . . . So I shaved my hairline back about an inch and a half, grew a beard and put on thirty pounds. And when we told Warners that we were going to do it for no money, it's hard to say no to that."

The weight gain that so drastically altered Clooney's classic leading-man good looks also crucially affected his physical stability. Gaining the weight so quickly had left Clooney off balance, and during the harrowing, cringe-inducing scene in which Barnes is taped to a chair and tortured, Clooney fell over in the chair and hit his head hard on the floor.

The pain was immediate, but the seriousness of the injury was not immediately apparent. Clooney continued to work on the movie, taking pain medication but still fully functioning in the role through the film's wrap in January 2005. Not only that, but he was already lining up funding for his next film, his long-in-development Edward R. Murrow passion project *Good Night, and Good Luck*.

Producer Jeff Skoll had started his Participant Productions company with some of the funds that had made him wealthy, as the first paid employee of eBay. Skoll flew to Dubai, one of *Syriana*'s filming locations, to meet with Clooney. Still in excruciating pain, which he'd later describe as comparable to having a "severe ice cream brain freeze that lasted twenty-four hours a day"—Clooney nevertheless wowed Skoll with a description of the movie he planned to make, scene by scene, detail by detail, right down to the music he wanted to use and the archival news footage he wanted to base much of the story around.

It would take a modest budget to get the movie made, Clooney told Skoll, and he was willing to cut his own director's salary to $1 to get the cameras rolling. He'd add on another $1 to take an acting role, as CBS producer Fred Friendly, and Clooney's obvious dedication to the project, as well as his finely tuned vision for it, led Skoll to agree to finance the film.

"About five or six years ago, I tried pitching a story about Murrow as a TV movie for CBS, but thankfully they turned it down," Clooney said. "And then, a few years ago, when I was getting beaten up for being unpatriotic by guys like Bill O'Reilly, I started getting frustrated. So I looked at the footage some more—Senator Joseph McCarthy calling Murrow a terrorist and Murrow's speech about not confusing dissent with disloyalty—and I started to see an idea. I thought, I have to find a way to do this as *The Crucible*."

Just one obstacle stood in Clooney's way: the injury. His back pain continued, and after shooting was wrapped on *Syriana*, the full extent of the injury was diagnosed. He'd torn his dura mater, the wrapping around his spine. In other words, he'd suffered a serious brain injury, he was leaking spinal fluid, and, after enduring biweekly injections of blood into his spine, followed by several surgeries, he'd still live with pain for many months afterward.

The pain even forced him to conclude that he would fail the insurance physical he needed to secure the financing for *Good Night, and Good Luck* to begin production. But, after years of trying to get the movie made and finally seeing its start date so close within his grasp, Clooney says he did the only thing he could. He put up his beloved Casa de Clooney as collateral to insure the *Good Night* production.

"The only thing that could go wrong is I couldn't finish the film," Clooney told *LOOK* magazine. "And there's no way, *no way*, that was going to happen unless I died.

"And if I did die, hey, I wouldn't really need the house anyway."

Jokes aside, Clooney was in considerable pain as he began his second directorial effort just a month after back surgery. "Directing a movie a month out of surgery was pretty rough," he said. "I usually just run on energy. I'm like the Pete Rose of directors. What I lack in talent, I try to make up for in hustle. But I didn't have a whole lot of energy."

No one could argue that his physical limitations showed on set or in the final product, though. By all accounts, the production was a pleasant one, as befits Clooney's philosophy of directing. "Here's what I believe as a director," he told *Variety*'s *VLife*. "Cast the right people. Period. Then let the right people do their jobs."

As for the cast, the main role of legendary CBS newsman Edward R. Murrow went to David Strathairn, a talented, scene-stealing character actor who'd been nominated for several Independent Spirit Awards but hadn't carried such a high-profile film before. That didn't shake Clooney's faith that Strathairn was the perfect man for the job—rather than, as many had suggested, Clooney himself.

"The secret to Murrow is that there is a sadness to him," Clooney said. "You always felt that he was carrying the weight of the world on his shoulders, and that's not something that you can act, it's something that you just sort of are. David Strathairn has it . . . that sense that everything he does he'll do for your benefit, but it hurts. No one thinks that way of me. Also David's face; there's this elegance to him that's not pretty at all, but it's stunning."

In the movie's other main roles, Robert Downey Jr. and Patricia Clarkson were cast as Joseph and Shirley Wershba, the secretly married members of Murrow's staff; Frank Langella portrayed CBS chief executive William Paley; Jeff Daniels was CBS News head Sig Mickelson; Grant Heslov portrayed Murrow's *See It Now* program director Don Hewitt; and Ray Wise portrayed Don Hollenbeck, a fellow CBS journalist who, like Murrow, had come under fire for his investigations of Senator McCarthy.

Clooney, though committed to not pushing his actors through take after take unnecessarily (a process he had grown to resent during his days on the *Three Kings* set with David O. Russell), did employ some Method-type acting techniques to help the stars prepare for their roles. Every morning, when the supporting cast got to the set, Clooney would give them copies of the day's newspapers and have them sit down in front of vintage manual typewriters and copy stories for ninety minutes. Then, he'd conduct morning news meetings, during which the actors, as their characters, would pretend to pitch story ideas for the day's broadcast.

He was also secretly taping the mock news meeting sessions, and later, when showing them to his newsman father, Clooney got the ultimate compliment.

"Dad and I, neither of us are good at taking compliments," he said. "And [after watching the tapes], he got up and just patted me on the shoulder and said, 'You got it right.'" All those years spent following his father around the news sets had clearly paid off—and his experience on the *Syriana* and *Good Night, and Good Luck* sets would soon pay off, too.

Reviews for both movies were overwhelmingly positive, with critics Roger Ebert and fellow TV critic Richard Roeper putting *Syriana* (released on December 9, 2005) and *Good Night, and Good Luck* number two and one, respectively, on their lists of the year's best movies. Clooney's performance, in particular, was singled out, and left few people questioning that he would receive some sort of recognition, several nominations at the least, when Hollywood awards season rolled around.

"Clooney suffers for his art here, but he and writer and director Stephen Gaghan do deliver the art: a film that transcends its obvious timeliness to say some elemental things about personal loyalty and institutional betrayal," *New York* magazine's Ken Tucker wrote of *Syriana*.

"This is Clooney doing a De Niro, growing a beard and cocooning himself in flab," wrote *Time* reviewer Richard Corliss. "The actor must want to prove that his star quality is more than just Cary Grant looks and a stud's sly aplomb. It is. Here he seduces the viewer into looking closer, to catch the eye glint of skeptical intelligence, the interior burden that a samurai for the CIA bears with weary grace, and for reasons he may have forgotten or never known."

Wrote *Rolling Stone* reviewer Peter Travers: "This is the best acting Clooney has ever done . . . he's hypnotic, haunting and quietly devastating."

The reviews for *Good Night, and Good Luck* were just as positive, and Clooney's direction was the focus of many of the accolades.

Wrote *Newsweek*'s David Ansen: "It's a passionate, serious, impeccably crafted movie tackling a subject Clooney cares about deeply: the duty of journalism to speak truth to power. It also happens to be the most compelling American movie of the year so far. . . . In his life, and in his movies, Clooney is fascinated by male camaraderie. His elaborate choreography of the teamwork that goes into television journalism is unsurpassed. The period detail is impeccable, from the ubiquitous cigarette smoking to the courtly male chauvinism. . . . You can feel the influence of Robert Altman in the playful overlapping dialogue and the sinuous, roving camera that darts from studio to studio."

From *USA Today*: "Flip, you say? Well, this viable awards contender isn't. So even-keeled that it allows McCarthy to play himself, using kinescopes from the era, *Luck* gleans extra depth from being the best movie ever about the in-bred tension between newsfolk and their advertisers. As such, George Clooney's second directorial outing couldn't be more topical, though the events it chronicles occurred over half a century ago."

Wrote Roger Ebert in the *Chicago Sun-Times*, "As a director, Clooney does interesting things. One of them is to shoot in black and white, which is the right choice for this material, lending it period authenticity and a matter-of-factness. . . . Clooney shoots close, showing men (and a few women) in business dress, talking in anonymous rooms. Everybody smokes all of the time. When they screen footage, there is an echo of

Citizen Kane. Episodes are separated by a jazz singer (Dianne Reeves), who is seen performing in a nearby studio; her songs don't parallel the action, but evoke a time of piano lounges, martinis and all those cigarettes."

Filming in black and white was less of a conscious decision than a necessity, Clooney would later say. Once he had decided to incorporate the actual footage of Joseph McCarthy, which was in black and white, the rest of the movie had to follow. Still, it was a key part of the movie's success, both because the black-and-white look added to how authentic Clooney's version of events felt, and also because, as he pointed out, no one could possibly have been as effective in portraying the ideas of Joseph McCarthy than McCarthy himself.

"I knew right off the bat that we wanted the old footage of McCarthy, because I thought no actor could play him," Clooney said. "No one would believe that anyone in that situation could be that much of a buffoon. No one could giggle like a hyena and be believable. So we wanted to use the real footage, in the same way Murrow used the footage of McCarthy to hang him. That meant we were shooting in black and white."

As for the fallout of making two very politically charged movies in one year, the controversy never reached the pitch Clooney and company expected it might.

Especially given his recent run-ins with conservative Fox TV host Bill O'Reilly and the opinions of some political writers who felt Clooney was both unqualified to speak about politics in general, and specifically wrong to criticize the Bush administration at the beginning of the war in Iraq, the actor had braced himself for a storm of negative feedback about his 2005 big-screen projects, and welcomed whatever his detractors might throw his way. "It was fun to be doing stuff I really believed in," Clooney said. "You want to raise a little hell while you can."

Political pundits on the right did take some issue with some of the implied politics of *Syriana*. Syndicated conservative columnist and frequent Fox News commentator Charles Krauthammer dismissed the movie as being nothing more than a piece of propaganda used to tout the liberal viewpoints of Clooney and other Hollywood left-wingers.

"Most liberalism is angst- and guilt-ridden, seeing moral equivalence everywhere," Krauthammer wrote. "*Syriana* is of a different species entirely—a pathological variety that burns with the certainty of its malign anti-Americanism. Osama bin Laden could not have scripted this film with more conviction."

Still, the movie was widely praised, and, because Edward R. Murrow is a hero to journalists of all political beliefs, *Good Night, and Good Luck* also failed to provoke much negative sentiment.

"I think that the temperature of the country changed," Clooney later explained. "When we were shooting [*Syriana*], there was nobody that wanted us to make that film. Because anybody who talked about oil policies was a traitor to his country. What's happened in the last year, especially since Katrina, people are less able to wrap themselves in the flag and say, 'For God and country.' Which suddenly makes it less controversial, which is good. I'm happy it's less controversial, because it means that people are actually having open discussions about things."

Instead, Clooney and company would have to be content with those reviews, and, beginning in January 2006, a slew of honors from their peers.

23

The Future

I mean, how much money do you actually need? My house is paid off and it's beautiful . . . I've made it Shangri-La. I drive up my driveway and I laugh. I'm in a position right now where I can live off the interest for the rest of my life and live ridiculously well. So then it comes down to, what is your legacy going to be? What are you going to stand for when you get hit by a bus? You want to be able to say you made a couple of good movies.

—George Clooney

With the Oscar win for *Syriana*, and nominations for both *Syriana* and *Good Night, and Good Luck*, his passion project, Clooney's foreseeable future in the industry promises to be a good one.

Though his first post–Oscar win project, the Steven Soderbergh-directed noir war thriller *The Good German*, wasn't the critical or box office hit the duo might have hoped it would be, it did succeed as another testament to the friends' original vision for the Section Eight production company: to make interesting movies that don't necessarily fit into a preconceived studio mold for the kind of films an A-list director and an A-list actor should be making.

The Onion A.V. Club's Scott Tobias wrote in his review of *The Good German*: "The film has more in common with the romantic cynicism of

Casablanca and *The Third Man* than other period works that commented on the war. With a few self-conscious exceptions, Soderbergh makes an earnest attempt to return to that place and time in both history and American filmmaking, and his risk-taking pays fascinating dividends."

The *Washington Post's* Stephen Hunter wrote: "Of *The Good German*, it can be said that the operation was a brilliant success, even if the patient is not merely dead but most sincerely dead. The movie, in other words, lies there as if on a slab in a morgue, while you admire the corpse for its beauty."

And Lou Lumenick wrote in the *New York Post*, "While Clooney and especially [Cate] Blanchett give solid performances, and [Tobey] McGuire plays effectively against type, the movie is best appreciated as an exercise in vintage Hollywood style." Clooney and Soderbergh have actually wrapped up their professional partnership, for now, with the 2007 legal thriller *Michael Clayton*, starring Clooney, as the final Section Eight production. Despite gossip that the company is dissolving because the two friends have fallen out, Clooney says it's nothing so salacious. "Two years ago, we announced we were only going to run till 2006," he told *Vanity Fair*. "We just felt things have a beginning, a middle and an end."

Clooney is also quick to point out what an influence Soderbergh has been and continues to be, on his career. "He's by far the biggest influence creatively I've had," the multi-hyphenate Hollywood star told the *Hollywood Reporter*. "Here's the thing: I got to get firsthand, up-close and personal lessons on writing, storytelling, directing, producing, with someone who will be remembered as one of the greats. And I got to do it on a daily basis for years. He's a huge influence on the way I write, on the way I direct films, on everything—and a great, great friend."

The end of Section Eight, then, also meant the beginning of Smoke House, Clooney's new production company, which pairs him with *Good Night, and Good Luck* cowriter (and member of The Boys club) Grant Heslov. The name is an homage to one of Clooney's favorite haunts, the Smoke House restaurant, the retro joint across the street from the

Warner Bros. studio lot where he filmed *ER* and where he once helped save the life of costar Anthony Edwards' baby.

With Smoke House, Clooney plans to continue fleshing out the kinds of projects he and Soderbergh sought for Section Eight, producing them with pal Heslov, who also understands the industry from a unique standpoint, having worked as an actor, writer, producer and executive for Section Eight.

"We'd like to keep it along the same vision," Clooney says of Smoke House, "which is to try to infuse [the movies] with the things we've learned over the years from independent and foreign films into the studio system, because they have the best resources. That's the same sort of philosophy Steven and I had with Section Eight."

And the beat goes on, as Clooney doesn't look to be tapering off his career anytime soon. In fact, if anything, his schedule is only getting busier, packed with more high-profile projects.

The last half of 2007 includes the release of *Ocean's Thirteen*, *Michael Clayton* and *Leatherheads*.

The latest *Ocean's* flick, one of the most anticipated movies for summer 2007, finds the entire cast, minus Julia Roberts, reunited for a very special reason: revenge. Even their old nemesis Terry Benedict throws in with Danny and the gang to defy a new, even more powerful Vegas baddie: Willie Banks, played by Oscar winner Al Pacino.

Next, Clooney is New York attorney Michael Clayton in the film of the same name. The movie, scheduled for release in September 2007, revolves around a lawyer who's about to have one very bad day, and a very bad case of karma slapping him in the face, when fifteen years of covering up for his shady clients comes back to bite him. Clooney filmed the movie on location in Manhattan and upstate New York, where he stayed at a budget hotel and supped and drank with the locals.

December 2007 finds the Oscar winner back on screen and back in the director's chair with *Leatherheads*, a long-in-development romantic comedy set in the world of professional football in the 1920s. A pigskin team owner, Jimmy Connelly (Clooney), finds himself locked in a love triangle with All-American college football star Carter Rutherford (*The Office* star John Krasinski) and Rutherford's fiancée, Lexi (Clooney's one-time real-life fling, Oscar winner Renée Zellweger).

Among the actor/director/producer's other upcoming projects:

36 (2008), a remake of the French crime thriller *36 Quai des Orfèvres*, about two detectives—Clooney and fellow Oscar winner Robert De Niro—who are competing against each other to solve a recent car theft ring, with the winner earning a promotion within the department.

Burn After Reading (2008), a dark comedy that will reunite Clooney with directors Joel and Ethan Coen and *Ocean's* movies co-star Brad Pitt. Clooney will play a quirky killer in the movie, about a CIA agent who's writing a memoir recalling his government exploits, and who has to retrieve the computer disc it's stored on after he loses it.

The Fantastic Mr. Fox (2008), an animated comedy based on the classic kids' book by Roald Dahl. The story revolves around a hapless farmer who plots to get rid of Mr. Fox (Clooney) and Mrs. Fox (Cate Blanchett), who are stealing the farmer's chickens.

White Jazz (2009), a crime thriller based on a James Ellroy novel and starring Clooney as a 1950s LAPD cop who has to expose the corruption within the department to save himself after he's framed by some of his unscrupulous coworkers.

Tishomingo Blues, a crime dramedy based on an Elmore Leonard novel and directed by and starring Don Cheadle. Clooney is executive producer on the movie, which also stars Matthew McConaughey. It's a classic Leonard story, about a high diver (McConaughey) at the Tishomingo Lodge & Casino who befriends a Detroit con man (Cheadle), after which they both become involved with a wacky scheme involving the local Dixie mafia and a group of Civil War re-enactors.

The Innocent Man, the movie version of author John Grisham's nonfiction book about a man who's finally cleared after spending eleven years on death row for a murder he didn't commit. Clooney and Smoke House Productions partner Grant Heslov purchased the movie rights to the project and plan to produce the movie.

The Diamond Age, a Sci Fi Channel miniseries, based on the Hugo Award-winning novel of the same name by Neal Stephenson, to be produced by Smoke House.

The Belmont Boys, a 2008 heist movie to be directed by Clooney. In a plot that sounds like "Ocean's Eleven: The Retirement Years," the movie will revolve around seven of the world's most successful thieves, who almost pull off a major heist, then reunite thirty years later to finish the job. In another *Ocean's* tie-in, the movie will be produced by *Ocean's* producer Jerry Weintraub.

Garland Bunting, a comedy, coproduced by Clooney, that sounds like a cross between *The Dukes of Hazzard* and *O Brother, Where Art Thou?* The story revolves around the titular real-life Bunting, a colorful, legendary character who worked as an officer for the Alcoholic Beverage Control board, catching wily North Carolina moonshine runners in the 1950s.

Jennifer Government, based on the satirical novel by author Max Berry, about a futuristic world in which corporations rule the world, taxes are illegal, and employees use their company's name as their surname. The main characters include John Nike, Hack Nike, Georgia Saints Nike (she also volunteers at the Church of Latter-Day Saints), Billy NRA (the NRA has become a publicly traded corporation), Buy Mitsui, Hayley McDonald's and Jennifer Government, a former ad exec turned government agent who has a barcode tattoo under her eye. Clooney is a coproducer on the movie.

Our Brand Is Crisis, a remake of the 2005 documentary about American political campaigning policies, focusing on the efforts of political consultant James Carville in the 2002 Bolivian presidential election. Clooney is signed on as an executive producer on the Smoke House/Warner Bros. production, with the option of directing and/or taking a starring role in the movie, as well.

An untitled HBO sitcom about an NBA expansion team, with Clooney, Steven Soderbergh and Grant Heslov as executive producers. The improv series follows the coaches and players of a fictional team throughout their first season in the NBA.

"I'm trying to put myself in a position where I can be creative for as long as I can," Clooney says. "To be able to die my own death. . . . You know, one day, I might be allowed to direct a film without being forced to act in it, which would be nice."

Clooney says he's not counting on his leading man looks to carry him throughout the rest of his career, either. "Eventually my looks will fall apart and I'll have to give [acting] up," he says. "You [direct] to have some control over your career when people say, 'I don't want to see you act anymore.' Paul Newman is acting almost into his eighties, but name another one. Robert Duvall? Fine. But he's Robert Duvall! He did *To Kill a Mockingbird*. I did *Batman & Robin*. He did *Network*. I did *Battle of the Network Stars*."

And then there's the actor's new commitment to enjoying the fruits of his considerable labors. He stopped smoking as his 2007 New Year's resolution, he told Jay Leno on *The Tonight Show*. "It was either that or give up drinking, and I'm not going to do that," he joked.

He's still driving his cool toys: the motorcycles, on which he enjoys long rides with The Boys every weekend he's not off on some movie set; the Tango, a small black electric car that looks like a golf cart and seats two people (one in front, one in back) but can go up to 130 mph, Clooney says; and even the Jaguar, which, at a hefty price, he had totally refitted with a hybrid engine. "If you're doing a movie about oil consumption, you can't just talk the talk," he told *Vanity Fair*. "You gotta walk the walk."

And he's fully committed to making the most of his Lake Como villa. "I find [the villa on Lake Como] part of an extension of my life, because all my friends come there," the actor told *Fade In*.

> Go there once and you understand the appeal: the food, the wine, the people are so friendly, it's the architecture, the land, the art . . . they don't get rid of things. . . . The best way for me to describe what kind of peace you get from being there is (this): I was sitting out looking over the road the other day . . . And I saw these old construction workers, looking just like every other construction worker—their shirts off, pants hanging low—coming home from work. They had a bottle of wine, a roll of bread, some flowers in their hands, and they were singing as they walked. And I thought, "We don't do that." They live their lives better than we do. The Italians taught me the one thing I never learned how to do, especially when you get success later in life. You're terrified as an actor of being unemployed still, so you just don't stop. This little town on this little lake taught me for the first time in my life, "OK, stop. Just stop. Relax. Sit on the side of the lake and listen to other people and eat great food and drink great wine and understand that you can actually not have to worry for a minute that the world has passed you by and you're not going to get another job. And even if it does, you could still afford to live there for a while and to really enjoy it."

That newfound philosophy of learning to enjoy his life will, of course, include more leisurely trips to Lake Como, and, with his fiftieth birthday still a few years off, maybe, finally, the woman who can replace work as the number one priority in his life. Despite the fact that he's proclaimed, for years, in interview after interview, that he will not remarry, and that even his closest friends and family members say they don't foresee him jumping into another marriage, more recently Clooney has seemed to soften his resolve a bit. "I made the mistake of saying [that I wouldn't get married again] a month after I got famous," Clooney recalls of his infamous interview with Barbara Walters. "Then for five years I played a rogue on *ER*. It was probably not the smartest thing to say, because the truth is, I'm not looking to be a bachelor my whole life. I happened to have just gotten through a divorce.

"I should have just cried," he joked about the Walters chat. "It would have been easier."

He may also consider a new pet, since his beloved Max, the potbellied pig he repeatedly referred to as the longest relationship of his life, died in December 2006. The rascally, nineteen-year-old swine, who had survived being accidentally run over by a car driven by Clooney pal Tom Hinckley, being put on a strict diet by his owner when his weight spun out of control, and numerous Clooney girlfriends and temporary and long-term houseguests, died peacefully, of natural causes, while Clooney was on the road promoting *The Good German*.

The loss was such a blow to the actor that his father, Nick Clooney, devoted an entire entry of his *Cincinnati Post* column to the piggie. "Though he started his life as a cute little porker, he grew to be a full-sized boar with a distinct personality," Nick Clooney wrote. "Like every friend you and I have, he had his quirks. He could be loud. In fact, he could go from a grunt to a shrill squeal and back again at every volume level imaginable. While this had a downside if it happened in the middle of a dinner conversation, it also had an upside. Max was the greatest watch-pig in California. No one set foot on the property at any hour of the day or night without Max raising a ruckus."

Clooney himself, who grew teary as he talked to a newspaper reporter about Max at *The Good German* premiere in Hollywood, said he couldn't point to one single best memory of life with his pig. "Oh, there are plenty of them. He got me in a lot of trouble, that pig, in general, and scared the hell out of a lot of delivery people, too," Clooney recalled.

On the other hand, new pets and potential Mrs. Clooneys may not be in the cards, as most of the actor's movie down time in the last couple of years has been reserved for humanitarian projects. Clooney, in partnership with many of his fellow celebrities and his father, the original inspiration for his civic-mindedness, is heavily involved with efforts to educate people about and help stop the inhumane treatment of the citizens of war-ravaged Darfur. Clooney and his father traveled to the country in April 2006, and the resulting documentary of their trip, *A Journey to Darfur*, painted a shockingly bleak picture of life for the refugees of the country. Clooney and his father point out that the refugees' lives are heartbreaking not only because of the state of the world they live in, but because they remain bravely optimistic in the face of such adversity. "I will remember forever how the people there were hanging from such a thin thread, and there were so many ways for them to die and yet they were optimistic," Clooney said. Added Nick Clooney, "We couldn't figure out why so few of these stories were on the front page. We were trying to think of ways that we could affect that. George obviously has this currency of his own—his enormous celebrity—and so he said, 'Pop why don't we go over there.'"

Shortly after returning from Darfur, Clooney made a trip to Washington, D.C., where he talked to government officials and urged them to intervene in Darfur, and later spoke at a rally at the National Mall, where seventy-five thousand people gathered to demand the refugees in Darfur become a priority. "If we turn our heads and look away and hope that it will all disappear, then they will," the actor told the crowd. "An entire generation of people."

In September 2006, Clooney and Nobel Peace Prize winner Elie Wiesel addressed the United Nations in New York, asking that aid to Darfur be stepped up, lest the world's governments allow a repeat of the 1994 Rwanda genocide to go unchecked. Before Christmas 2006, Clooney and his *Ocean's* movie series costar Don Cheadle made trips to Beijing and Cairo, to talk with government representatives in those countries about the genocide. Clooney and his contingency hoped to convince the Chinese and Egyptian officials, whose countries have close ties to the Sudanese government, that they needed to intervene in the continuing tragedy, which has, so far, left more than 450,000 refugees dead, and another 2.5 million displaced. Also along for the trip: a human rights attorney, a United Nations sports ambassador, and U.S. Olympic gold medalist speed skater Joey Cheek, whose presence, it was hoped, might suggest to the Chinese government that a boycott of the 2008 Beijing Olympics might be in order if the situation in Darfur continued.

His continuing humanitarian efforts, as well as his commitment to environmentally responsible living, his willingness to step to the forefront of fundraising efforts at times of national crisis and his affinity for sharing his opinions on all things political, have sparked pundits to suggest that Clooney will, and in the case of some politicos, should, run for political office himself someday.

The actor, by his own admission, is a political junkie, and clearly enjoys mingling with national, and thanks to his humanitarian works, even international political movers and shakers. He's publicly thrown his support in the 2008 presidential election behind Senator Barack Obama, saying he's impressed with the Illinois candidate's interactions with voters. "We were at a rally on Darfur. People were standing around backstage," Clooney says. "All of a sudden, Obama walks out and steps onto the stage. Everyone stopped to hear what he had to say. . . . I've never been around anyone who can literally take someone's breath away."

Yet, when chatter arises about his own potential candidacy—admirers have suggested he would make a fine congressman representing his home state, Kentucky—Clooney deflects it in his typical, self-deprecating manner.

"No, no, no," he told newswoman Diane Sawyer when she asked him if a political run might be in his future. "Done too many bad things in my life. I would literally have to run on the ticket of, 'Yes, I did it.' 'Wasn't it true that . . . ?' 'Yes, I did.' And, 'Weren't you with . . . ?' 'Yes, I think, I believe I was. And I drank the bong water at the time.'"

Even when reporters at a 2006 California rally to discourage investors from funneling money toward Sudan asked Clooney if he might have political aspirations like his *Batman & Robin* costar, and now California governor, Arnold Schwarzenegger, he brushed them off with a quip. "That's a bad idea," he said. "[Schwarzenegger]'s gone on to be governor, and I still think I'm Batman."

Though the actor does relish his involvement in the political machine of the United States, he's already cautious because of his father's failed congressional bid. He also says he doesn't feel throwing his own hat into the political ring is the best way to affect change.

"He started to wonder with what devils he would find himself sleeping," says Nick Clooney of his son's ultimate decision not to parlay his "currency" as an international movie star into a political career.

"I saw what [a political campaign] did to [my dad], "Clooney told *Esquire*. "I watched him getting the crap beaten out of him, and I realized how incompatible my personality is with the job. There are so many concessions you have to make, even with your own side of the fight."

"You can get a lot more done when you're not in politics, I think," Clooney re-iterated, to *USA Today*. "I'm not good with compromises."

With a thriving, award-winning career built on the idea of doing things his own way, it's hard to argue with his logic.

Filmography

Predator: The Concert[1] a.k.a. ***Grizzly II: The Predator*** (1987)
Writer: Harvey Flaxman, Joan McCall, David Sheldon
Cast: George Clooney, Charlie Sheen, Laura Dern, Jonathan Rhys-Davies
Rating: PG-13
Studio: Film Ventures International

Return to Horror High (1987)
Director: Bill Froehlich
Writer: Bill Froehlich, Mark Lisson, Dana Escalante, Greg H. Sims
Cast: George Clooney, Alex Rocco, Philip McKeon, Maureen McCormick
Running time: 95 minutes
Rating: R
Studio: New World Pictures

Return of the Killer Tomatoes! (1988)
Director: John De Bello
Writer: Stephen F. Andrich, John De Bello, Costa Dillon, J. Stephen Peace
Cast: George Clooney, John Astin
Running time: 98 minutes
Rating: PG
Studio: New World Pictures

[1] Movie was never released

Red Surf (1990)
Director: H. Gordon Boos
Writer: H. Gordon Boos, Brian Gamble, Jason Hoffs, Vincent Robert
Cast: George Clooney, Doug Savant, Gene Simmons, Dedee Pfeiffer, Philip McKeon
Running time: 104 minutes
Rating: R
Studio: Arrowhead Films

The Magic Bubble a.k.a ***Unbecoming Age*** (1992)
Director: Deborah Ringel, Alfredo Ringel
Writer: Meridith Baer, Geof Prysirr
Cast: George Clooney, Wallace Shawn, Bill Irwin, Michael Boatman, Don Diamont, Priscilla Pointer, Colleen Camp
Running time: 92 minutes
Rating: PG-13
Studio: Castle Hill Productions

Without Warning: Terror in the Towers[2] (1993)
Director: Alan J. Levi
Writer: Stephen Downing, Duane Poole
Cast: George Clooney, Andre Braugher, Fran Drescher, John Karlen, James Avery, Susan Ruttan, Robin Thomas
Running time: 96 minutes
Studio: NBC Television

The Harvest (1993)
Director: David Marconi
Writer: David Marconi
Cast: George Clooney, Miguel Ferrer, Harvey Fierstein
Running time: 97 minutes
Rating: R
Studio: Curb/Musifilm

---

[2] Made-for-TV movie that aired on NBC

From Dusk Till Dawn (1996)
Director: Robert Rodriguez
Writer: Robert Kurtzman, Quentin Tarantino
Cast: George Clooney, Quentin Tarantino, Harvey Keitel, Salma Hayek, Juliette Lewis, Cheech Marin, Danny Trejo, Kelly Preston
Running time: 108 minutes
Rating: R
Studio: Dimension Films
Awards: Saturn Award: Best Actor (Clooney), Best Horror Film; MTV Movie Awards: Best Breakthrough Performance (Clooney)

One Fine Day (1996)
Director: Michael Hoffman
Writer: Terrel Seltzer, Ellen Simon
Cast: George Clooney, Michelle Pfeiffer, Mae Whitman, Alex D. Linz, Charles Durning, Pete Hamill, Anna Maria Horsford, Robert Klein, Amanda Peet, Bitty Schram, Holland Taylor
Running time: 108 minutes
Rating: PG
Studio: Fox
Awards: Blockbuster Entertainment Awards: Favorite Actress - Comedy/Romance (Pfeiffer); Young Artist Awards: Best Family Feature - Musical or Comedy, Best Performance in a Feature Film - Actress Age Ten or Under (Whitman)

Batman & Robin (1997)
Director: Joel Schumacher
Writer: Bob Kane, Akiva Goldsman
Cast: George Clooney, Arnold Schwarzenegger, Uma Thurman, Chris O'Donnell, Alicia Silverstone, John Glover, Michael Gough, Pat Hingle, Elle Macpherson, Vivica A. Fox, Jesse Ventura, Coolio, Nicky Katt

Running time: 125 minutes
Rating: PG-13
Studio: Warner Bros.
Awards: Blockbuster Entertainment Awards: Favorite Actress - Sci-Fi (Thurman), Favorite Supporting Actor - Sci-Fi (O'Donnell); Kids Choice Awards: Favorite Movie Actress (Silverstone); Razzie Awards: Worst Supporting Actress (Silverstone)

The Peacemaker (1997)
Director: Mimi Leder
Writer: Leslie Cockburn, Andrew Cockburn, Michael Schiffer
Cast: George Clooney, Nicole Kidman, Marcel Iures, Michael Boatman, Goran Visnjic, Matt Adler, Thom Matthews, Aleksandr Baluyev, René Medvešek, Gary Werntz, Armin Mueller-Stahl, Randall Batinkoff
Running time: 124 minutes
Rating: R
Studio: DreamWorks SKG

Out of Sight (1998)
Director: Steven Soderbergh
Writer: Elmore Leonard, Scott Frank
Cast: George Clooney, Jennifer Lopez, Ving Rhames, Don Cheadle, Albert Brooks, Isaiah Washington, Dennis Farina, Luis Guzmán, Catherine Keener, Steve Zahn, Nancy Allen, Paul Calderon, Samuel L. Jackson,[3] Michael Keaton[4]
Running time: 123 minutes
Rating: R
Studio: Universal
Awards: ALMA Awards: Outstanding Actress in a Feature Film in a Crossover Role (Lopez); Boston Society of Film Critics Awards: Best Film, Best Screenplay (Frank); Edgar Allen Poe Awards: Best

[3] Uncredited
[4] Uncredited

Screenplay (Leonard, Frank); Golden Trailer Awards: Best Music; National Society of Film Critics Awards: Best Film, Best Director (Soderbergh), Best Screenplay (Frank); Online Film Critics Society Awards: Best Screenplay, Adapted (Frank); Southeastern Film Critics Association Awards: Best Adapted Screenplay (Frank); Writers Guild of America: Best Screenplay Based on Material Previously Produced or Published (Frank)

The Thin Red Line (1998)
Director: Terrence Malick
Writer: James Jones, Terrence Malick
Cast: George Clooney, Adrien Brody, Sean Penn, John Cusack, Jim Caviezel, John Travolta, Nick Nolte, Elias Koteas, Ben Chaplin, Dash Mihok, Kirk Acevedo, Woody Harrelson, Paul Gleeson, Thomas Jane, Jared Leto, Tim Blake Nelson, John C. Reilly, John Savage, Nick Stahl, Donal Logue[5]
Running time: 170 minutes
Rating: R
Studio: Fox
Awards: ALMA Awards: Outstanding Actor in a Supporting Role in a Feature Film (Acevedo); American Society of Cinematographers Award: Outstanding Achievement in Cinematography in Theatrical Releases (John Toll); Chicago Film Critics Association Awards: Best Director (Malick), Best Cinematography (Toll); Film Critics Circle of Australia Awards: Best Foreign Film; New York Film Critics Circle Awards: Best Director (Malick), Best Cinematography (Toll); Satellite Awards: Best Director of a Motion Picture (Malick), Best Motion Picture - Drama (producers Robert Michael Geisler, Grant Hill, John Roberdeau), Best Motion Picture Cinematography (Toll), Best Motion Picture Score (Hans Zimmer), Special Achievement Award - Outstanding Motion Picture Ensemble

---

[5] Uncredited

South Park: Bigger, Longer & Uncut (1999)
Director: Trey Parker
Writer: Trey Parker, Matt Stone, Pam Brady
Cast: George Clooney, Trey Parker, Matt Stone, Mary Kay Bergman, Isaac Hayes, Brent Spiner, Minnie Driver, Dave Foley, Eric Idle, Nick Rhodes, Stewart Copeland, Mike Judge
Running time: 81 minutes
Rating: R
Studio: Paramount
Awards: Chicago Film Critics Association Awards: Best Original Score (Parker, Marc Shaiman); Los Angeles Film Critics Association Awards: Best Music (Parker, Shaiman); MTV Movie Awards: Best Musical Performance (Parker, Stone, for the song "Uncle Fucka"); New York Film Critics Circle Awards: Best Animated Film; Online Film Critics Society Awards: Best Original Score (Shaiman)

Three Kings (1999)
Director: David O. Russell
Writer: David O. Russell, John Ridley
Cast: George Clooney, Mark Wahlberg, Ice Cube, Spike Jonze, Nora Dunn, Jamie Kennedy, Judy Greer, Mykelti Williamson, Saïd Taghmaoui, Liz Stauber, Alia Shawkat, Jim Gaffigan, Brian Bosworth
Running time: 114 minutes
Rating: R
Studio: Warner Bros.
Awards: Blockbuster Entertainment Awards: Favorite Action Team (Clooney, Wahlberg, Ice Cube); Boston Society of Film Critics Awards: Best Film, Best Director (Russell); Broadcast Film Critics Association Awards: Breakthrough Artist (Jonze)

Fail Safe[6] (2000)
Director: Stephen Frears
Writer: Eugene Burdick, Harvey Wheeler, Walter Bernstein

[6] Live, made-for-TV movie that aired on CBS

Cast: George Clooney, Don Cheadle, Richard Dreyfuss, Harvey Keitel, Noah Wyle, Brian Dennehy, Sam Elliott, James Cromwell, Hank Azaria, John Diehl, Norman Lloyd, Bill Smitrovich, Matt Adler, Tommy Hinkley, Thom Mathews, Grant Heslov
Running time: 86 minutes
Studio: Maysville Pictures/Warner Bros. Television
Awards: Saturn Award: Best Single Genre Television Presentation

The Perfect Storm (2000)
Director: Wolfgang Petersen
Writer: Sebastian Junger, William D. Wittliff
Cast: George Clooney, Mark Wahlberg, Diane Lane, John Hawkes, John C. Reilly, William Fichtner, Mary Elizabeth Mastrantonio, Cherry Jones, Karen Allen, Christopher McDonald, Rusty Schwimmer, Allen Payne, Dash Mihok, Josh Hopkins, Michael Ironside, Sebastian Junger[7]
Running time: 130 minutes
Rating: PG-13
Studio: Warner Bros.
Awards: British Academy of Film and Television Arts (BAFTA) Awards: Best Achievement in Special Visual Effects; World Stunt Awards: Best Water Work

O Brother, Where Art Thou? (2000)
Director: Ethan Coen, Joel Coen
Writer: Ethan Coen, Joel Coen, Homer
Cast: George Clooney, John Turturro, Tim Blake Nelson, John Goodman, Holly Hunter, Charles Durning, Michael Badalucco, Ray McKinnon, Stephen Root, Gillian Welch
Running time: 106 minutes
Rating: PG-13
Studio: Buena Vista/Touchstone Pictures/Universal
Awards: Golden Globes: Best Performance by an Actor in a Motion

[7] Uncredited as a patron at the Crow's Nest

Picture - Comedy/Musical (Clooney); Florida Film Critics Circle Awards: Best Soundtrack and Score (T-Bone Burnett, Carter Burwell); Grammy Awards: Best Compilation Soundtrack Album for a Motion Picture, Television or Other Visual Media

Spy Kids (2001)
Director: Robert Rodriguez
Writer: Robert Rodriguez
Cast: George Clooney, Antonio Banderas, Carla Gugino, Alexa Vega, Daryl Sabara, Alan Cumming, Teri Hatcher, Tony Shaloub, Mike Judge, Richard Linklater, Danny Trejo, Robert Patrick, Cheech Marin, Dick Clark
Running time: 88 minutes
Rating: PG
Studio: Dimension
Awards: ALMA Awards: Outstanding Director of a Motion Picture (Rodriguez)

Ocean's Eleven (2001)
Director: Steven Soderbergh
Writer: George Clayton Johnson, Jack Golden Russell, Harry Brown, Charles Lederer, Ted Griffin
Cast: George Clooney, Brad Pitt, Matt Damon, Julia Roberts, Bernie Mac, Carl Reiner, Don Cheadle, Andy Garcia, Elliott Gould, Casey Affleck, Scott Caan, Eddie Jemison, Shaobo Qin, Scott L. Schwartz, Lennox Lewis, Jerry Weintraub, Eydie Gormé, Angie Dickinson, Steve Lawrence, Wayne Newton, Roy Horn, Siegfried Fischbacher, Jim Lampley, Topher Grace, Joshua Jackson, Shayne West, Holly Marie Combs, Barry Watson
Running time: 116 minutes
Rating: PG-13
Studio: Warner Bros.

Awards: ALMA Awards: Outstanding Supporting Actor in a Motion Picture (Garcia)

Welcome to Collinwood (2002)
Director: Anthony Russo, Joe Russo
Writer: Anthony Russo, Joe Russo
Cast: George Clooney, William H. Macy, Isaiah Washington, Sam Rockwell, Patricia Clarkson, Michael Jeter, Luis Guzmán, Jennifer Esposito, Gabrielle Union
Running time: 86 minutes
Rating: R
Studio: Warner Bros.

Solaris (2002)
Director: Steven Soderbergh
Writer: Stanislaw Lem, Steven Soderbergh
Cast: George Clooney, Natascha McElhone, Viola Davis, John Cho, Jeremy Davies
Running time: 99 minutes
Rating: PG-13
Studio: Fox

Confessions of a Dangerous Mind (2002)
Director: George Clooney
Writer: Chuck Barris, Charlie Kaufman
Cast: George Clooney, Sam Rockwell, Drew Barrymore, Michael Cera, Dick Clark, Maggie Gyllenhaal, Brad Pitt, Matt Damon, Julia Roberts, Jim Lange, Rutger Hauer, Richard Kind, Krista Allen, Michael Ensign, Chuck Barris, James Urbaniak, Tommy Hinkley, Akiva Goldsman, Jerry Weintraub
Running time: 113 minutes
Rating: R

Studio: Miramax
Awards: Berlin International Film Festival: Best Actor (Rockwell); Broadcast Film Critics Association Awards: Best Writer (Kaufman); Chicago Film Critics Association Awards: Most Promising Performer (Gyllenhaal); Las Vegas Film Critics Society Awards: Best Picture; National Board of Review: Best Screenplay (Kaufman)

Spy Kids 3-D: Game Over (2003)
Director: Robert Rodriguez
Writer: Robert Rodriguez
Cast: George Clooney, Antonio Banderas, Carla Gugino, Alexa Vega, Daryl Sabara, Ricardo Montalban, Holland Taylor, Sylvester Stallone, Mike Judge, Salma Hayek, Ryan Pinkston, Elijah Wood, Cheech Marin, Danny Trejo, Alan Cumming, Tony Shalhoub, Steve Buscemi, Bill Paxton
Running time: 84 minutes
Rating: PG
Studio: Dimension
Awards: Razzie Awards: Worst Supporting Actor (Stallone)

Intolerable Cruelty (2003)
Director: Ethan Coen, Joel Coen
Writer: Robert Ramsey, Matthew Stone, John Romano, Ethan Coen, Joel Coen
Cast: George Clooney, Catherine Zeta-Jones, Geoffrey Rush, Edward Herrmann, Billy Bob Thornton, Cedric the Entertainer, Paul Adelstein, Julia Duffy, Richard Jenkins, Tom Aldredge, Kristin Datillo, Bruce Campbell
Running time: 100 minutes
Rating: PG-13
Studio: Universal

Ocean's Twelve (2004)
Director: Steven Soderbergh
Writer: George Nolfi, George Clayton Johnson, Jack Golden Russell
Cast: George Clooney, Brad Pitt, Matt Damon, Julia Roberts, Bernie Mac, Carl Reiner, Don Cheadle, Catherine Zeta-Jones, Andy Garcia, Elliott Gould, Casey Affleck, Scott Caan, Eddie Jemison, Shaobo Qin, Vincent Cassel, Eddie Izzard, Jerry Weintraub, Cherry Jones, Scott L. Schwartz, Albert Finney, Topher Grace, Bruce Willis
Running time: 125 minutes
Rating: PG-13
Studio: Warner Bros.

Good Night, and Good Luck (2005)
Director: George Clooney
Writer: George Clooney, Grant Heslov
Cast: George Clooney, David Strathairn, Robert Downey Jr., Patricia Clarkson, Jeff Daniels, Frank Langella, Tate Donovan, Reed Diamond, Glenn Morshower, Alex Borstein, Matt Ross, Thomas McCarthy, Ray Wise, Grant Heslov, Robert Knepper, Peter Jacobson
Running time: 93 minutes
Rating: PG
Studio: Warner Independent Pictures
Awards: National Board of Review: Best Picture; Online Film Critics Society Awards: Best Screenplay - Original (Clooney, Heslov); PGA (Producers Guild of America) Golden Laurel Awards: Stanley Kramer Award (Heslov); San Francisco Film Critics Circle: Best Screenplay (Clooney, Heslov); Satellite Awards: Outstanding Screenplay - Original (Clooney, Heslov), Special Achievement Award for an Auteur (Clooney); Venice Film Festival: FIPRESCI Prize (Clooney), Best Screenplay (Clooney, Heslov), Human Rights Film Network Award - Special Mention (Clooney), Best Film (Clooney), Best Actor (Strathairn)

Syriana (2005)
Director: Stephen Gaghan
Writer: Stephen Gaghan, Robert Baer
Cast: George Clooney, Matt Damon, Chris Cooper, Robert Foxworth, Jeffrey Wright, Amanda Peet, Max Minghella, Amr Waked, Kayvan Novak, Jamey Sheridan, Thomas McCarthy, Tim Blake Nelson, Alexander Siddig, David Clennon, William Hurt, Viola Davis
Running time: 126 minutes
Rating: R
Studio: Warner Bros.
Awards: Academy Awards: Best Performance by an Actor in a Supporting Role (Clooney); Golden Globes: Best Performance by an Actor in a Supporting Role in a Motion Picture (Clooney); Boston Society of Film Critics Awards: Best Ensemble Cast; Edgar Allan Poe Awards: Best Motion Picture Screenplay (Gaghan, Baer); National Board of Review: Best Screenplay - Adapted (Gaghan)

The Good German (2006)
Director: Steven Soderbergh
Writer: Paul Attanasio, Joseph Kanon
Cast: George Clooney, Cate Blanchett, Tobey Maguire, Beau Bridges, Leland Orser, Jack Thompson, Robin Weigert, Tony Curran, Dave Power, Dominic Comperatore, Don Pugsley
Running time: 105 minutes
Rating: R
Studio: Warner Bros.

Ocean's Thirteen (2007)
Director: Steven Soderbergh
Writer: Brian Koppelman, David Levien, George Clayton Johnson, Jack Golden Russell
Cast: George Clooney, Brad Pitt, Matt Damon, Al Pacino, Andy Garcia, Don Cheadle, Bernie Mac, Elliott Gould, Carl Reiner, Ellen Barkin, Casey Affleck, Scott Caan, Shaobo Qin, Eddie Jemison, Scott L. Schwartz
Rating: PG-13
Studio: Warner Bros.

The George Clooney Timeline

1961 George Timothy Clooney is born on May 6 in Lexington, Kentucky, to parents Nick and Nina Clooney.

1966 Unofficially begins his showbiz career on St. Patrick's Day, dressing up as a leprechaun on *The Nick Clooney Show*, a local talk show in Cincinnati.

1974 After years spent moving all around Columbus and Cincinnati, Ohio, for Nick's jobs, the Clooney family settles in Augusta, Kentucky.

1975 While sitting in church one Sunday, Clooney feels the left side of his face go numb. He'll suffer from Bell's palsy for the next nine months.

1978 Is an uncredited extra in the NBC miniseries *Centennial*, which films scenes in Kentucky.

1979 Graduates from Augusta High School in Augusta, Kentucky.

Tries out for the Cincinnati Reds; doesn't make the cut.

Enrolls as a broadcast journalism major at Northern Kentucky University.

1982 Is invited by cousin Miguel Ferrer to spend several months in Lexington, working as an extra on the movie *And They're Off*.

Decides to move to Hollywood and pursue an acting career.

Spends a summer cutting tobacco to save $300, which he uses to drive his jalopy, "Danger Car," across country.

Moves in with his aunt Rosemary Clooney in Beverly Hills.

While taking acting classes and auditioning for TV and movie roles, works construction jobs and acts as Tony Bennett's chauffeur.

1983 Moves in with pal Thom Mathews, living in Mathews' closet, after Aunt Rosemary kicks him out of her house.

Mathews becomes the first member of "The Boys," Clooney's now-famous group of friends from his early days in Hollywood.

1984 Plays a kidnapper in an episode of the NBC drama *Riptide*.

Lands his first regular TV series job, on a CBS medical sitcom called *E/R*, with his future *Ocean's Eleven* costar Elliott Gould.

Is a finalist for the *Breakfast Club* role that eventually goes to Judd Nelson.

Turns down a $1,400/week role on the now-defunct daytime soap opera *Santa Barbara*.

1985 Is cast as the resident hunk on *The Facts of Life*.

Guest stars on TV series *Street Hawk* and *Crazy Like a Fox*.

1986 Guest stars in episodes of *Hotel* and *Throb*, and stars in the made-for-TV movie *Combat High*.

1987 Stars in his first major movie, *Predator: The Concert*, a sequel to the movie *Grizzly*. The flick, costarring Charlie Sheen, is never released.

Stars in *Return to Horror High*.

Guest stars on TV shows *Hunter*; *Murder, She Wrote* and *The Golden Girls*.

Quits *The Facts of Life*.

Stars in an NBC sitcom pilot called *Bennett Brothers*, where he costars with his future best friend, Richard Kind. The pilot doesn't air.

1988 Is cast as the resident hunk on *Roseanne*.

Stars in *Return of the Killer Tomatoes!*

Meets actress Kelly Preston at a party; less than a month later, they buy a $1 million house together.

Clooney and Preston get engaged.

Clooney buys Max, a Vietnamese black bristled potbellied pig, as a gift for Preston.

1989 Breaks up with Preston; gets the house and custody of Max the pig.

Marries actress Talia Balsam.

Quits *Roseanne*.

1990 Auditions several times for the role of J.D. the drifter in *Thelma & Louise*, eventually losing out on the career-changing role to Brad Pitt.

Stars as a drug-dealing surfer in *Red Surf*.

Stars in the ABC drama pilot *Sunset Beat*, as a cop undercover as a motorcycle gang member; it isn't picked up by the network.

Lands lead role in *Baby Talk*, an ABC sitcom based on the hit movie *Look Who's Talking*.

Clooney's great-uncle George, the man he was named after,

dies in a VA hospital in Cincinnati, with Clooney at his bedside.

After a public confrontation on the set of *Baby Talk* with producer Ed Weinberger, Clooney quits the show.

Four days after quitting *Baby Talk*, another producer, aware of Clooney's difficulties with Weinberger, offers Clooney a lead role in the NBC sitcom pilot *Knights of the Kitchen Table*; it isn't picked up by the network.

1991 *Baby Talk* premieres in March, and is voted the worst show on TV in a critics poll.

1992 Stars in the movie *The Magic Bubble* (a.k.a. *Unbecoming Age*).

Stars in the short-lived CBS cop drama *Bodies of Evidence*.

1993 Divorce from Talia Balsam becomes final.

Stars in the NBC movie *Without Warning: Terror in the Towers*, about the 1993 World Trade Center bombing.

Plays a lip-synching transvestite in the movie *The Harvest*, which also stars his cousin, Miguel Ferrer.

Is cast as the resident hunk on *Sisters*.

1994 Signs on for his breakout role as pediatrician Doug Ross on NBC's hit medical drama *ER*.

ER's series debut ratings make it one of the top-rated shows of the week, and the show's first season is second only to *Seinfeld* in the Nielsen ratings.

Clooney's Aunt Rosemary guest stars on two episodes of *ER*.

Clooney is sound asleep when the Northridge earthquake hits, and only incessant squealing by Max the pig awakens him and gets him out of the house before it's shaken off its foundation.

1995 Buys the eight-bedroom Hollywood Hills home that will be nicknamed Casa de Clooney, and which will serve as hangout central for The Boys.

Guest stars on *Friends*, with *ER* costar Noah Wyle, playing a doctor.

Nominated for Outstanding Lead Actor in a Drama Emmy for *ER*.

Rosemary Clooney is nominated for Outstanding Guest Actress in a Drama Series for her guest role on *ER*.

Clooney signs on to a movie version of radio show and comic book series *The Green Hornet*.

1996 Stars in *From Dusk Till Dawn*, gets great reviews, a Saturn Award for Best Actor and a $250,000 salary for his first major movie role since *ER* debuted.

Meets twenty-one-year-old Céline Balitran while vacationing in Paris; they begin dating after he invites her to visit him in Los Angeles.

Balitran moves to L.A. and into Casa de Clooney.

Stars in the romantic comedy *One Fine Day* with Michelle Pfeiffer.

Nominated for Outstanding Lead Actor in a Drama Emmy for *ER*; takes Balitran as his date to the Emmy ceremony.

Pfeiffer famously bets Clooney $10,000 that he'll be a father by the time he turns forty.

Nominated for Best Performance by an Actor in a TV Series - Drama Golden Globe Award for *ER*.

Nominated for Outstanding Performance by a Male Actor in a Drama Series Screen Actors Guild Award for *ER*.

1997 Voted *People* magazine's Sexiest Man Alive.

Replaces Val Kilmer as the big-screen Caped Crusader in *Batman & Robin*; makes $10 million salary for the movie.

After *Batman & Robin* tanks at the box office, Clooney quips, "Well, I killed that franchise!"

Guest stars on *South Park* as Sparky, the gay dog.

Launches his own production company, Maysville Productions, named after his father's Kentucky birthplace.

After *ER* producer Steven Spielberg pulls strings to get him out of his contract to star in *The Green Hornet*, Clooney stars with Nicole Kidman in *The Peacemaker*, the first feature from Spielberg's newly formed DreamWorks studio.

Kidman also bets Clooney $10,000 that he'll be a father by the time he turns forty.

Upon Clooney and costar Anthony Edwards' suggestion, the fourth season premiere of *ER* airs live.

Famously launches a boycott of tabloid TV show *Entertainment Tonight* after *ET* sister show *Hard Copy* runs a story on him; several A-list stars join the boycott.

Nominated for Best Performance by an Actor in a TV Series Drama Golden Globe Award for *ER*.

Nominated for Outstanding Performance by a Male Actor in a Drama Series Screen Actors Guild Award for *ER*; wins Outstanding Performance by an Ensemble in a Drama Series Screen Actors Guild Award with *ER* cast.

1998 Guest stars on *Murphy Brown*.

Stars in *Out of Sight*, his first collaboration with future production-company partner Steven Soderbergh.

Films a role in Terrence Malick's all-star war drama *The Thin Red*

Line, but the part is cut down to a minor appearance in editing.

Nominated for Best Performance by an Actor in a TV Series - Drama Golden Globe Award for *ER*.

Wins Outstanding Performance by an Ensemble in a Drama Series Screen Actors Guild Award with *ER* cast.

1999 Fulfills five-year contract with *ER*, then leaves the show to focus on movie career full-time.

Plays Dr. Doctor in the *South Park: Bigger, Longer & Uncut* movie.

Stars in *Three Kings*; gets into major fisticuffs with director David O. Russell during the contentious production.

Wins Outstanding Performance by an Ensemble in a Drama Series Screen Actors Guild Award with *ER* cast.

He and Balitran break up; she's reportedly frustrated that he's not interested in marriage and children.

2000 Produces and stars in a live CBS remake of the nuclear war thriller *Fail Safe* (a coproduction of Clooney's now-defunct Maysville Pictures production company).

Makes a guest appearance on *ER*, during costar Julianna Margulies' final episode.

Stars in *O Brother, Where Art Thou?*, his first collaboration with filmmaker brothers Joel and Ethan Coen; accepts a $500,000 salary in an effort to help get the low-budget movie made.

Stars in *The Perfect Storm*; makes $8 million salary.

2001 Turns forty.

Michelle Pfeiffer and Nicole Kidman each send him $10,000 checks as payoff on the bets they lost with him; he sends the checks back with notes that say "Double or nothing" by his fiftieth birthday.

Launches Section Eight Productions company with Steven Soderbergh.

Films a role in Robert Rodriguez's *Spy Kids*.

Clooney pal Tommy Hinkley accidentally runs over Max the pig with his car; Max survives.

Section Eight produces, Steven Soderbergh directs and Clooney leads an all-star cast in a remake of the Rat Pack heist movie classic *Ocean's Eleven*; cast takes a lower upfront salary in exchange for a piece of the profits. Clooney's share is estimated at $20 million.

Wins Best Performance by an Actor in a Motion Picture - Comedy/Musical Golden Globe Award for *O Brother, Where Art Thou?*

Acts as executive producer on pal Mark Wahlberg's drama *Rock Star* (a coproduction of Maysville Pictures).

Helps organize *America: A Tribute to Heroes*, a star-studded telethon that kicks off a campaign that ultimately raises $130 million for the victims of the 9/11 attacks.

Engages in war of words with conservative TV host Bill O'Reilly after O'Reilly charges that the celebrities involved with *A Tribute to Heroes* aren't taking responsibility for making sure the funds raised are dispersed quickly enough.

2002 Makes his directorial debut with and stars in *Confessions of a Dangerous Mind*, accepting a $500,000 salary for both jobs as part of a deal with Miramax to get the movie made.

Begins dating actress Krista Allen, on and off, following her appearance as an extra in *Confessions of a Dangerous Mind*.

Acts as executive producer for and stars in *Welcome to Collinwood* (a Section Eight coproduction).

Stars in *Solaris* for director Steven Soderbergh.

Serves as a pallbearer at the funeral of his aunt Rosemary Clooney, who died of lung cancer.

Acts as executive producer on the Al Pacino/Robin Williams thriller *Insomnia* (a Section Eight coproduction).

Acts as executive producer on the Oscar-nominated Julianne Moore drama *Far From Heaven* (a Section Eight coproduction).

Buys Villa Oleandra, a fifteen-room, eighteenth-century mansion he discovered in Lake Como, Italy, while on a motorcycle trip through Europe.

Hosts fundraisers for his father in his dad's losing bid to win a Kentucky congressional seat; his opponent, Geoff Davis, claims that he represents "heartland values," while Clooney represents the liberal values of Hollywood.

A *TV Guide* poll names Clooney as the sexiest male star in television history.

2003 Stars in *Spy Kids 3-D: Game Over*.

Stars in second movie for Joel and Ethan Coen, *Intolerable Cruelty*, at a salary of $15 million.

Acts as executive producer of the HBO political dramedy series *K Street*, which stars his ex-wife, Talia Balsam, and her new husband, John Slattery (a Section Eight coproduction).

2004 Stars in *Ocean's Twelve*, directed by Steven Soderbergh (a Section Eight coproduction).

Acts as producer on the crime dramedy *Criminal* (a Section Eight coproduction).

2005 Directs, cowrites and stars in *Good Night, and Good Luck*, coproduced by Section Eight.

Takes a $1 salary for writing *Good Night, and Good Luck*, and a $1 salary for directing the movie, so most of the film's $7 million budget can be funneled into production.

Stars in *Syriana*; also acts as an executive producer on the movie; suffers a temporarily debilitating spinal cord injury during filming.

Acts as producer on the sci-fi thriller *The Jacket* (a Section Eight coproduction).

Becomes involved with the One Campaign, the "effort by Americans to rally Americans—ONE by ONE—to fight the emergency of global AIDS and extreme poverty," and personally recruits televangelist Pat Robertson to join the campaign.

Co-creator and acts as executive producer of the HBO improvised dramedy *Unscripted*, which stars his on-again, off-again girlfriend Krista Allen (a Section Eight coproduction).

Acts as executive producer on the Jennifer Aniston romantic dramedy *Rumor Has It . . .* (a Section Eight coproduction).

Sister Ada's husband dies unexpectedly of a heart attack.

Grandmother Dica Warren dies.

Becomes the owner of the first Electric Tango Spied, known as an "electric muscle car."

2006 Nominated for three Oscars: Best Supporting Actor for *Syriana*, Best Writing, Original Screenplay (with Grant Heslov), and Best Director for *Good Night, and Good Luck*; wins Best Supporting Actor.

Nominated for three Golden Globe Awards: Best Performance by an Actor in a Supporting Role in a Motion Picture for *Syriana*, Best Screenplay - Motion Picture (with Grant Heslov), and Best Director - Motion Picture for *Good Night, and Good Luck*; wins Best Performance by an Actor in a Supporting Role.

Nominated for Director's Guild of America Award for *Good Night, and Good Luck*.

Nominated for Writer's Guild of America Award (with Grant Heslov) for *Good Night, and Good Luck*.

Nominated for Outstanding Performance by a Cast in a Motion Picture Screen Actors Guild Award with cast of *Good Night, and Good Luck*.

Acts as executive producer on the Richard Linklater sci-fi thriller *A Scanner Darkly* (a Section Eight coproduction).

Acts as executive producer on the drama *The Half Life of Timofey Berezin* (a Section Eight coproduction).

Beloved pet potbellied pig Max dies.

Beloved pet bulldog Bud dies.

Asks former president George Bush Sr. to join him in an effort to raise funds to rebuild a New Orleans hospital ravaged by Hurricane Katrina.

Stars in *The Good German*, directed by Steven Soderbergh (a Section Eight coproduction).

Announces he and Steven Soderbergh are disbanding Section Eight Productions to work on other projects.

George and Nick Clooney travel to Sudan, where they witness and document the plight of the refugees from war-torn Darfur.

Both Clooneys speak at the Save Darfur Coalition rally in Washington, D.C., on April 30, and George addresses the United Nations Security Council in September to urge more humanitarian aid for the millions of refugees.

Is awarded the twenty-first annual American Cinematheque Award.

Forms Smoke House Productions with longtime friend and *Good Night, and Good Luck* cowriter Grant Heslov.

Voted *People* magazine's Sexiest Man Alive (only second person—along with Brad Pitt—to be named Sexiest Man Alive twice).

Tops AskMen.com's "manly men" list as the best representative of the male gender.

2007 Stars in and acts as executive producer for *Ocean's Thirteen*, directed by Steven Soderbergh (a Section Eight coproduction).

Acts as executive producer on the horror flick *Wind Chill* (a Section Eight coproduction).

Stars in and acts as executive producer for legal drama *Michael Clayton*, the final Section Eight production.

Acts as executive producer on pal Don Cheadle's Elmore Leonard crime dramedy *Tishomingo Blues*.

Directs, cowrites, produces and stars in football-themed romantic comedy *Leatherheads*, the first production from his Smoke House Productions venture.

Supports the presidential candidacy of Senator Barack Obama.

George Clooney's Top 100 Films

In December 2004, George Clooney gave his closest friends and family members a very personal gift: DVDs of his one hundred favorite movies from the years 1964–1976, what he considers to be the golden age of cinema. The actor's favorites, as printed in *Entertainment Weekly's LOOK* magazine, provide insight into his inspirations as an actor, producer, director and writer. Among his favorites are movies starring, written and directed by future Clooney collaborators, including Harvey Keitel, Terrence Malick, Al Pacino, Robert De Niro, Elliott Gould and Steven Spielberg, and others, including directors Sidney Lumet, Alan Pakula, Martin Scorsese and Mike Nichols, whom Clooney has cited as informing his own directorial efforts.

1. ***Alfie*** (1966)
   Director: Lewis Gilbert
   Writer: Bill Naughton
   Cast: Michael Caine, Shelley Winters, Vivien Merchant

2. ***Alice Doesn't Live Here Anymore*** (1974)
   Director: Martin Scorsese
   Writer: Robert Getchell
   Cast: Ellen Burstyn, Kris Kristofferson, Vic Tayback, Diane Ladd, Jodie Foster, Harvey Keitel

3. ***All the President's Men*** (1976)
Director: Alan Pakula
Writer: William Goldman, based on Carl Bernstein and Bob Woodward's book
Cast: Dustin Hoffman, Robert Redford, Jason Robards, Jane Alexander

4. ***Alphaville*** (1965)
Director: Jean-Luc Godard
Writer: Jean-Luc Godard
Cast: Eddie Constantine, Anna Karina

5. ***American Graffiti*** (1973)
Director: George Lucas
Writer: George Lucas, Gloria Katz, Willard Huyck
Cast: Richard Dreyfuss, Ron Howard, Harrison Ford, Candy Clark, Cindy Williams, Paul Le Mat

6. ***Badlands*** (1973)
Director: Terrence Malick
Writer: Terrence Malick
Cast: Martin Sheen, Sissy Spacek

7. ***The Bad News Bears*** (1976)
Director: Michael Ritchie
Writer: Bill Lancaster
Cast: Walter Matthau, Tatum O'Neal, Jackie Earle Haley

8. ***Bang the Drum Slowly*** (1973)
Director: John D. Hancock
Writer: Mark Harris
Cast: Robert De Niro, Vincent Gardenia, Michael Moriarty

9. ***Blazing Saddles*** (1974)
Director: Mel Brooks
Writer: Mel Brooks, Richard Pryor, Norman Steinberg, Alan Uger

Cast: Gene Wilder, Cleavon Little, Mel Brooks, Harvey Korman, Madeline Kahn, Dom DeLuise

10. ***Blowup*** (1966)
    Director: Michelangelo Antonioni
    Writer: Julio Cortazar, Michelangelo Antonioni, Tonino Guerra, Edward Bond
    Cast: David Hemmings, Vanessa Redgrave, Sarah Miles, John Castle, Jane Birkin

11. ***Bonnie and Clyde*** (1967)
    Director: Arthur Penn
    Writer: Robert Benton, David Newton (Robert Towne—uncredited)
    Cast: Warren Beatty, Faye Dunaway, Gene Hackman, Estelle Parsons, Michael J. Pollard

12. ***Bound for Glory*** (1976)
    Director: Hal Ashby
    Writer: Robert Getchell, Woody Guthrie
    Cast: David Carradine, Melinda Dillon

13. ***Butch Cassidy and the Sundance Kid*** (1969)
    Director: George Roy Hill
    Writer: William Goldman
    Cast: Paul Newman, Robert Redford, Katharine Ross

14. ***Cabaret*** (1972)
    Director: Bob Fosse
    Writer: Jay Presson Allen
    Cast: Liza Minnelli, Joel Grey, Michael York

15. ***The Candidate*** (1972)
    Director: Michael Ritchie
    Writer: Jeremy Larner
    Cast: Robert Redford, Peter Boyle, Melvyn Douglas

16. ***Carnal Knowledge*** (1971)
Director: Mike Nichols
Writer: Jules Feiffer
Cast: Jack Nicholson, Art Garfunkel, Candice Bergen, Ann-Margret

17. ***Cat Ballou*** (1965)
Director: Elliot Silverstein
Writer: Walter Newman, Frank Pierson, Roy Chanslor
Cast: Jane Fonda, Lee Marvin, Michael Callan, Dwayne Hickman, Nat King Cole

18. ***Catch-22*** (1970)
Director: Mike Nichols
Writer: Buck Henry, Joseph Heller
Cast: Alan Arkin, Richard Benjamin, Martin Balsam, Art Garfunkel, Bob Newhart, Anthony Perkins, Martin Sheen, Paula Prentiss, Jon Voight, Norman Fell, Orson Welles, Jack Gilford

19. ***Chinatown*** (1974)
Director: Roman Polanski
Writer: Robert Towne
Cast: Jack Nicholson, Faye Dunaway, John Huston

20. ***A Clockwork Orange*** (1971)
Director: Stanley Kubrick
Writer: Stanley Kubrick, Anthony Burgess
Cast: Malcolm McDowell

21. ***The Conversation*** (1974)
Director: Francis Ford Coppola
Writer: Francis Ford Coppola
Cast: Gene Hackman, John Cazale, Teri Garr, Harrison Ford

22. ***Cool Hand Luke*** (1967)
Director: Stuart Rosenberg

Writer: Donn Pearce, Frank Pierson
Cast: Paul Newman, George Kennedy, Dennis Hopper, Harry Dean Stanton

23. ***The Day of the Jackal*** (1973)
Director: Fred Zinnemann
Writer: Kenneth Ross, Frederick Forsythe
Cast: Edward Fox

24. ***Deliverance*** (1972)
Director: John Boorman
Writer: James Dickey
Cast: Burt Reynolds, Ned Beatty, Jon Voight, Ronny Cox

25. ***Dog Day Afternoon*** (1975)
Director: Sidney Lumet
Writer: Frank Pierson
Cast: Al Pacino, John Cazale, Chris Sarandon, Charles Durning

26. ***Don't Look Back*** (1967)
Director: D.A. Pennebaker
Writer: D.A. Pennebaker
Cast: Bob Dylan, Joan Baez, Donovan, Alan Price, Albert Grossman, Bob Neuwirth, Marianne Faithfull, John Mayall

27. ***Don't Look Now*** (1973)
Director: Nicolas Roeg
Writer: Daphne Du Maurier, Allan Scott, Chris Bryant
Cast: Julie Christie, Donald Sutherland

28. ***Dr. Strangelove or: How I Learned to Stop Worrying and Love the Bomb*** (1964)
Director: Stanley Kubrick
Writer: Stanley Kubrick, Terry Southern, Peter George
Cast: Peter Sellers, George C. Scott, Sterling Hayden

29. ***Easy Rider*** (1969)
Director: Dennis Hopper
Writer: Peter Fonda, Dennis Hopper, Terry Southern
Cast: Peter Fonda, Dennis Hopper, Phil Spector, Jack Nicholson

30. ***Everything You Always Wanted to Know About Sex (But Were Afraid to Ask)*** (1972)
Director: Woody Allen
Writer: Woody Allen, David Reuben
Cast: Woody Allen, Louise Lasser, John Carradine, Tony Randall, Burt Reynolds, Gene Wilder, Lynn Redgrave, Regis Philbin

31. ***The Exorcist*** (1973)
Director: William Friedkin
Writer: William Peter Blatty
Cast: Linda Blair, Ellen Burstyn, Jason Miller, Max von Sydow, Lee J. Cobb, Kitty Winn

32. ***Fail-Safe*** (1964)
Director: Sidney Lumet
Writer: Walter Bernstein, Eugene Burdick, Harvey Wheeler
Cast: Henry Fonda, Larry Hagman, Walter Matthau, Dan O'Herlihy

33. ***Five Easy Pieces*** (1970)
Director: Bob Rafelson
Writer: Bob Rafelson, Carole Eastman
Cast: Jack Nicholson, Karen Black

34. ***The French Connection*** (1971)
Director: William Friedkin
Writer: Ernest Tidyman, Robin Moore
Cast: Gene Hickman, Roy Scheider, Fernando Rey, Tony Lo Bianco

35. ***The Front*** (1976)
 Director: Martin Ritt
 Writer: Walter Bernstein
 Cast: Woody Allen, Zero Mostel, Michael Murphy, Danny Aiello, Andrea Marcovicci

36. ***The Godfather*** (1972)
 Director: Francis Ford Coppola
 Writer: Francis Ford Coppola, Mario Puzo
 Cast: Marlon Brando, Al Pacino, James Caan, Robert Duvall, John Cazale, Diane Keaton, Talia Shire, Abe Vigoda

37. ***The Godfather II*** (1974)
 Director: Francis Ford Coppola
 Writer: Francis Ford Coppola, Mario Puzo
 Cast: Al Pacino, Robert De Niro, Robert Duvall, John Cazale, Diane Keaton, Talia Shire, Abe Vigoda, Dominic Chianese

38. ***The Graduate*** (1967)
 Director: Mike Nichols
 Writer: Buck Henry, Calder Willingham, Charles Webb
 Cast: Dustin Hoffman, Anne Bancroft, Katharine Ross, William Daniels

39. ***The Great Gatsby*** (1974)
 Director: Jack Clayton
 Writer: Francis Ford Coppola, F. Scott Fitzgerald
 Cast: Robert Redford, Mia Farrow, Bruce Dern, Karen Black, Sam Waterston, Edward Herrmann, Scott Wilson

40. ***A Hard Day's Night*** (1964)
 Director: Richard Lester
 Writer: Alun Owen
 Cast: John Lennon, Paul McCartney, Ringo Starr, George Harrison

41. ***Harold and Maude*** (1971)
Director: Hal Ashby
Writer: Colin Higgins
Cast: Ruth Gordon, Bud Cort

42. ***High Plains Drifter*** (1973)
Director: Clint Eastwood
Writer: Ernest Tidyman
Cast: Clint Eastwood

43. ***The Hot Rock*** (1972)
Director: Peter Yates
Writer: William Goldman, Donald E. Westlake
Cast: Robert Redford, Ron Leibman, George Segal, Moses Gunn

44. ***I Am Cuba*** (1964)
Director: Mikheil Kalatozishvili
Writer: Enrique Pineda Barnet, Yevgeni Yevtushenko
Cast: Sergio Corrieri, Salvador Wood

45. ***In Cold Blood*** (1967)
Director: Richard Brooks
Writer: Richard Brooks, Truman Capote
Cast: Robert Blake, Scott Wilson, John Forsythe, Paul Stewart

46. ***In the Heat of the Night*** (1967)
Director: Norman Jewison
Writer: Stirling Silliphant
Cast: Sidney Poitier, Rod Steiger, Lee Grant

47. ***Jaws*** (1975)
Director: Steven Spielberg
Writer: Peter Benchley, Carl Gottlieb
Cast: Roy Scheider, Richard Dreyfuss

48. ***Jeremiah Johnson*** (1972)
    Director: Sydney Pollack
    Writer: John Milius, Edward Anhalt
    Cast: Robert Redford, Will Geer

49. ***The King of Marvin Gardens*** (1972)
    Director: Bob Rafelson
    Writer: Bob Rafelson, Jacob Brackman
    Cast: Jack Nicholson, Bruce Dern, Ellen Burstyn, Scatman Crothers

50. ***Klute*** (1971)
    Director: Alan Pakula
    Writer: Andy Lewis, Dave Lewis
    Cast: Jane Fonda, Donald Sutherland, Roy Scheider, Charles Cioffi

51. ***The Ladykillers*** (1955)
    Director: Alexander Mackendrick
    Writer: William Rose
    Cast: Alec Guiness, Cecil Parker, Peter Sellers, Danny Green, Herbert Lom, Jack Warner, Katie Johnson

52. ***The Last Detail*** (1973)
    Director: Hal Ashby
    Writer: Robert Towne, Darryl Ponicsan
    Cast: Jack Nicholson, Randy Quaid

53. ***The Last Picture Show*** (1971)
    Director: Peter Bogdanovich
    Writer: Peter Bogdanovich, Larry McMurty
    Cast: Jeff Bridges, Timothy Bottoms, Cybill Shepherd, Ben Johnson, Cloris Leachman, Ellen Burstyn, Randy Quaid

54. ***Last Tango in Paris*** (1972)
    Director: Bernardo Bertolucci
    Writer: Bernardo Bertolucci, Franco Arcalli, Agnès Varda
    Cast: Marlon Brando, Maria Schneider

55. ***Lenny*** (1974)
    Director: Bob Fosse
    Writer: Julian Barry
    Cast: Dustin Hoffman, Valerie Perrine

56. ***The Life and Times of Judge Roy Bean*** (1972)
    Director: John Huston
    Writer: John Milius
    Cast: Paul Newman, Richard Farnsworth, Jacqueline Bisset, Ned Beatty, Stacy Keach, Victoria Principal, Anthony Perkins, Ava Gardner

57. ***The Lion in Winter*** (1968)
    Director: Anthony Harvey
    Writer: James Goldman
    Cast: Peter O'Toole, Katharine Hepburn, Anthony Hopkins

58. ***Little Murders*** (1971)
    Director: Alan Arkin
    Writer: Jules Feiffer
    Cast: Elliott Gould, Doris Roberts, Vincent Gardenia, Marcia Rodd

59. ***The Longest Yard*** (1974)
    Director: Robert Aldrich
    Writer: Albert Ruddy, Tracy Keenan Wynn
    Cast: Burt Reynolds, Eddie Albert, Bernadette Peters, James Hampton

60. ***The Long Goodbye*** (1973)
    Director: Robert Altman
    Writer: Leigh Brackett, Raymond Chandler
    Cast: Elliott Gould

61. ***A Man and a Woman*** (1966)
    Director: Claude Lelouch
    Writer: Pierre Uytterhoeven, Claude Lelouch
    Cast: Anouk Aimée, Jean-Louis Trintignant

62. ***Marathon Man*** (1976)
    Director: John Schlesinger
    Writer: William Goldman
    Cast: Dustin Hoffman, Laurence Olivier, Roy Scheider, William Devane

63. ***M*A*S*H*** (1970)
    Director: Robert Altman
    Writer: Ring Lardner Jr., Richard Hooker
    Cast: Donald Sutherland, Elliot Gould, Tom Skerritt, Robert Duvall, Sally Kellerman, Roger Bowen, Gary Burghoff, René Auberjonois

64. ***McCabe & Mrs. Miller*** (1971)
    Director: Robert Altman
    Writer: Robert Altman, Brian McKay, Edmund Naughton
    Cast: Warren Beatty, Julie Christie, René Auberjonois

65. ***Mean Streets*** (1973)
    Director: Martin Scorsese
    Writer: Martin Scorsese, Mardik Martin
    Cast: Harvey Keitel, Robert De Niro, David Proval, Amy Robinson

66. ***Midnight Cowboy*** (1969)
Director: John Schlesinger
Writer: Waldo Salt, James Leo Herlihy
Cast: Jon Voight, Dustin Hoffman, Sylvia Miles

67. ***Monty Python and the Holy Grail*** (1975)
Director: Terry Gilliam, Terry Jones
Writer: Terry Gilliam, Terry Jones, John Cleese, Graham Chapman, Eric Idle, Michael Palin
Cast: Terry Gilliam, Terry Jones, John Cleese, Graham Chapman, Eric Idle, Michael Palin

68. ***Murder on the Orient Express*** (1974)
Director: Sidney Lumet
Writer: Paul Dehn, Agatha Christie
Cast: Albert Finney, Lauren Bacall, Sean Connery, Ingrid Bergman, Michael York, Vanessa Redgrave, Jacqueline Bisset, Richard Widmark

69. ***My Fair Lady*** (1964)
Director: George Cukor
Writer: Alan Jay Lerner, George Bernard Shaw
Cast: Rex Harrison, Audrey Hepburn, Stanley Holloway, Gladys Cooper

70. ***Nashville*** (1975)
Director: Robert Altman
Writer: Joan Tewkesbury
Cast: Ned Beatty, Keith Carradine, Shelley Duvall, Scott Glenn, Geraldine Chaplin

71. ***Network*** (1976)
Director: Sidney Lumet
Writer: Paddy Chayefsky
Cast: Faye Dunaway, William Holden, Robert Duvall, Peter Finch, Ned Beatty, Beatrice Straight

72. ***The Odd Couple*** (1968)
    Director: Gene Saks
    Writer: Neil Simon
    Cast: Jack Lemmon, Walter Matthau

73. ***The Omen*** (1976)
    Director: Richard Donner
    Writer: David Seltzer
    Cast: Gregory Peck, Lee Remick, Harvey Stephens, Billie Whitelaw

74. ***One Flew Over the Cuckoo's Nest*** (1975)
    Director: Milos Forman
    Writer: Ken Kesey, Lawrence Hauben, Bo Goldman
    Cast: Jack Nicholson, Louise Fletcher, Brad Dourif

75. ***Paper Moon*** (1973)
    Director: Peter Bogdanovich
    Writer: Alvin Sargent, Joe David Brown
    Cast: Ryan O'Neal, Tatum O'Neal, Madeline Kahn

76. ***Papillon*** (1973)
    Director: Franklin J. Schaffner
    Writer: Dalton Trumbo, Lorenzo Semple Jr., Henri Charriere
    Cast: Steve McQueen, Dustin Hoffman

77. ***The Parallax View*** (1974)
    Director: Alan Pakula
    Writer: David Giler, Lorenzo Semple Jr., Loren Singer
    Cast: Warren Beatty, William Daniels, Hume Cronyn, Paula Prentiss

78. ***The Party*** (1968)
    Director: Blake Edwards
    Writer: Blake Edwards, Frank Waldman, Tom Waldman
    Cast: Peter Sellers, Gavin McLeod, Claudine Longet, Marge Champion, Steve Franken

79. ***Patton*** (1970)
Director: Franklin J. Schaffner
Writer: Francis Ford Coppola, Edmund North, Omar Bradley, Ladislas Farago
Cast: George C. Scott, Karl Malden

80. ***The Pawnbroker*** (1964)
Director: Sidney Lumet
Writer: Morton Fine, David Friedkin
Cast: Rod Steiger, Geraldine Fitzgerald, Brock Peters

81. ***The Producers*** (1968)
Director: Mel Brooks
Writer: Mel Brooks
Cast: Gene Wilder, Zero Mostel, Renée Taylor

82. ***Rosemary's Baby*** (1968)
Director: Roman Polanski
Writer: Roman Polanski, Ira Levin
Cast: Mia Farrow, John Cassavetes, Ruth Gordon, Sidney Blackmer

83. ***Serpico*** (1973)
Director: Sidney Lumet
Writer: Waldo Salt, Norman Wexler, Peter Maas
Cast: Al Pacino, Tony Roberts, John Randolph, M. Emmet Walsh, Bernard Barrow

84. ***Seven Days in May*** (1964)
Director: John Frankenheimer
Writer: Rod Serling, Fletcher Knebel, Charles W. Bailey II
Cast: Kirk Douglas, Burt Lancaster, Fredric March, Ava Gardner, Edmond O'Brien

85. ***Shampoo*** (1975)
Director: Hal Ashby

Writer: Warren Beatty, Robert Towne
Cast: Warren Beatty, Julie Christie, Goldie Hawn, Lee Grant, Jack Warden, Carrie Fisher, Tony Bill

86. ***Sleeper*** (1973)
Director: Woody Allen
Writer: Woody Allen, Marshall Brickman
Cast: Woody Allen, Diane Keaton

87. ***Smile*** (1975)
Director: Michael Ritchie
Writer: Jerry Belson
Cast: Bruce Dern, Barbara Feldon

88. ***The Spy Who Came in From the Cold*** (1965)
Director: Martin Ritt
Writer: Paul Dehn, Guy Trosper, John le Carré
Cast: Richard Burton, Oskar Werner

89. ***The Sting*** (1973)
Director: George Roy Hill
Writer: David S. Ward
Cast: Robert Redford, Paul Newman, Robert Shaw, Charles Durning, Eileen Brennan

90. ***Straw Dogs*** (1971)
Director: Sam Peckinpah
Writer: Sam Peckinpah, Savid Zelag Goodman, Gordon Williams
Cast: Dustin Hoffman, Susan George

91. ***The Taking of Pelham One Two Three*** (1974)
Director: Joseph Sargent
Writer: Peter Stone, John Godey
Cast: Walter Matthau, Jerry Stiller, Martin Balsam, Robert Shaw

92. ***Taxi Driver*** (1976)
Director: Martin Scorsese
Writer: Paul Schrader
Cast: Robert De Niro, Jodie Foster, Harvey Keitel, Cybill Shepherd, Peter Boyle, Albert Brooks

93. ***The Thomas Crown Affair*** (1968)
Director: Norman Jewison
Writer: Alan Trustman
Cast: Steve McQueen, Faye Dunaway

94. ***Three Days of the Condor*** (1975)
Director: Sydney Pollack
Writer: David Rayfiel, Lorenzo Semple Jr., James Grady
Cast: Robert Redford, Faye Dunaway, Cliff Robertson, Max von Sydow, John Houseman

95. ***2001: A Space Odyssey*** (1968)
Director: Stanley Kubrick
Writer: Stanley Kubrick, Arthur C. Clarke
Cast: Keir Dullea, Gary Lockwood, William Sylvester

96. ***Wait Until Dark*** (1967)
Director: Terence Young
Writer: Robert Carrington, Frederick Knott
Cast: Audrey Hepburn, Alan Arkin, Efrem Zimbalist Jr.

97. ***The Way We Were*** (1973)
Director: Sydney Pollack
Writer: Arthur Laurents
Cast: Barbra Streisand, Robert Redford

98. ***Who's Afraid of Virginia Woolf?*** (1966)
Director: Mike Nichols
Writer: Ernest Lehman, Edward Albee

Cast: Elizabeth Taylor, Richard Burton, George Segal, Sandy Dennis

99. ***Young Frankenstein*** (1974)
    Director: Mel Brooks
    Writer: Mel Brooks, Gene Wilder, Mary Shelley
    Cast: Gene Wilder, Peter Boyle, Teri Garr, Cloris Leachman, Madeline Kahn, Marty Feldman

100. ***Z*** (1969)
    Director: Costa-Gavras
    Writer: Jorge Semprún, Vassilis Vassilikos
    Cast: Jean-Louis Trintignant, Yves Montand, Irene Papas, Jacques Perrin

Notes

Prologue

ix "They've asked me to present . . .": Karger, Dave. "'Luck' Is on His Side." *Entertainment Weekly*, January 20, 2006.

xi "severe ice cream brain freeze": Millar, John. "Exclusive: George Clooney on the Injury That Threatened His Career." *Sunday Mail* (U.K.), February 19, 2006.

xi "There was not one thing that was fun about it . . .": Stein, Joel. "The Whiz of Showbiz." *Time*, December 6, 2004.

xiii "Wow. Wow. All right, so I'm not winning . . .": Oscars.org Web site; http://www.oscars.org/78academyawards/winners/02_supp_actor.html.

xiv "I said, 'Oh, Lord! How stupid is that? . . .": Shone, Tom. "Here Comes Trouble." *Men's Vogue*, September 2005.

xiv "We jumped up and down like teenagers . . .": Clooney, Nick. "Sizing Up the Oscars with Dust Now Settled." *Cincinnati Post*, March 13, 2006.

xv "We had almost nodded off when . . .": Clooney, Nick. "Sizing Up the Oscars with Dust Now Settled." *Cincinnati Post*, March 13, 2006.

Chapter 1

1 "I remember asking him, when he was only five or six . . .": Rhodes, Joe. "What's Up Doc?" *US*, April 1995.

1 "not pictures, houses": Clooney, Rosemary, with Barthel, Joan. *Girl Singer: An Autobiography*. New York: Doubleday, 1999.

3 "The audition was Betty's idea . . .": Clooney, Rosemary, with Barthel, Joan. *Girl Singer: An Autobiography*. New York: Doubleday, 1999.

3 "That was the only time I ever won . . .": Clooney, Rosemary, with Barthel, Joan. *Girl Singer: An Autobiography*. New York: Doubleday, 1999.

4 "Betty smiled brightly . . .": Clooney, Rosemary, with Barthel, Joan. *Girl Singer: An Autobiography*. New York: Doubleday, 1999.

4 "'You know you wouldn't have been able . . .": Clooney, Rosemary, with Barthel, Joan. *Girl Singer: An Autobiography*. New York: Doubleday, 1999.

Chapter 2

9 "I said, 'Would you please pass the butter . . .": Wang, Cynthia. "Talking with Nick Clooney." *People*, February 17, 1997.

10 "I was determined that my kids . . .": Dougan, Andy. *The Biography of George Clooney*. London: Boxtree, 1997.

11 "a mansion to a trailer—literally a trailer": DePaulo, Lisa. "Catch Him If You Can." *Vogue*, June 2000.

11 "Going out to eat with my family . . .": Clooney, George. Interview by Cal Fussman. *Esquire*, January 2005.

Chapter 3

13 "It was like *Gulliver's Travels* . . .": Rhodes, Joe. "What's Up Doc?" *US*, April 1995.

13 "One day in English . . .": Kiesewetter, John and McGurk, Margaret A. "Curious, Funny, Ambitious George." *Cincinnati Enquirer*, March 5, 2006.

14 "I was convinced I had Lou Gehrig's disease . . .": "American Idol." *Midwest Today*, 2006.

14 "Yeah, all twenty-two of them": DePaulo, Lisa. "Catch Him If You Can." *Vogue*, June 2000.

14 "I only lacked skill . . .": "American Idol." *Midwest Today*, 2006.

14–15 "I was there for three years . . .": Weinraub, Bernard. "George Clooney: ER's Rogue in Residence." *Cosmopolitan*, March 1996.

15 "I had studied broadcasting . . .": Clooney, George. Interview by Bernard Weinraub. *Playboy*, July 2000.

15 "I got a bit part . . .": AOL chat, June 27, 2000.

15 " I said, 'Are you crazy, George?' . . .": Rhodes, Joe. "What's Up Doc?" *US*, April 1995.

Chapter 4

17 "There's this thing about guys that is attractive . . .": DePaulo, Lisa. "Catch Him If You Can." *Vogue*, June 2000.

18 "I will never really be over the sense of how humiliated I was . . .": Friend, Tom. "The Doctor Is In." *Premiere*, December 1995.

18 "My mother has a way . . .": Noden, Merrell. *People Profiles: George Clooney*. New York: Time, Inc., 2000.

18–19 "He ran pretty wild . . .": Conant, Jennet. "Heartthrob Hotel." *Vanity Fair*, December 1996.

20 "I could never understand how . . .": Rhodes, Joe. "What's Up Doc?" *US*, April 1995.

20 " Richard was in the middle. . .": Newman, Bruce. "This Time, It's Personal." *Los Angeles Times*, September 7, 1997.

Chapter 5

21 "One day I decided to audition . . .": Richmond, Peter. "The Keeper of the Flame." *GQ*, October 1997.

22 "Actors go into auditions thinking . . .": Clooney, George. Interview by Bernard Weinraub. *Playboy*, July 2000.

23 "This goddamn Dracula thing's comin' in here . . .": Richardson, John H. "The Common Touch of the Leading Man." *Esquire*, October 1999.

Chapter 6

25 "There comes a point where you go . . .": Spines, Christine. "How Cool Is George Clooney?" *Premiere*, January 2002.

26 "She was hysterical . . .": Noden, Merrell. *People Profiles: George Clooney*. New York: Time, Inc., 2000.

27 "It's very easy to sit in a room at twenty-three . . .": Conant, Jennet. "Heartthrob Hotel." *Vanity Fair*, December 1996.

28 "At thirty-one, I still looked like a young man . . .": Clooney, George. Interview by Bernard Weinraub. *Playboy*, July 2000.

29 "George gave me a ride on his Harley . . .": *People*, February 13, 1989.

30 "I was living with someone . . .": Clooney, George. Interview by Bernard Weinraub. *Playboy*, July 2000.

30 "I had gotten out of a relationship . . .": Conant, Jennet. "Heartthrob Hotel." *Vanity Fair*, December 1996.

32 "He was a bomber . . .": Rader, Dotson. "It's Finally and Friendship and Loyalty." *Parade*, June 7, 1998.

32 "As he was dying . . .": Lynch, Lorrie. "The Clooney File." *USA Weekend*, September 26-28, 1997.

33 "Ed, that's enough . . ." Dougan, Andy. *The Biography of George Clooney*. London: Boxtree, 1997.

33 "I was unhappy with him . . .": Conant, Jennet. "Heartthrob Hotel." *Vanity Fair*, December 1996.

33 "To this day, I think that's when I grew up . . .": Newman, Bruce. "This Time, It's Personal." *Los Angeles Times*, September 7, 1997.

33 "What Ed lacked in couth . . .": Clooney, George. Interview by Michael Fleming. *Movieline*, October 2000.

34 "I asked them why they were doing this . . .": Hudson, Jeff. *George Clooney: A Biography*. London: Virgin, 2003.

34 "He's the guy who takes care of eveything . . .": Kiesewetter, John and McGurk, Margaret A. "Curious, Funny, Ambitious George." *Cincinnati Enquirer*, March 5, 2006.

Chapter 7

37 "If I get hit by a truck . . .": Frostrup, Mariella. "Bedside Manner." *Observer* (U.K.), January 20, 2002.

37 "[It's not that] I didn't love and adore . . .": Clooney, George. Interview by Cal Fussman. *Esquire*, January 2005.

38 "The great thing I have in my life . . .": Clooney, George. Interview by Cal Fussman. *Esquire*, January 2005.

38 "George is not the sort . . .": Johnston, Jenny. "My Hell as a Boy Monster." *Mirror* (London), March 1, 2003.

38 "I think he really made an effort . . .": O'Neill, Anne-Marie. "Boy George." *People*, May 7, 2001.

39 "I would say to Talia . . .": Conant, Jennet. "Heartthrob Hotel." *Vanity Fair*, December 1996.

40 "Talia is a lovely girl . . .": Wagener, Leon. "Revealed—the Terrible Fears That Hold Him Back from Love." *News of the World* Sunday magazine, September 11, 2005.

40 "George always coveted my '59 Corvette . . .": Hudson, Jeff. *George Clooney: A Biography*. London: Virgin, 2003.

Chapter 8

43 "I did some really bad . . .": Nashawaty, Chris. "The Last Great Movie Star." *LOOK*, December 2005.

44 "I always felt it was in a special category . . .": Dougan, Andy. *The Biography of George Clooney*. London: Boxtree, 1997.

45 "Yeah, it was a great mistake . . .": *Dateline NBC* interview with Stone Phillips, May 6, 2003.

Chapter 9

47 "I remember saying to my friends . . .": Lynch, Lorrie. "The Clooney File." *USA Weekend*, September 26–28, 1997.

49 " I really fought for the show . . .": "Clooney Finds His Niche in New *ER*." *Austin American-Statesman*, October 9, 1994.

49 "I like the flaws in this guy . . .": Cawley, Janet. "George Clooney: Taking Summer by Storm." *Biography*, June 2000.

49 "The alcoholic thing is funny . . .": Brodie, John. "Playing Doctor." *GQ*, March 1995.

50 "There is, with George . . .": Hudson, Jeff. *George Clooney: A Biography*. London: Virgin, 2003.

50 "He was terrific . . .": Hudson, Jeff. *George Clooney: A Biography*. London: Virgin, 2003.

50 “the albatross in getting . . .”: Smith, Sean and Ansen, David. “Prize Fighters.” *Newsweek*, February 6, 2006.

50 “I just got a career”: Stanton, Doug. “Why George Clooney Never Sleeps.” *Men’s Journal*, July 2000.

Chapter 10

51 “I give [George] a lot of credit . . .”: Kiesewetter, John. “Clooney’s Last Shift.” *Cincinnati Enquirer*, February 18. 1999.

54 “The powers that be at the time . . .”: *CNN* interview with Larry King, June 27, 1998.

56 “If you stuck a mannequin in my part . . .”: People.com. http://www.people.com/people/george_clooney/biography.

57 “Right around the third weekend . . .”: Brodie, John. “Playing Doctor.” *GQ*, March 1995.

Chapter 11

60 “This was something I never thought . . .”: Rensin, David. “Young Doctors in Love.” *TV Guide*, October 14, 1995.

60 “Probably the one thing . . .”: Richmond, Peter. “The Keeper of the Flame.” *GQ*, October 1997.

61 “George is definitely the most loyal . . .”: Schneller, Johanna. “On the Brink.” *US Weekly*, April 17, 2000.

61 “It’s a very tough show to do . . .”: *CNN* interview on *Larry King Live*, June 27, 1998.

61 “There are times when . . .”: Rhodes, Joe. “What’s Up Doc?” *US*, April 1995.

62 “I said, ‘It’s too bad Julianna dies’ . . .”: Rensin, David. “Young Doctors in Love.” *TV Guide*, October 14, 1995.

62 “He called me just in time . . .”: Rensin, David. “Young Doctors in Love.” *TV Guide*, October 14, 1995.

62 “If I was stuck somewhere . . .”: Meyers, Kate. “Playing Doctor.” *Entertainment Weekly*, December 9, 1994.

62 “George is like . . .”: Conant, Jennet. “Heartthrob Hotel.” *Vanity Fair*, December 1996.

63 “he has this box in his hand . . .”: Gliatto, Tom. “The End of an ER-A.” *People*, February 22, 1999.

64 “Eriq wanted to go after *TV* Guide . . .”: Clooney, George. Interview by Michael Fleming. *Movieline*, October 2000.

64 “I’ve fought my whole life . . .”: Watson, Bret. “What’s Up, Docs?” *Entertainment Weekly*, September 22, 1995.

64 "I'm prouder of that . . .": Gliatto, Tom. "The End of an ER-A." *People*, February 22, 1999.

Chapter 12

65 "The chasm between television . . .": Vincent, Mal. *Virginian-Pilot*, June 21, 1998.

66 "When I was doing *Roseanne* with Laurie Metcalfe . . .": Daly, Steve. "Clooney Steps Up to Bat." *Entertainment Weekly*, January 26, 1996.

67 "big payday, got a lot of attention . . .": Daly, Steve. "Clooney Steps Up to Bat." *Entertainment Weekly*, January 26, 1996.

67–68 "That's the danger, you inhale . . .": *Primetime Live* interview with Diane Sawyer, December 31, 1997.

68 "The goal was to recognize . . .": Spines, Christine. "How Cool Is George Clooney?" *Premiere*, January 2002.

68 "I've made it difficult . . .": Brady, Shirley. "Top 100: America's Most Wanted." *People*, July 10, 2000.

69 "If George is on a movie set . . .": Daly, Steve. "Clooney Steps Up to Bat." *Entertainment Weekly*, January 26, 1996.

69 "I read for the Michael Madsen dancing around scene . . .": Clooney, George. Interview by Michael Fleming. *Movieline*, October 2000.

70 "There was a turning point . . .": Clooney, George. Interview by Michael Fleming. *Movieline*, October 2000.

70 " He was just sitting back and brooding . . .": Dougan, Andy. *The Biography of George Clooney*. London: Boxtree, 1997.

Chapter 13

72 "The thing I really respect about George . . .": Spines, Christine. "How Cool Is George Clooney?" *Premiere*, January 2002.

74 "You would have thought . . .": Noden, Merrell. *People Profiles: George Clooney*. New York: Time, Inc., 2000.

74 "It's a horror movie/action movie . . .": Noden, Merrell. *People Profiles: George Clooney*. New York: Time, Inc., 2000.

74–75 "He was already on TV . . .": *Total Film*, May 28, 1999.

75 "The script was so good . . .": Clooney, George. Interview by Michael Fleming. *Movieline*, October 2000.

75 "This is horror with a wink . . .": Savlov, Marc. *From Dusk Till Dawn* review. *Austin Chronicle*, January 19, 1996.

75 "Quentin Tarantino and Robert Rodriguez had . . .": LaSalle, Mick. *From Dusk Till Dawn* review. *San Francisco Chronicle*, January 19, 1996.

75 "Clooney makes a terrific debut . . .": Thomson, Desson. *From Dusk Till Dawn* review. *Washington Post*, January 19, 1996.

75 “tremendously smooth”: Giles, Jeff. *From Dusk Till Dawn* review. *Newsweek*, January 29, 1996.
75 “truly dashing”: Maslin, Janet. *From Dusk Till Dawn* review. *New York Times*, January 19, 1996.
75 “What demands attention . . .”: McCarthy, Todd. *From Dusk Till Dawn* review. *Austin Chronicle*, January 22, 1996.
76 “I was scared to death . . .”: TV interview, *Flicks* (Australia), 1996.
77 “All of those girls loved him . . .”: Sanz, Cynthia. “Sexiest Man Alive 1997.” *People*, November 17, 1997.
77 “ You had to tell [George] where . . .”: Sanz, Cynthia. “Sexiest Man Alive 1997.” *People*, November 17, 1997.
77 “I don’t think Harvey’s ever laughed . . .”: Friend, Tom. “The Doctor Is In.” *Premiere*, December 1995.
78 “I worked seven days a week . . .”: Daly, Steve. “Clooney Steps Up to Bat.” *Entertainment Weekly*, January 26, 1996.
78 “On the movie set . . .”: Friend, Tom. “The Doctor Is In.” *Premiere*, December 1995.
78 “The first few days on the set of the film . . .”: Kronke, David. “The Actor Is In.” *Los Angeles Times*, January 14, 1996.

Chapter 14

81 “The world changed . . .”: Clooney, George. Interview by Michael Fleming. *Movieline*, October 2000.
83 “You know, I have a . . .”: Whipp, Glenn. “Clooney Steps Up to Bat.” *Los Angeles Daily News*, July 3, 1998.
84 “There’s something that women call . . .”: Sanz, Cynthia. “Sexiest Man Alive 1997.” *People*, November 17, 1997.
84 “It became clear to me . . .”: *One Fine Day* press junket interview with Michelle Pfeiffer. Audio clip at http://thetwilightzone.xs4all.nl/MPPG/Data/_Interviews/Interview_02.mp3.
85 “I just wanted [Seth Gecko] to look like . . .”: Clooney, George. Interview by Noah Wyle. *US Weekly*, January 22, 2001.
86 “I just went bats . . .”: Friend, Tom. “The Doctor Is In.” *Premiere*, December 1995.
86 “I don’t care about a man taking my picture . . .”: Rader, Dotson. “It’s Finally About Friendship and Loyalty.” *Parade*, June 7, 1998.
87 “She said I stood around the set . . .”: Friend, Tom. “The Doctor Is In.” *Premiere*, December 1995.
87 “They printed the story . . .”: Hudson, Jeff. *George Clooney: A Biography*. London: Virgin, 2003.
88 “I’m an Irish-American . . .”: Hudson, Jeff. *George Clooney: A Biography*. London: Virgin, 2003.

88–89 "[He] should have won [the Emmy] . . .": Rensin, David. "Young Doctors in Love." *TV Guide*, October 14, 1995.

89 "We were all in our doctor's smocks . . .": Smith, Sean and Ansen, David. "Prize Fighters." *Newsweek*, February 6, 2006.

90 "One reason our show took off . . .": Rensin, David. "Young Doctors in Love." *TV Guide*, October 14, 1995.

Chapter 15

91 "Look, if I'm walking out of a cathouse . . .": E! Online interview, 1997.

92 "I just picture George's brain . . .": Rochlin, Margy. "George Clooney." *US*, July 1997.

92 "Every single day, some photographer . . .": Weinraub, Bernard. "George Clooney: ER's Rogue in Residence." *Cosmopolitan*, March 1996.

93 "I walked outside with a girl . . .": Weinraub, Bernard. "George Clooney: ER's Rogue in Residence." *Cosmopolitan*, March 1996.

94 "I said, 'Look, you guys' . . .": Fisher, Carrie. *George*, June 1997.

95 "I was still shooting *ER* at the time . . .": Hruska, Bronwen. "Just Another Manci 'Day.'" *Los Angeles Times*, July 28, 1996.

95 "Jack's a bit of an idiot . . .": Newman, Bruce. "This Time, It's Personal." *Los Angeles Times*, September 7, 1997.

96 "George is all talk . . .": Slotek, Jim. "One Fine Guy." Canoe.com, 1996.

96 "I'm a fun uncle . . .": Noden, Merrell. *People Profiles: George Clooney*. New York: Time, Inc., 2000.

96 "He's like watching Cary Grant . . .": Conant, Jennet. "Heartthrob Hotel." *Vanity Fair*, December 1996.

96 "Oh my God . . .": Macpherson, Andrew. "Soaring as a Hollywood Superhero, He Comes Down Hard on Star Exploitation." *People*, December 30, 1996.

96 "uninspired formula movie": Ebert, Roger. *One Fine Day* review. *Chicago Sun-Times*, December 20, 1996.

96 "bedraggled": Zacharek, Stephanie. *One Fine Day* review. Salon.com, December 1996.

96 "lacks focus and direction": Berardinelli, James. *One Fine Day* review. ReelViews.net, December 1996.

97 "the rare major actor . . .": McCarthy, Todd. *One Fine Day* review. Variety.com, April 6, 1997.

97 "rakish, rumpled and effortlessly . . .": Zacharek, Stephanie. *One Fine Day* review. Salon.com, December 1996.

98 "It was extremely difficult . . .": *Premiere*, April 1997.

98 "You understand why he's doing it . . .": *CNN* interview with Larry King, 1997.

99 "What *The Peacemaker* doesn't do well . . .": Turan, Kenneth. *The Peacemaker* review. *Los Angeles Times*, September 26, 1997.

99 "essential spark of surprise . . .": Gleiberman, Owen. *The Peacemaker* review. *Entertainment Weekly*, October 10, 1997.

100 "A ticket to terminal boredom.": Groen, Rick. *The Peacemaker* review. *Globe and Mail* (Toronto), September 26, 1997.

100 "[what] he doesn't have much of is variety . . .": Shulgasser, Barbara. *The Peacemaker* review. *San Francisco Examiner*, September 26, 1997.

100 "his rugged good looks spell movie . . .": LaSalle, Mick. *The Peacemaker* review. *San Francisco Chronicle*, September 26, 1997.

100 "naturally well cast . . .": Maslin, Janet. *The Peacemaker* review. *New York Times*, September 26, 1997.

100 "Both Kidman and Clooney give dependable . . ." Turan, Kenneth. *The Peacemaker* review. *Los Angeles Times*, September 26, 1997.

Chapter 16

101 "I basically buried . . .": "Stormy Weather." *Cinescape*, May–June 2000.

103 "I thought it was a bad script . . .": Clooney, George. Interview by Michael Fleming. *Movieline*, October 2000.

105 "Although the movie's fun to do . . .": E! Online interview, 1997.

105 "It's a gee-whiz kiddie movie . . .": McDonagh, Maitland. *Batman & Robin* review. *TV Guide*, June 1997.

105 "Screenwriter Akiva Goldsman has written . . .": Ansen, David. *Batman & Robin* review. *Newsweek*, June 30, 1997.

105–06 "It looks bad: cluttered surfaces . . .": Ross, Alex. *Batman & Robin* review. *Slate*, June 22, 1997.

106 "*Batman & Robin* drags itself . . .": Kempley, Rita. *Batman & Robin* review. *Washington Post*, June 20, 1997.

106 "Clooney fails to make much . . .": Phipps, Keith. *Batman & Robin* review. *Onion A. V. Club*, June 1997.

106 "A non-brooding Batman? . . .": Shulgasser, Barbara. *Batman & Robin* review. *San Francisco Examiner*, June 20, 1997.

106 "Physically, Clooney is unquestionably . . .": McCarthy, Todd. *Batman & Robin* review. *Variety*, June 16, 1997.

107 "The next day he calls . . .": Schindehette, Susan. "Too Busy for Love?" *People*, September 27, 1999.

107 "Between George and me . . .": Schindehette, Susan. "Too Busy for Love?" *People*, September 27, 1999.

108 "Val is the most psychologically troubled . . .": *Premiere*, April 1997.

108 "Please leave my penis out of it": Rochlin, Margy. "George Clooney." *US*, July 1997.

108 "what you see is what you get": Svetkey, Benjamin. "Holy Happy Set!" *Entertainment Weekly*, July 12, 1996.
109 "So now we begin . . .": *Variety*, October 1996.
110 "I'm not punching anybody . . .": *Los Angeles Times*, 1996.
111 "They pay you to do publicity . . .": Clooney, George. Interview by Michael Fleming. *Movieline*, October 2000.

Chapter 17

113 "I wouldn't have been prepared for the down period . . .": Edwards, Gavin. "George Clooney: Renegade of the Year." *Rolling Stone*, December 15, 2005.
115 "This is it. This is the end": Noden, Merrell. *People Profiles: George Clooney*. New York: Time, Inc., 2000.
115 "We really hit it off . . .": Pringle, Gill. "Why I'm Not Ready to Marry." *Sunday Mirror* (London), July 19, 1998.
116 "It's essential for the film . . .": "George Clooney: Man of the Moment." *She*, October 1998.
116 "It became a game . . .": Pringle, Gill. "Why I'm Not Ready to Marry." *Sunday Mirror* (London), July 19, 1998.
116 "To be bad in front . . .": Noden, Merrell. *People Profiles: George Clooney*. New York: Time, Inc., 2000.
117 "They're saying a very nice thing . . .": Access Hollywood interview, circa November 1997.
117 "Clooney is the most impressive . . .": Hunter, Stephen. *Out of Sight* review. *Washington Post*, June 26, 1998.
117 "Clooney finally comes to his own . . .": Levy, Emanuel. *Out of Sight* review. *Variety*, June 22, 1998.
117 "This is Clooney's wiliest . . .": Gleiberman, Owen. *Out of Sight* review. *Entertainment Weekly*, June 1998.
118 "Looking leaner and hungrier . . .": Ansen, David. *Out of Sight* review. *Newsweek*, June 29, 1998.
118 "What I liked most about George . . .": *People*, June 1998.
118 "I call it the Jack Kennedy syndrome . . .": Jones, Chris. "It's More Fun to Be the Painter Than the Paint." *Esquire*, December 2006.
118 "It didn't do well, but that wasn't our fault . . .": *Movieline*, 2000.

Chapter 18

119 "Life's too short.": *CNN* interview with Larry King, February 16, 2006.
120 "weird masterpiece . . .": Ebert, Roger. *Three Kings* review. *Chicago Sun-Times*, October 4, 1999.
120 "It's a black comedy . . .": Barnes and Noble.com interview, July 11, 2000.

121 "He opened the door . . .": Nashawaty, Chris. "Three the Hard Way." *Entertainment Weekly*, October 8, 1999.

121 "I worked until four-thirty . . .": Goldstein, Gregg. "King's Ransom." *Premiere*, November 1999.

122 "You have a lot of habits . . .": Waxman, Sharon. *Rebels on the Backlot: Six Maverick Directors and How They Conquered the Hollywood Studio System*. New York: HarperCollins, 2005.

122 "I want you to be very still . . .:" Waxman, Sharon. *Rebels on the Backlot: Six Maverick Directors and How They Conquered the Hollywood Studio System*. New York: HarperCollins, 2005.

123 "because I don't think you're going . . .": Waxman, Sharon. *Rebels on the Backlot: Six Maverick Directors and How They Conquered the Hollywood Studio System*. New York: HarperCollins, 2005.

124 "You have created the most . . .": Waxman, Sharon. *Rebels on the Backlot: Six Maverick Directors and How They Conquered the Hollywood Studio System*. New York: HarperCollins, 2005.

125 "Don't you push . . .": Waxman, Sharon. *Rebels on the Backlot: Six Maverick Directors and How They Conquered the Hollywood Studio System*. New York: HarperCollins, 2005.

125 "grabbed me by the waist . . .": Clooney, George. Interview by Bernard Weinraub. *Playboy*, July 2000.

125 "Some days George was right . . .": Goldstein, Gregg. "King's Ransom." *Premiere*, November 1999.

126 "are friends . . .": Goldstein, Gregg. "King's Ransom." *Premiere*, November 1999.

126 "would not stand for [Russell] . . .": Zeman, Ned. "The Admirable Clooney." *Vanity Fair*, October 2003.

126 "George Clooney can . . .": Zeman, Ned. "The Admirable Clooney." *Vanity Fair*, October 2003.

126 "That tape has been going around . . .": Collis, Clark. "*Huckabees* Whacks." *Entertainment Weekly*, April 20, 2007.

127 "I felt bad for Lily . . .": Collis, Clark. "*Huckabees* Whacks." *Entertainment Weekly*, April 20, 2007.

127 "weirdo": Nashawaty, Chris. "Three the Hard Way." *Entertainment Weekly*, October 8, 1999.

Chapter 19

129 "I can't sleep; I can't breathe . . .": DePaulo, Lisa. "Catch Him If You Can." *Vogue*, June 2000.

130 "(George) didn't cheat the network . . .": Bickley, Claire. "Planning Clooney's *ER* Exit." Jam! Showbiz, July 22, 1998.

130–31 "It was all very sneaky . . .": Reiter, Amy. "Nothing Personal." Salon.com, May 17, 2000.

131 "It was Camelot . . .": Kaylin, Lucy. "Man with a Mission." *TV Guide*, April 8, 2000.

132 "People will watch us . . .": Bassom, David. *George Clooney: An Illustrated Story*. London: Reed Consumer Books, 1998.

133 "The truth is . . .": Richardson, John H. "The Common Touch of the Leading Man." *Esquire*, October 1999.

134 "I wanted to have a real family . . .": Shone, Tom. "Here Comes Trouble." *Men's Vogue*, September 2005.

134 "You're getting the French dip . . .": DePaulo, Lisa. "Catch Him If You Can." *Vogue*, June 2000.

134 "She pulled up roots . . .": DePaulo, Lisa. "Catch Him If You Can." *Vogue*, June 2000.

135 "If you hang out with George . . .": Schindehette, Susan. "Too Busy for Love?" *People*, September 27, 1999.

Chapter 20

137 "His head is shaped like a star's . . .": *Premiere*, October 2003.

138 "It's all about my hair . . .": Richardson, John H. "The Common Touch of the Leading Man." *Esquire*, October 1999.

139 "My Uncle Jack has a tobacco farm . . .": Clooney, George. Interview by Noah Wyle. *US Weekly*, January 22, 2001.

139 "People talk about George . . .": Tracy, Jennifer. "Will George Clooney Ever Settle Down?" *McCalls*, October 2000.

139 "We were both staring . . .": *OK!* magazine (UK), January 12, 2001.

140 "I finally got it when Mel fell out . . .": DePaulo, Lisa. "Catch Him If You Can." *Vogue*, June 2000.

140 "It's guys like Clooney . . .": DePaulo, Lisa. "Catch Him If You Can." *Vogue*, June 2000.

140–41 "Some of the movie was shot . . .": Clooney, George. Interview by Bernard Weinraub. *Playboy*, July 2000.

141 "For the actors . . .": Cawley, Janet. "George Clooney: Taking Summer by Storm." *Biography*, June 2000.

142 "The tricky part about . . .": ClooneyNetwork.com, http://www.clooneynetwork.com/articles2/viewarticle.php?articleid=75.

142 "We were shooting at sea . . .": Cawley, Janet. "George Clooney: Taking Summer by Storm." *Biography*, June 2000.

144 "The movie . . .": Alspector, Lisa. *The Perfect Storm* review. *Chicago Reader*, June 2000.

144 "With the exception . . .": McCarthy, Todd. *The Perfect Storm* review. *Variety*, June 2000.

144 "Mr. Clooney conveys . . .": Holden, Stephen. *The Perfect Storm* review. *New York Times*, June 30, 2000.

Chapter 21

145 "Clooney—in his roles and in his life . . .": DePaulo, Lisa. "Catch Him If You Can." *Vogue*, June 2000.

146 "We're friends, and we share similar . . .": Clooney, George. Interview by Michael Fleming. *Movieline*, October 2000.

146 "I like what he does . . .": Rebello, Stephen. "Steven Soderbergh Is So Money" *Movieline*, January 2002.

146–47 "Steven calls me . . .": Clooney, George. Interview by Michael Fleming. *Movieline*, October 2000.

148 "It's a scrumptious . . .": Gleiberman, Owen. *Ocean's Eleven* review. *Entertainment Weekly*, December 5, 2001.

149 "When you're at thirty thousand feet . . .": Spines, Christine. "How Cool Is George Clooney?" *Premiere*, January 2002.

149 "I had this feeling . . .": Rebello, Stephen. "Steven Soderbergh Is So Money" *Movieline*, January 2002.

150 "The studio was panicked . . .": Karger, Dave. "This Ones Goes to Twelve." *Entertainment Weekly*, December 10, 2004.

150 "*Ocean's Thirteen* . . .": Cohen, Rich. "Already a Classic." *Vanity Fair*, November 2006.

151 "One of the benefits . . .": Swanson, Tim. "Jokers Wild." *Premiere*, December 2004.

151 "the best thing I've ever done . . .": Clooney, George. Sexiest Man Alive Interview by Elizabeth Leonard. *People*, November 27, 2006.

152 "[These were painted] before . . .": *Primetime Live* interview with Diane Sawyer, October 16, 2005.

152 "Clooney and company work . . .": Travers, Peter. *Ocean's Twelve* review. *Rolling Stone*, December 10, 2004.

152 "They're more fun to play": Cohen, Rich. "Already a Classic." *Vanity Fair*, November 2006.

153 "This will be my third idiot . . .": Cohen, Rich. "Already a Classic." *Vanity Fair*, November 2006.

154 "I think 'stole' . . .": Kotler, Steven. "George Clooney." *Variety VLife*, Oscar portfolio 2006.

154 "It was really nice . . .": Clooney, George. Interview by Cal Fussman. *Esquire*, January 2005.

155 "I didn't have time . . .": Reiter, Amy. "Nothing Personal." Salon.com, July 2, 2001.

156 "[Miramax head] Harvey Weinstein . . .": Shone, Tom. "Here Comes Trouble." *Men's Vogue*, September 2005.

156 "I demand my right . . .": Kotler, Steven. "George Clooney." *Variety VLife*, Oscar portfolio 2006.

Chapter 22

159 "*Syriana* isn't an attack . . .": Kotler, Steven. "George Clooney." *Variety VLife*, Oscar portfolio 2006.

160 "When we started [*Syriana*] . . .": Svetkey, Benjamin. "Hollywood Pulls the Trigger" *Entertainment Weekly*, December 2, 2005.

161 "People talk about cutting . . .": Nashawaty, Chris. "The Last Great Movie Star." *LOOK*, December 2005.

161–62 "I bulked up to 207 pounds . . .": Whittell, Cassie. "*Good Night, And Good Luck*." *DVD Review*, August 2006.

162 "The studio was willing . . .": Edwards, Gavin. "George Clooney: Renegade of the Year." *Rolling Stone*, December 15, 2005.

162 "severe ice cream brain freeze . . .": Millar, John. "Exclusive: George Clooney on the Injury That Threatened His Career." *Sunday Mail* (U.K.), February 19, 2006.

163 "About five or six years . . .": Svetkey, Benjamin. "Hollywood Pulls the Trigger" *Entertainment Weekly*, December 2, 2005.

163–64 "The only thing . . .": Nashawaty, Chris. "The Last Great Movie Star." *LOOK*, December 2005.

164 "Directing a movie . . .": Kotler, Steven. "George Clooney." *Variety VLife*, Oscar portfolio 2006.

164 "Here's what I believe . . .": Kotler, Steven. "George Clooney." *Variety VLife*, Oscar portfolio 2006.

164 "The secret to Murrow . . .": Brockes, Emma. "I've Learned How to Fight." *Guardian*, February 10, 2006.

165 "Clooney suffers for his art . . .": Tucker, Ken. *Syriana* review. *New York*, November 28, 2005.

165–66 "This is Clooney doing . . .": Corliss, Richard. *Syriana* review. *Time*, November 21, 2005.

166 "This is the best acting . . .": Travers, Peter. *Syriana* review. *Rolling Stone*, November 17, 2005.

166 "It's a passionate, serious . . .": Ansen, David. *Good Night, and Good Luck* review. *Newsweek*, October 10, 2005.

166 "Flip, you say?": Clark, Mike. *Good Night, and Good Luck* review. *USA Today*, October 6, 2005.

166–67 "As a director, Clooney does . . .": Ebert, Roger. *Good Night, and Good Luck* review. *Chicago Sun-Times*, October 21, 2005.

167 "I knew right off the bat . . .": Kotler, Steven. "George Clooney." *Variety VLife*, Oscar portfolio 2006.

167 "It was fun to be doing stuff . . .": Edwards, Gavin. "George Clooney: Renegade of the Year." *Rolling Stone*, December 15, 2005.

168 "Most liberalism is angst . . .": Krauthammer, Charles. "Oscars for Osama." *Washington Post*, March 3, 2006.

168 "I think that the temperature . . .": Karger, Dave. "'Luck' Is on His Side." *Entertainment Weekly*, January 20, 2006.

Chapter 23

169 "I mean, how much money . . .": Nashawaty, Chris. "Three the Hard Way." *Entertainment Weekly*, October 8, 1999.

169–70 "The film has more in common . . .": Tobias, Scott. *The Good German* review. *Onion A.V. Club*, December 14, 2006.

170 "Of *The Good German* . . .": Hunter, Stephen. *The Good German* review. *Washington Post*, December 22, 2006.

170 "While Clooney and especially . . .": Lumenick, Lou. *The Good German* review. *New York Post*, December 15, 2006.

170 "Two years ago . . .": Cohen, Rich. "Already a Classic." *Vanity Fair*, November 2006.

170 "He's by far the biggest influence . . .": McIntyre, Gina. "Q&A with George Clooney." *Hollywood Reporter*, October 25, 2006.

171 "We'd like to keep it . . .": McIntyre, Gina. "Q&A with George Clooney." *Hollywood Reporter*, October 25, 2006.

174 "I'm trying to put myself . . .": Jones, Chris. "It's More Fun to Be the Painter Than the Paint." *Esquire*, December 2006.

174 "Eventually my looks . . .": Cruz, Anne Marie. "The Aging Process." *People*, February 7, 2003.

174 "It was either that . . .": Silverman, Stephen M. "George Clooney's New Year: A Date with Dorothy." People.com, January 3, 2007.

175 "If you're doing a movie . . .": "The Green Team." *Vanity Fair*, May 2006.

175 "I find [the villa on Lake Como] . . .": Fleming, Michael. "Candid Crusader." *Fade In*, October 2005.

176 "I made the mistake of saying . . .": Souter, Ericka. "Singular Sensation." *People*, December 23, 2002.

176 "Though he started his life . . .": Clooney, Nick. "Moment of Silence for Max." *Cincinnati Post*, December 11, 2006.

177 "Oh, there are plenty of them . . .": Keegan, Rebecca Winters. "Contemplating Hog Heaven with George." *Time*, December 18, 2006.

177 "I will remember forever . . .": "Clooney Darfur documentary to air Monday." *USA Today*, January 11, 2007.

177 "We couldn't figure out . . .": "Clooney Darfur documentary to air Monday." *USA Today*, January 11, 2007.

177 "If we turn our heads . . .": Hananel, Sam. "Actor Clooney Urges More Aid, Intervention in Darfur." *San Diego Union-Tribune*, April 27, 2006.

178 "We were at a rally . . .": Daunt, Tina. " Clooney Steps Cautiously into Obama's Camp." *Los Angeles Times*, March 30, 2007.

179 "No, no, no . . .": *Primetime Live* interview with Diane Sawyer, October 16, 2005.

179 "That's a bad idea . . .": Associated Press, September 25, 2006.

179 "He started to wonder . . .": Jones, Chris. "It's More Fun to Be the Painter Than the Paint." *Esquire*, December 2006.

179 "I saw what [a political campaign] . . .": Jones, Chris. "It's More Fun to Be the Painter Than the Paint." *Esquire*, December 2006.

179 "You can get a lot more done . . .": Freydkin, Donna. "Mr. Clooney goes to the United Nations." *USA Today*, September 14, 2006.

George Clooney's Top 100 Films

207–23 List: Nashawaty, Chris. "The Last Great Movie Star." *LOOK*, December 2005.

Bibliography

BOOKS

Bassom, David. *George Clooney: An Illustrated Story*. London: Reed Consumer Books, 1998.

Clooney, Rosemary, with Barthel, Joan. *Girl Singer: An Autobiography*. New York: Doubleday, 1999.

Dougan, Andy. *The Biography of George Clooney*. London: Boxtree, 1997.

Hudson, Jeff. *George Clooney: A Biography*. London: Virgin, 2003.

Keenleyside, Sam. *Bedside Manners: George Clooney and ER*. Toronto: ECW Press, 1998.

Noden, Merrell. *People Profiles: George Clooney*. New York: Time, Inc., 2000.

Waxman, Sharon. *Rebels on the Backlot: Six Maverick Directors and How They Conquered the Hollywood Studio System*. New York: HarperCollins, 2005.

PERIODICALS

Access Hollywood interview, circa November 1997.

"American Idol." *Midwest Today*, 2006.

Alspector, Lisa. *The Perfect Storm* review. *Chicago Reader*, June 2000.

Ansen, David. *Batman & Robin* review. *Newsweek*, June 30, 1997.

Ansen, David. *Good Night, and Good Luck* review. *Newsweek*, October 10, 2005.

Ansen, David. *Out of Sight* review. *Newsweek*, June 29, 1998.

AOL chat, June 27, 2000.

Associated Press, September 25, 2006.

Austin American-Statesman, October 9, 1994.

Barnes and Noble.com interview, July 11, 2000.

Berardinelli, James. *One Fine Day* review. ReelViews.net, December 1996.

Bickley, Claire. "Planning Clooney's *ER* Exit." Jam! Showbiz, July 22, 1998.

Brady, Sara. "Catching Up with . . . George Clooney." *Premiere*, October 2005.

Brady, Shirley. "Top 100: America's Most Wanted." *People*, July 10, 2000.

Brockes, Emma. "I've Learned How to Fight." *The Guardian*, February 10, 2006.

Brodie, John. "Playing Doctor." *GQ*, March 1995.

Brodie, John. "George Clooney." *GQ*, December 2003.

Cawley, Janet. "George Clooney: Taking Summer by Storm." *Biography*, June 2000.

Cinescape, May/June 2000. "Stormy Weather."

Clark, Mike. *Good Night, and Good Luck* review. *USA Today*, October 6, 2005.

Clooney, George. Interview by Michael Fleming. *Movieline*, October 2000.

Clooney, George. Interview by Cal Fussman. *Esquire*, January 2005.

Clooney, George. Interview by Bernard Weinraub. *Playboy*, July 2000.

Clooney, George. Sexiest Man Alive Interview by Elizabeth Leonard. *People*, November 27, 2006.

Clooney, George. Interview by Noah Wyle. *US Weekly*, January 22, 2001.

Clooney, Nick. "Moment of Silence for Max." *Cincinnati Post*, December 11, 2006.

Clooney, Nick. "Sizing Up the Oscars With Dust Now Settled." *Cincinnati Post*, March 13, 2006.

CNN interview with Larry King, 1997.

CNN interview with Larry King, June 27, 1998.

CNN interview with Larry King, February 16, 2006.

Cohen, Rich. "Already a Classic." *Vanity Fair*, November 2006.

Collis, Clark. "*Huckabees* Whacks." *Entertainment Weekly*, April 20, 2007.

Conant, Jennet. "Heartthrob Hotel." *Vanity Fair*, December 1996.

Corliss, Richard. *Syriana* review. *Time*, November 21, 2005.

Cruz, Anne Marie. "The Aging Process." *People*, February 7, 2003.

Cruz, Clarissa. "By George He's Got It." *Entertainment Weekly*, December 14, 2001.

Daly, Steve. "Clooney Steps Up to Bat." *Entertainment Weekly*, February 1996.

Dateline NBC interview with Stone Phillips, May 6, 2003.

Daunt, Tim. "Clooney Steps Cautiously into Obama's Camp." *Los Angeles Times*, March 30, 2007.

DePaulo, Lisa. "Catch Him If You Can." *Vogue*, June 2000.

Dreben, Jed. "George Clooney Recalls Beloved Pet Pig." *USA Today*, December 5, 2006.

E! Online interview, 1997.

Ebert, Roger. *Good Night, and Good Luck* review. *Chicago Sun-Times*, October 21, 2005.

Ebert, Roger. *One Fine Day* review. *Chicago Sun-Times*, December 20, 1996.

Ebert, Roger. *Three Kings* review. *Chicago Sun-Times*, October 4, 1999.

Edwards, Gavin. "George Clooney: Renegade of the Year." *Rolling Stone*, December 15, 2005.

Fisher, Carrie. *George*, June 1997.

Fleming, Michael. "Candid Crusader." *Fade In*, October 2005.

Flicks (Australia), TV interview, 1996.

Freydkin, Donna. "Mr. Clooney Goes to the United Nations." *USA Today*, September 14, 2006.

Friend, Tom. "The Doctor Is In." *Premiere*, December 1995.

Frostrup, Mariella. "Bedside Manner." *The Observer* (U.K.), January 20, 2002.

Gliatto, Tom. "The End of an ER-A." *People*, February 22, 1999.

Giles, Jeff. *From Dusk Till Dawn* review. *Newsweek*, January 29, 1996.

Gleiberman, Owen. *Ocean's Eleven* review. *Entertainment Weekly*, December 5, 2001.

Gleiberman, Owen. *Out of Sight* review. *Entertainment Weekly*, June 1998.

Gleiberman, Owen. *The Peacemaker* review. *Entertainment Weekly*, October 10, 1997.

Goldstein, Gregg. "King's Ransom." *Premiere*, November 1999.

Groen, Rick. *The Peacemaker* review. (Toronto) *Globe and Mail*, September 26, 1997.

Hananel, Sam. "Actor Clooney Urges More Aid, Intervention in Darfur." *San Diego Union-Tribune*, April 27, 2006.

Hoban, Phoebe. "The Perfect Storm: Clooney Steers Bestseller to Screen." *US Weekly*, May 22, 2000.

Holden, Stephen. *The Perfect Storm* review. *New York Times*, June 30, 2000.

Horn, John. "George Clooney Rolls the Dice." *Newsweek*, December 17, 2001.

Hruska, Bronwen. "Just Another Manci 'Day.'" *Los Angeles Times*, July 28, 1996.

Hunter, Stephen. *The Good German* review. *Washington Post*, December 22, 2006.

Hunter, Stephen. *Out of Sight* review. *Washington Post*, June 26, 1998.

Johnston, Jenny. "My Hell as a Boy Monster." (London) *Mirror*, March 1, 2003.

Jones, Chris. "It's More Fun to Be the Painter Than the Paint." *Esquire*, December, 2006.

Karger, Dave. "'Luck' Is on His Side." *Entertainment Weekly*, January 20, 2006.

Karger, Dave. "This One Goes to Twelve." *Entertainment Weekly*, December 10, 2004.

Kaylin, Lucy. "Man with a Mission." *TV Guide*, April 8, 2000.

Keegan, Rebecca Winters. "Contemplating Hog Heaven With George." *Time*, December 18, 2006.

Kempley, Rita. *Batman & Robin* review. *Washington Post*, June 20, 1997.

Kennedy, Colin. "O, Lucky Man!" *Empire*, March, 2003.

Kiesewetter, John. "Clooney's Last Shift." *Cincinnati Enquirer*, February 18. 1999.

Kiesewetter, John and McGurk, Margaret A. "Curious, Funny, Ambitious George." *Cincinnati Enquirer*, March 5, 2006.

Kotler, Steven. "George Clooney." *Variety Life*, Oscar portfolio 2006.

Krauthammer, Charles. "Oscars for Osama." *Washington Post*, March 3, 2006.

Kronke, David. "The Actor Is In." *Los Angeles Times*, January 14, 1996.

LaSalle, Mick. *From Dusk Till Dawn* review. *San Francisco Chronicle*, January 19, 1996.

LaSalle, Mick. *The Peacemaker* review. *San Francisco Chronicle*, September 26, 1997.

Levy, Emanuel. *Out of Sight* review. *Variety*, June 22, 1998.

Lumenick, Lou. *The Good German* review. *New York Post*, December 15, 2006.

Lynch, Lorrie. "The Clooney File." *USA Weekend*, September 26–28, 1997.

Macpherson, Andrew. "Soaring as a Hollywood Superhero, He Comes Down Hard on Star Exploitation." *People*, December 30, 1996.

Maslin, Janet. *From Dusk Till Dawn* review. *New York Times*, January 19, 1996.

Maslin, Janet. *The Peacemaker* review. *New York Times*, September 26, 1997.

McCarthy, Todd. *Batman & Robin* review. *Variety*, June 16, 1997.

McCarthy, Todd. *From Dusk Till Dawn* review. *Austin Chronicle*, January 22, 1996.

McCarthy, Todd. *One Fine Day* review. Variety.com, April 6, 1997.

McCarthy, Todd. *The Perfect Storm* review. *Variety*, June 2000.

McDonagh, Maitland. *Batman & Robin* review. *TV Guide*, June 1997.

McIntyre, Gina. "Q&A with George Clooney." *The Hollywood Reporter*, October 25, 2006.

Meyers, Kate. "Playing Doctor." *Entertainment Weekly*, December 9, 1994.

Millar, John. "Exclusive: George Clooney on the Injury That Threatened His Career." (U.K.) *Sunday Mail*, February 19, 2006.

Nashawaty, Chris. "Three the Hard Way." *Entertainment Weekly*, October 8, 1999.

Nashawaty, Chris. "The Last Great Movie Star." *LOOK*, December 2005.

Neumaier, Joe. "Out of the Past." *New York Daily News*, December 10, 2006.

Newman, Bruce. "This Time, It's Personal." *Los Angeles Times*, September 7, 1997.

OK! magazine (UK), January 12, 2001.

One Fine Day press junket interview with Michelle Pfeiffer. Audio clip at http://thetwilightzone.xs4all.nl/MPPG/Data/_Interviews/Interview_02.mp3.

O'Neill, Anne-Marie. "Boy George." *People*, May 7, 2001.

Oscars.org Website; http://www.oscars.org/78academyawards/winners/02_supp_actor.html.

People, February 13, 1989.

People, June 1998.

People.com. http://www.people.com/people/george_clooney/biography.

Phipps, Keith. *Batman & Robin* review. *The Onion A.V. Club*, June 1997.

Premiere, April 1997.

Premiere, October 2003.

Primetime Live interview with Diane Sawyer, December 31, 1997.

Primetime Live interview with Diane Sawyer, October 16, 2005.

Pringle, Gill. "Why I'm Not Ready to Marry." *(London) Sunday Mirror*, July 19, 1998.

Rader, Dotson. "It's Finally About Friendship and Loyalty." *Parade*, June 7, 1998.

Rebello, Stephen. "Steven Soderbergh Is So Money" *Movieline*, January 2002.

Reiter, Amy. "Nothing Personal." Salon.com, May 17, 2000.

Rensin, David. "Young Doctors in Love." *TV Guide*, October 14, 1995.

Rhodes, Joe. "What's Up Doc?" *US*, April 1995.

Richardson, John H. "The Common Touch of the Leading Man." *Esquire*, October 1999.

Richmond, Peter. "The Keeper of the Flame." *GQ*, October 1997.

Rochlin, Margy. "George Clooney." *US*, July 1997.

Ross, Alex. *Batman & Robin* review. *Slate*, June 22, 1997.

Sanz, Cynthia. "Sexiest Man Alive 1997." *People*, November 17, 1997.

Savlov, Marc. *From Dusk Till Dawn* review. *Austin Chronicle*, January 19, 1996.

Schneller, Johanna. "On the Brink" *US Weekly*, April 17, 2000.

Schindehette, Susan. "Too Busy for Love?" *People*, September 27, 1999.

She, October 1998. "George Clooney: Man of the Moment."

Shone, Tom. "Here Comes Trouble." *Men's Vogue*, September 2005.

Shulgasser, Barbara. *Batman & Robin* review. *San Francisco Examiner*, June 20, 1997.

Shulgasser, Barbara. *The Peacemaker* review. *San Francisco Examiner*, September 26, 1997.

Silverman, Stephen M. "George Clooney's New Year: A Date with Dorothy." People.com, January 3, 2007.

Slotek, Jim. "One Fine Guy." Canoe.com, 1996.

Smith, RJ. "American Idol." *Los Angeles*, February 2006.

Smith, Sean and Ansen, David. "Prize Fighters." *Newsweek*, February 6, 2006.

Souter, Ericka. "Singular Sensation." *People*, December 23, 2002.

Spines, Christine. "How Cool Is George Clooney?" *Premiere*, January 2002.

Stanton, Doug. "Why George Clooney Never Sleeps." *Men's Journal*, July 2000.

Stein, Joel. "The Whiz of Showbiz." *Time*, December 6, 2004.

Svetkey, Benjamin. "Hollywood Pulls the Trigger" *Entertainment Weekly*, December 2, 2005.

Svetkey, Benjamin. "Holy Happy Set!" *Entertainment Weekly*, July 12, 1996.

Swanson, Tim. "Jokers Wild." *Premiere*, December 2004.

Thomson, Desson. *From Dusk Till Dawn* review. *Washington Post*, January 19, 1996.

Tobias, Scott. *The Good German* review. *The Onion A.V. Club*, December 14, 2006.

Total Film, May 28, 1999.

Tracy, Jennifer. "Will George Clooney Ever Settle Down?" *McCalls*, October 2000.

Travers, Peter. *Ocean's Twelve* review. *Rolling Stone*, December 10, 2004.

Travers, Peter. *Syriana* review. *Rolling Stone*, November 17, 2005.

Tucker, Ken. *Syriana* review. *New York*, November 28, 2005.

Turan, Kenneth. *The Peacemaker* review. *Los Angeles Times*, September 26, 1997.

USA Today, January 11, 2007. "Clooney Darfur Documentary to Air Monday."

Vanity Fair, May 2006. "The Green Team."

Variety, October 1996.

Vincent, Mal. *Virginian Pilot*, June 21, 1998.

Wagener, Leon. "Revealed—the Terrible Fears That Hold Him Back from Love." *News of the World* Sunday magazine, September 11, 2005.

Wang, Cynthia. "Talking with Nick Clooney." *People*, February 17, 1997.

Watson, Bret. "What's Up, Docs?" *Entertainment Weekly*, September 22, 1995.

Weinraub, Bernard. "George Clooney: ER's Rogue in Residence." *Cosmopolitan*, March 1996.

Wells, Jeffrey. "A Tights Squeeze." *Entertainment Weekly*, March 8, 1996.

Whipp, Glenn. "Clooney Steps Up to Bat." *Los Angeles Daily News*, July 3, 1998.

Whittell, Cassie. "*Good Night, And Good Luck.*" *DVD Review*, August 2006.

Wioszczyna, Susan. "A Choosier George Clooney Forges His Career Strategy." *USA Today*, December 13, 2006.

Wioszczyna, Susan. "Clooney: A True Friend to the Piggish." *USA Today*, December 4, 2006.

Zacharek, Stephanie. *One Fine Day* review. Salon.com, December 1996.

Zeman, Ned. "The Admirable Clooney." *Vanity Fair*, October 2003.

"George Clooney: Man of the Moment." *She*, October 1998.

"Clooney Darfur Documentary to Air Monday." Associated Press, January 11, 2007.

WEBSITES

The Clooney Network

www.clooneynetwork.com

Features an extensive video library of Clooney's work, including clips from early work like *Riptide*, *E/R*, *The Facts of Life* and the infamous *Baby Talk*.

Clooney Studio

www.clooneystudio.com

Features a large library of Clooney photos, including childhood photos, family pictures and early career photographs.

George Clooney Sights and Sounds

www.sightssounds.net

Features a large archive of Clooney audio and video clips.

Clooney Files

www.clooneyfiles.com

Features a large archive of Clooney photos and articles.

Index